Alain-Fournier

Twayne's World Authors Series
French Literature

David O'Connell, Editor
University of Illinois

TWAS 790

ALAIN-FOURNIER, 1913
Paris studio portrait by Dornac,
courtesy of Alain Rivière

Alain-Fournier

By Stephen Gurney

Bemidji State University

Twayne Publishers
A Division of G. K. Hall & Co. • Boston

Alain-Fournier

Stephen Gurney

Copyright © 1987 by G.K. Hall & Co.
All Rights Reserved
Published by Twayne Publishers
A Division of G.K. Hall & Co.
70 Lincoln Street
Boston, Massachusetts 02111

Copyediting supervised by Lewis DeSimone
Book production by Elizabeth Todesco
Book design by Barbara Anderson

Typeset in 11 pt. Garamond
by Modern Graphics, Inc., Weymouth, Massachusetts

Printed on permanent/durable acid-free paper
and bound in the United States of America

Library of Congress Cataloging in Publication Data

Gurney, Stephen.
    Alain-Fournier.

    (Twayne's World authors series; TWAS 790. French literature)
    Bibliography: p. 162
    Includes index.
    1. Alain-Fournier, 1886–1914.   2. Novelists,
French—20th century—Biography.   I. Title.
II. Series: Twayne's world authors series; TWAS 790.
III. Series: Twayne's world authors series. French
literature.
PQ2611.085Z68   1987   843'.912   86–18476
ISBN 0-8057-6642-1

To my mother and father,
with admiration and love

Contents

About the Author

Stephen Gurney received his Ph.D. in 1978 from the University of Maryland where he was strongly influenced by the critical thought of George A. Panichas. He formerly taught at St. Mary's Seminary and University in Baltimore, Maryland, and is now professor of English at Bemidji State University in northern Minnesota. Through the assistance of two grants from the National Endowment for the Humanities he has been able to prosecute his studies on Alain-Fournier in the context of seminars at Princeton University under the respective directorships of Albert Sonnenfeld and U. C. Knoepflmacher.

He has published numerous articles and reviews on Keats, Browning, D. G. Rossetti, Flaubert, Henry James, Walter Pater, Alexander Pope, Elias Canetti, John Ruskin, Tractarian verse, Heideggerian poetics, Tennyson, Arnold, Hesse, Mann, the criticism of George A. Panichas, and the aesthetics of Jacques Maritain in the following journals: *Studies in Browning and His Circle, Soundings, Hartford Studies in English, Romanticism Past and Present, Comparative Literature Studies, Modern Age, Victorian Britain, Germanic Notes,* and *Studies in the Literary Imagination.*

Preface

"There is probably no work more harmoniously matured than *Le Grand Meaulnes*," observes Robert Champigny.[1] "*Le Grand Meaulnes* is to the art of fiction what *Les Fleurs du Mal* is to the art of poetry . . . a unique and supremely complete construction," writes M. A. Ruff.[2] And Harold Nicolson, the esteemed British critic, unhesitatingly avers that "were I asked what was the most impressive novel published in France during my lifetime, I should answer 'Alain-Fournier's *Le Grand Meaulnes.*'" He further adds: "certainly I should place this novel among those which every literate person should have read."[3]

The following study is intended to examine the reasons for the critical accolades that have established Fournier's novel as a classic of modern French literature; to provide a distillation of the principal critical views that have developed since its publication in 1913; to examine the biographical events in a life that has itself the quality of a spiritual allegory; to develop a coherent and integrated reading of a novel that is among the most distinguished examples of literary modernism; and, it is hoped, to stimulate a new generation of readers to seek out and discover a book that must be credited as one of the most cunning and superlative examples of fictional art to come out of France in the years immediately before the First World War.

"*Le Grand Meaulnes*," writes Robert Gibson, "is an exploration of that fleeting period of life . . . between the end of youth and the beginning of full manhood, when life itself is a mingling of dream and reality, love, adventure, and chivalry. It is a time . . . when youth seeks a shrine at which to worship . . . and . . . is fired with longing for perfection and the Absolute."[4] Disappearing on the field of battle at the age of twenty-eight and in the second month of the Great War, Alain-Fournier (née Henri Alban Fournier) has become to generations of his countrymen the incarnate image of a world in which the qualities Gibson describes were still a sought for and cherished ideal. In the perfection of his only completed novel and the pathos of his aspiring but ravished youth, Alain-Fournier appears to us as a figure from another world—a world that seems far more distant to us, as if seen through the wrong end of a telescope, than the actual lapse of years would apparently warrant. For Fournier belongs to that period which George A. Panichas speaks of as "the end of the lamplight,"—that is to say, the period of prewar innocence, ingenuous faith, and traditional loveliness that existed before the world, as Aleksandr Solzhenitsyn describes it in *August 1914*, devolved "into a new era," where "the entire atmosphere of the planet—its oxygen content, its rate of combustion, the mainspring pressure in all its clocks—had somehow changed." To read *Le Grand Meaulnes* allows one, at least on an historical level, to enter an era of spacious and magnanimous sensibility, where horizons seem remote and magically beckoning; youth, poignantly credulous and altruistically aspiring; and love, radiantly pure and incorruptibly beautiful.

Fournier, who was deeply influenced by British poetry and fiction and who, through his pupil T. S. Eliot, had some influence himself on the course of British literature, is apt to remind Anglo-Saxon readers of the youthful Keats or Shelley. His early death and undefeated idealism elicit, at least, a comparable poignancy. Yet his work, which shows a thorough knowledge and canny appreciation of both the naturalist and symbolist elements in early twentieth-century literature, is itself an amalgam of two strains in French prose that are often seen as antagonistic to one another.

Fournier, writes Cyril Connolly, "was determined to create a magical world that was only just around the corner, plausible in space and time."[5] In doing this, he cut through the boundaries of realism and romance and discovered a common frontier in which, for once, they perfectly and indissolubly blend. France is famous for aesthetic manifestoes and for authors who adhere rigidly to the confines of an aesthetic formula. Fournier's flexibility, in this regard, seems more British than French in origin. The tension in the nineteenth century between the realistic novels of Balzac and the romances of George Sand, the naturalism of Zola and the rarefied ether of the symbolists, was even further exacerbated as the twentieth century arrived by opposing schools whose very existence constituted a repudiation of their opposite numbers: hence, the existentialists increasingly narrowed their field of vision to the prison-house of individual consciousness while the surrealists, losing all touch with the actualities of real life, engaged in the pursuit of occult chimeras. *Le Grand Meaulnes* is one of the few novels of the modern age that hold these antagonistic extremes in equilibrium and keep faith with the real world while expressing at the same time those genuine human impulses that impel us to look beyond it.

Despite its structural cohesiveness and thematic unity, *Le Grand Meaulnes* is in this regard virtually unclassifiable. In its combination of familiar homeliness and fantastic adventure, it defies categorization and stands by itself—exhaling an aura of symbolist sorcery and yet reposing on a bedrock of solid values and sober common sense. Readers who hanker after exotic thrills, fabulous quests, and fantastic adventures will be disappointed to find that the novel subordinates these elements to a realistic evocation of the French midlands and a sober fidelity to the laws of human limit. Others who eschew all vagaries in their fiction and prefer a universe purged of metaphysical vapors will be equally dismayed by the haunting suggestiveness and prescient lyricism of Fournier's book. For this reason, perhaps, it has been somewhat neglected outside its native land—at least in comparison to other French works that are generally recognized, if only in name, by the nonspecialist. It is hoped that this study will assist in developing for *Le Grand Meaulnes* the wider readership that it deserves; though we hasten to add that the number of critical studies of Alain-Fournier in France, England, and America, demonstrates that in academic circles this readership is fairly healthy. In the recently published sixth volume of *A Critical Bibliography of French Literature* (1980), Alain-Fournier is one of a handful of modern French writers, including Proust, Gide, and Malraux, considered weighty enough to occupy separate chapters of their own. The critical entries on Fournier extend in small print over nineteen, double-columned pages.

Finally, there is an element in Fournier's writing that is hard to define but necessary to suggest in any preface to his works. The definition of this element requires us, for the moment, to engage in a short divigation on some comments made by C. S. Lewis in his autobiography—for it is through these comments that we can best attune ourselves to Alain-Fournier's special mode of sensibility.

At the beginning of his autobiography, Lewis describes a series of childhood experiences that decisively altered his perception of reality. Though attenuated by time and distance, these experiences remained for him more precious and far-reaching than any achievement or good fortune that graced his later years. The first experience came when, standing in a garden that at first held for him no peculiar interest, he was suddenly overcome by the memory of his brother constructing a diorama of a pastoral landscape. This memory seized him with a sense of irrepressible longing, a sudden stab of desire that passed through his body like a shudder. Yet what was it for? Assuredly not for a box of pressed flowers and withered plants, nor for his brother who was still his palpable playmate and companion. Though indefinable, this experience occurred again after a reading of Beatrix Potter's *Squirrel Nutkin:* the child suddenly found himself overwhelmed by what he later described as the "idea of Autumn."[6] The thrill and longing were there again, but again, for what? The "idea of Autumn" is certainly not a thing that can be held and grasped as a possession. On yet another occasion, Lewis experienced this sensation after stumbling on some lines about the death of Balder in a childhood version of the Norse myths. This time he was transported out of himself into a longing for something "cold, spacious, severe, pale, and remote."[7] But by now he was older and the sensation passed as instantaneously as it had come. For the first time, he found himself "falling out of the desire and wishing he were back in it."[8] But every attempt to willfully reproduce it resulted in its complete and utter extinction. One might say that virtually all of Lewis's mature philosophy derived from a contemplation of the significance of those childhood moments—that they became for him earmarks of a reality whose presence could only be sensed in the residue of that "sweet joy," as he later came to call it, which led him, in his mature reflections, to the threshold of eternity. It is precisely such an experience that Fournier adumbrates in *Le Grand Meaulnes*—its wizardry and magic bear the unmistakable traces of Lewis's "sweet joy."

There are doubtless many readers and critics who would dismiss such an experience as a form of emotional self-intoxication or regard it as a psychological quirk of dubious worth. For those, however, who have found themselves "surprised" by Lewis's "sweet joy" and have attempted, like Lewis, to investigate its origins and decipher its significance, *Le Grand Meaulnes* will be a welcome and revelatory text. For the experience it enshrines is something more than the sum of its structural parts and the tale it tells more marvelous than any critic's power to fully fathom.

Stephen Gurney

Bemidji State University

Acknowledgments

I wish to thank Alain Rivière, the nephew of Alain-Fournier, for the photograph of his uncle that serves as a frontispiece to this volume.

My debt, of course, is immense to the many critics who have commented on Fournier's life and works over the past several decades. Among these Martin Turnell, Stephen Ullmann, Mechthild Cranston and, above all, Robert Gibson—whose two magisterial biographies of Fournier are of permanent and priceless value—deserve especial mention.

A large percentage of the quotations from Fournier's letters and stories that appear in the volume generally follow the impeccable translations of Robert Gibson in *The Land without a Name* and *The Quest of Alain-Fournier*. I wish to thank Professor Gibson for his permission to use these as well as for his kind personal words of commendation. In those instances where I supply my own translations, I have endeavored to follow the spirit and letter of the original as closely as possible. Any errors in these are my own.

Of the three translations of *Le Grand Meaulnes* presently available, the most distinguished, accurate, and evocative, faithful to the original and yet a classic in its own right, is that of Frank Davison in the Penguin Modern Classics series. (*Le Grand Meaulnes* has also been translated as *The Wanderer* and *The Lost Domain*.) I wish to thank Oxford University Press for their permission to use Davison's translation, which originally appeared in 1959 in the World's Classics series.

To the librarians and staffs of Princeton University, Bemidji State University, and Salisbury State College, I want to express thanks for the assistance they gave me.

Two summer stipends from the National Endowment for the Humanities enabled me to pursue my research on Alain-Fournier in the context of seminars conducted respectively by U. C. Knoepflmacher and Albert Sonnenfeld at Princeton University. I am deeply grateful to both of these professors for their stimulus and support.

I wish especially to thank Dr. George A. Panichas for the example he has provided and the encouragement he has given me over the years. His three principal works, *The Reverent Discipline, The Courage of Judgment,* and *The Burden of Vision,* are invaluable examples of scholarly meditation and paradigms of critical thought. These books have been profoundly instrumental in shaping my own approach to literature.

Special thanks are due to David O'Connell for his faith in this project, his valuable suggestions, and enthusiastic support.

Mrs. Nickie Petrowske conscientiously typed and sensitively proofread the final draft of this book. Without her sustaining confidence and limitless patience my task would have been far more difficult.

Finally, to my parents, my wife, and my children, I owe more in the way of daily sustenance and inspiration than words can say. To Ingrid and Davy, in especial, I give thanks for their sustaining in me a sense of what Fournier described as "the other mysterious landscape—a landscape which the actual landscape makes me desire."

Chronology

1886   3 October, birth of Henri Alain-Fournier at La Chapelle-d'Angillon (Cher) in the house of his maternal grandmother.

1889   16 July, birth of Fournier's sister Isabelle at La Chapelle.

1891   In October, Fournier moves with his family to Epineuil-le-Fleuriel, where his parents teach in the local schoolhouse.

1898   Fournier attends the Lycée Voltaire in Paris.

1899   Fournier wins all the school prizes, including the *prix d'excellence.*

1901   Fournier enters the naval academy at Brest.

1902   Fournier leaves Brest in December to concentrate on philosophy at the Lycée de Bourges.

1903   In October, Fournier transfers to the Lycée Lakanal where, in his seventeenth year, he meets and begins his lifelong friendship with Jacques Rivière. He begins to write poetry in imitation of Francis Jammes.

1905   1 June, on leaving a contemporary art exhibit in Paris, Fournier meets Yvonne de Quiévrecourt—the inspiration of his novel and the model for Yvonne de Galais. In July, Fournier travels to London where he works as a clerk in a wallpaper firm. He extends his knowledge of English art and literature and writes "A Travers les étés"—the poem inspired by his meeting with Yvonne. The nine-year correspondence with Jacques Rivière begins at this time.

1906   In October, Fournier and his sister lodge with his grandmother in Paris. He attends the Lycée Fénelon.

1907   24 July, Fournier, preoccupied with the composition of *Le Grand Meaulnes,* fails to pass the national teacher's examination. He breaks down at a party during a recital of art songs by Debussy, and later learns that Yvonne de Quiévrecourt has married.

1908   Fournier is drafted into the army and enters the officer's training school. His father and mother are transferred to Paris.

1909   In April, Fournier is appointed Lieutenant of the 88th Infantry Regiment at Mirande. In May, he makes two trips to Lourdes; and, in July, he again fails to pass the national teacher's examination. In August, he completes his long prose poem "Madeleine." While at Mirande, he learns, in September, of the birth of Yvonne de Quiévrecourt's first child. Jacques Rivière marries Fournier's sister Isabelle in August. Fournier begins a liaison with Jeanne Bruneau.

1910   His military service finished, Fournier becomes a literary and cultural critic for the *Paris-Journal*. In December he writes "Le Miracle des trois dames de village" and "Le Miracle de la fermière," the latter of which appears in *La Grande Revue*, 25 May 1911.

1911   Fournier is present at the birth of his niece Jacqueline on 23 August. In September, his short story "Un Portrait" appears in the *Nouvelle Revue française*.

1912   In April, Fournier leaves the *Paris-Journal* in order to work as private secretary to Claude Casimir-Périer, the son of a former French president. In December, Fournier's friend René Bichet dies from an overdose of morphine. Fournier breaks permanently with Jeanne Bruneau.

1913   *Le Grand Meaulnes* completed, Fournier begins work on another novel: *Colombe Blanchet*. In May, he meets Yvonne de Quiévrecourt for a second time at an outing arranged by Rivière's brother Marc. She is happily married and the mother of two children. *Le Grand Meaulnes* appears, between July and October, in four numbers of the *Nouvelle Revue française*. At the end of October, it is published in book form by Emile Paul. Fournier begins a liaison with the actress Simone Casimir-Périer.

1914   22 September, Second Lieutenant Henri Alain-Fournier is reported missing in action during the Battle of the Marne.

Chapter One
Life and Times
Intellectual Background

During the lifetime of Alain-Fournier—that is to say, between 1886 and 1914—France was arguably the most vital center of cultural and artistic expression in western Europe. Music, painting, philosophy, poetry, dance, and the novel simultaneously flourished in an atmosphere of mutual awareness among the exponents of these arts. Picasso painted the sets for Diaghilev's *Russian Ballets* and Vuillard the backdrops for Debussy's post-Wagnerian opera based on the text of Maurice Maeterlinck's *Pelléas et Mélisande.* Nijinsky choreographed Debussy's tone poem *L'Après-midi d'un Faune,* which was itself a musical meditation on the symbolist poem of Stephane Mallarmé. The vibrating canvases of the impressionist painters gave visible expression to Bergson's philosophy of perpetual flux, while the opposing principles of aesthetic indulgence and spiritual renunciation were dramatized in the novels and plays of André Gide and Paul Claudel.

Paris drew the finest talents of various nations to its cultural heart, and became, in turn, the setting that nourished the music of Stravinsky and Ravel, the fiction of Joyce and Proust, and the poetry of Eliot and Apollinaire. The renewal and revitalization of English poetry, after a period of creative exhaustion and stultifying convention, would finally come from a young American expatriate who, around 1910, eagerly imbibed the atmosphere of Paris through the assistance of a private tutor who taught him the French language. The American was much affected by this "quiet-spoken, witty, elegant young man"[1] from the French provinces who worked as an art critic for the *Paris-Journal.* For, in addition to being an able and adept linguist, this attractive Frenchman had an apparently inexhaustible knowledge of English painting and literature—of Dickens, Hardy, Keats, Shelley, and the Pre-Raphaelites—and an infectious enthusiasm for the poetry of Jules LaForgue and the French symbolists, the painting of Cézanne and the postimpressionist ex-

1

perimenters, the choreography of Fokine, Nijinsky and the *Ballets russes,* and the novels of Dostoevsky, which had recently been translated into French. Moreover, he spoke of these things with a discriminating tact, critical judgment, and sympathetic insight of exceptional scope for one so young. The extent to which the twenty-three year old French tutor enabled his student—better known as T. S. Eliot—to absorb and transform these cultural influences, is now, of course, a matter of literary history. The tutor's name was Alain-Fournier. And it was, of course, in the midst of cultural modernism—that rich and significant interplay of the arts which took place in the Paris of *la belle époque*—that Fournier came of age.

What were some of the forces associated with this period and what effect did they have on a young Frenchman of rural background who responded with indefatigable zeal to this heady mixture of creative energy? Perhaps the most important attribute of the era was the manner in which one discipline interpenetrated and influenced another. At least two of the artistic movements that flourished in France at the turn of the century—symbolism and impressionism (with its several proliferating offshoots)—are terms that may be applied interchangeably to painting, music, and, in the case of the former, to literature. The ways in which musical and literary forms are related, the adaptation of compositional techniques or coloristic effects to literary genres, the manner in which thematic and philosophical concerns inhere in the methodologies of poet, painter, and composer, have an especial relevance to Fournier's oeuvre and to his letters, which, apart from their historical value and cultural significance, enable us to trace the growth of a novel and the maturation of an artist.

Wylie Sypher has observed that the structure of Gide's novel *Les Faux-Monnayeurs (The Counterfeiters),* was influenced by the cubists; in the same way Alain-Fournier's masterpiece, *Le Grand Meaulnes,* owes much to the example of the impressionists. It is, in fact, an impressionist novel—though its structural solidity and architectural weight give it an intellectual distinction akin to the canvases of Paul Cézanne, of whom Fournier spoke with discernment in his letters to Jacques Rivière. In any event, it bears witness to the synthetic, one might almost say, synaesthetic conception of the arts that underpins so many works of this period. Profoundly affected by the experiments of his contemporaries, Fournier endeavored to adapt the moods, themes, and effects germane to impressionist art and symbolist theory to the exigencies of narrative prose. Fournier's successful attempt "to insert the marvelous into reality,"[2] as he described it in a letter to Rivière, epitomizes his stance as an artist who absorbed the rival claims of symbolism and naturalism. And it is this that makes his novel, along with Proust's *Du Côté de chez Swann (Swann's Way)* (which appeared, incidentally, in the same year, 1913), an example of literary impressionism. As Henri Peyre observes, "Proust's *Du Côté de Chez Swann* and *Le Grand Meaulnes* whose influence on French fiction was to be felt for several decades . . . were [both] poetical novels of childhood, embodying what was most precious in the legacy of Symbolism and blending that airy fragrance with the earthy smells of Combray and the valley of the Cher."[3]

Impressionism itself was an attempt, in part, to fuse the opposing principles of naturalism and symbolism, of the actual and the ideal, reality and imagination, a life in time with a life of values. It reaches its culmination in the late water lily paintings of Monet and in Debussy's opera *Pelléas et Mélisande*—works, to be sure, in different mediums but similar in assumptions and effects. That Fournier, who attended Debussy's opera on numerous occasions, took to his heart and sympathetically intoned Mélisande's song of homesickness and longing—"Je ne suis pas d'ici, Je ne suis pas née là" (I am not from here, I was not born here)—and wrote astutely to Rivière on the orchestral means through which Debussy evoked the presence of the sea (itself an important symbol in *Le Grand Meaulnes*), was fully cognizant of these affinities and influences is without question. What Fournier shared with the impressionists was a desire to unite the symbolist search for an ultimate reality that transcends the senses with the naturalist's attention to the gritty textures of daily life and the poignant impermanence of the human condition.

For Fournier, however, naturalism, in itself, was a cul-de-sac. As epitomized by Emile Zola and his school, human nature was conceived of as strictly conditioned by social pressures, biological laws, and economic forces. This restrictive theory of portraying humanity denied metaphysical axioms, dispensed with the notion of interior psychology, and contradicted its own moral urge for social reform (which in itself bears witness to a sense of justice that transcends the mutations of history and environment). In this regard, Fournier, like the symbolists, saw the human subject in relation to forces, powers, and events that extend beyond the limited compass of workaday life into a realm of ultimate and unknowable mystery. But the symbolists often pursued this realm—as one sees in Mallarmé, who aspired to become but "an aptitude which the spiritual universe possesses to see itself," or Rimbaud, who followed a "long, immense, and reasoned out distraction of all the senses"—into an ether so rarified and an ecstasy of such questionable intensity, that they left behind the majority of their readers and the average concerns of common humanity. In this regard, Fournier found their procedures antagonistic to his own artistic goals. As he wrote to his friend Jacques Rivière: "Do you think I am in danger of divorcing the world of poetry from the living world, as so many others have done? On the contrary, it is only in the life of everyday that I can feel the sudden waves of impulse that lift me into the other" (*Corr. R-F*, 1:416). In the final analysis, Fournier characterized himself as being fundamentally a "peasant"—and it is his racy feel for the seasonal patterns of country life, his ability to evoke the melancholy monotone of an isolated village in the Cher valley and the dreary routines of a French provincial schoolroom, that give his art, even "as it strives," as he wrote, "towards the essential passage . . . those moments that are marked by grace" (*Corr. R-F*, 2:303), a solidity and weight far more compelling than the vaporous utterances of the symbolists who preceded him. What Fournier did share with the symbolists, however, was the sense that the Absolute is inexplicably disclosed in and intertwined with the fleeting phenomena of the sensuous world, the shifting panorama of scenes and events that Monet captured through short brushstrokes of primary color thrown vibrating one next to the other, or Debussy evoked through the novel use of the pentatonic scale articulated in timbres of matchless orchestral splendor. "Je veux être le Debussy de la littérature" (I wish to be the Debussy of literature), wrote Fournier at the height of his enthusiasm for *Pelléas et Mélisande*.[4]

The impressionists attained the symbolist awareness of a sovereign spiritual order not by circumventing the natural world of appearance—the manifold effects produced by a chance meeting of light and shade glimpsed briefly from a sudden and unexpected angle, the inextricable tangle and welter of lives consumed with desire or penitent with remorse, the sudden and rapid alternations of joy and sorrow, pleasure and pain, attraction and repulsion—but rather by seeking in these very things some hidden destiny or providential design that endows the most evanescent experience with a hierophantic grace.

In poetry, Baudelaire, Verlaine, and Rimbaud were the weightiest exponents of this vision—a vision that required nuance and suggestion rather than declamation and assertion for its perfect utterance. (In this regard, too, symbolism was as much a reaction against as an outgrowth of romanticism: the romantic school of Victor Hugo with its exaggerated emotions, tragic titanism, and bombastic rhetoric was inimical to that attitude of patient receptivity and self-effacing attention that the symbolists consciously cultivated.)

Yet it was not initially through the poetry of Baudelaire or Verlaine that Fournier found his vision of "the mysterious world I long for, the new and far-off landscape of my heart—mysteriously mingled with the world of my life, mysteriously suggested by it," (*Corr. R-F*, 1:415) delineated and confirmed, but rather through the minor symbolists, Francis Jammes and Henri de Régnier, whose melancholy landscapes, reticently beautiful though strangely augurous, recalled the world of his own childhood where the river Cher meandered among the pine forests, sandy wastes, abandoned châteaus, and isolated villages of central France.

But Fournier's affinity with the symbolists and impressionists is equally traceable to a common sense of being dispossessed of a childhood vision for which adult life offered no recompense. As his best friend, Jacques Rivière, wrote apropos of Fournier's inveterate nostalgia for the past: "Your childhood was so beautiful, so rich in dreams and so like paradise, that now you've left it behind, you're quite disillusioned by what seems to be the drabness of life. It's as though you've lived out your life already, as if there's nothing left for you to do except relive it in your memory, telling the same story to yourself over and over again" (*Corr. R-F*, 2:335).

Rivière's characterization of his friend is only partially accurate if we keep in mind that Fournier was finally able to transcend the feeling of nostalgia with which his works are so closely associated. As Marcel Proust observed, "You can recreate what you love only by giving it up." Be that as it may, this same inescapable feeling of regret for the child of pure unclouded brow and dreaming eyes of wonder, is as germane to the symbolist and impressionist school in general as it is to Fournier in particular (though here, as well, the influence of Wordsworth and the seventeenth-century metaphysical poets is equally pertinent). There are, for example, few portraits of children as exquisitely tender or evocative as those painted by Fournier's contemporaries, Auguste Renoir and Mary Cassatt. But even in those paintings of Renoir or Monet seemingly expressive of a joy at once pure and unalloyed (where the subject, though not necessarily of children, is nevertheless seen, as it were, through the enraptured eyes of childhood), the tacit sense of human transience and temporality is clear and unmistakable. Hence, a party of pleasure seekers steeped in the amber of a summer day, a shimmering sail streaking a distant horizon, or a humid atmosphere humming with life and motion are subjects that reveal to the impressionist artist the fugitive nature of mortal joy. As one critic, writing of the "delight" and "tragedy" implicit in Debussy's music, has observed apropos of the impressionist period: "The sense of the infirmity of life, the consciousness that it had no more than the signification of a dream with passing lights, or halting steps in the snow, or an old half-forgotten story, had mixed a deep wistfulness and melancholy into the very glamour of the globe, and become heavier itself for all the sweetness of earth. And Debussy has fixed the two in their confusion."[5]

And so, we might add, has Fournier in *Le Grand Meaulnes*. "There is," observes Fredrika Blair in her introduction to an English version of the novel, "through all Fournier's writing a feeling of homesickness . . . a consciousness, even in joyful moments, of the shortness of joy, which transforms the fields, houses, and people that Fournier describes, giving them a heightened intensity and poignance."[6]

It is fair to add, moreover, that part of the poignance associated with *Le Grand Meaulnes* has become, at least in France, indissolubly blended with the life of its author. As one of the first casualties of the Great War, Fournier has become, in the minds of his countrymen, the authentic embodiment of a generation and a way of life irretrievably silenced by the guns of August 1914. If Fournier, in his intellectual grasp, unerring sense of human motives and their effects, and assiduous craftsmanship, anticipates, on the one hand, the burgeoning forces of modernism that followed in the wake of the Great War, he is also among the last of that lost generation whose spacious aspirations, naive idealism, and delicate sentiments vanished in the debacle that redrew the lines of Europe and ushered in a new age of extremism in politics, disequilibrium in the arts, and confusion in human relations.

Fournier's present stature in France—which is indeed considerable—derives, in part, from his status as an allegorical figure, embodying the spirit of an age no longer amenable to the inhospitable atmosphere and brutal ideologies of the postwar era—that era which the German poet Rilke described as having "passed out of the hands of God into the hands of men." As one critic in a retrospective survey of modern French literature has observed apropos of *Le Grand Meaulnes*: "The whole of a generation . . . knew itself in this nostalgic narrative, which we can no longer read without seeing Alain-Fournier's chaste and rather grave smile delineated between the lines."[7] Apart from his outstanding achievement as the author of *Le Grand Meaulnes*, Fournier will remain, in the eyes of his compatriots and those who continue to cherish the "gentility, charm, urbanity, and chivalry"[8] of the prewar era, a figure of mythological proportions, prematurely violated "by the plunge of civilization" as Henry James described it, "into this abyss of blood and darkness."

The Landscape of Childhood

While Fournier's absorption in and indebtedness to the works of his contemporaries is unmistakable and his knowledge of French, English, and Russian literature of considerable sophistication, it would be wrong to consider him a poet's poet or a novelist's novelist. While his early works bear the imprint of many unassimilated influences—"too much of Renoiresque girls with white sunshades and the world's summers in their hair . . . and not nearly enough of the stink of a winter classroom in a small village school,"[9] as John Fowles wryly observes—Fournier found his own authentic voice when he eschewed the elaborate and self-conscious cadences of the symbolist prose poem and began, as he wrote in a letter to Rivière, "to write simply and directly, like one of my letters, in close little paragraphs full of feeling, a fairly straightforward story which could be mine" (*Corr. R-F*, 2:371).

It was then that he came into his artistic heritage and found the main theme and region of his song. And that theme was inextricably intertwined with reminiscences so personal, memories of childhood and feelings for a landscape of such intimate and ineffacable depth, and, above all, with an encounter so privileged in its grace that critics have justifiably compared it to Dante's meeting with Beatrice in *La Vita nuova (The New Life)*.

The reminiscences begin, as Robert Champigny observes, with "the [landscape] of Fournier's youth,"[10] itself a part of the region or "climate" of the symbolist period. Unlike the romantic poet who responded to the stupendous and sublime aspects of nature, the symbolists savored quiet retreats of unobtrusive charm: Proust's Combray or Monet's Argenteuil. Through these they were granted a delicate presage of what Fournier called, "the other mysterious landscape—a landscape which the actual landscape makes me desire" (*Corr. R-F*, 1:415–16). And indeed the Cher valley with its sandy marshlands, resinous forests of pine and fir, reedy mudbanks, desolate wastes, and limitless flat horizons, became, in Fournier's childhood imagination, a thing of unbounded wonder, haunted by an alien spirit of which it seemed a part, brooded over by some imponderable essence whose magic endowed the deserted wastes with a numinous and unaccustomed glow. Given his peculiar temperament and its consonance with the climate of the symbolist period, it seems almost providential that it was here, in the Loire basin, that Fournier was born on 3 October 1886.

The landscape of his childhood haunted him for the rest of his life and became, at once, the starting point and the goal of his subsequent aims as an artist. For, as he wrote to his parents in 1905, "I want to write books and books for you about all I have seen and felt in that little patch of land which was the world for us—and about that corner of my heart where I love to keep it still."[11]

More specifically, the "corner" of which Fournier speaks was Epineuil-le-Fleuriel, a small village with a single schoolhouse where his parents—Sylvan Baptiste Augustin Fournier and Albanie Barthe—presided over the pupils and lived in an adjacent dwelling overlooking the schoolyard. Between the ages of five and twelve, Fournier dwelt in this remote and humble village; and everything, down to the names of his fellow students in the class register, the drafty attic bedroom that his imagination transformed at nightfall into the groaning hull of a sea-laboring ship, the strolling players in gypsy caravans whose arrival dubiously coincided with a rash of stolen hens indignantly reported by the local farmers, and the country drawing rooms of neighbors and friends where "ladies used to play the piano while the children would sit on thick carpets, and browse through big books filled with adventures and carols,"[12] was transcribed, almost verbatim, into the early portions of his novel.

Similarly, the idiosyncrasies of his father and mother were given to Monsieur Seurel and his wife, Millie: the one, something of a boy himself who joined his students on their fishing expeditions and eternally hankered after a life of adventure and travel; the other a prudent and organized housekeeper, pious, exacting, neat as a pin, though warmly maternal. By the same token, his sister Isabelle would find some of her qualities translated into the character of François Seurel, the narrator of *Le Grand Meaulnes,* who shares her childhood limp and, as his name implies (*Soeur*-el), the sisterly qualities of loyalty and feminine solicitude. Isabelle would remain Fournier's devoted confidante, marry his closest friend, and cherish the memory of her brother throughout her life.

Fournier's attachment to Epineuil was equalled by his love for the home of his maternal grandparents at La Chapelle-d'Angillon where he was born. His grandmother Adèle regaled him with stories of her romantic youth: the country balls and elegant apparel of a courteous and sentimental age, and, most especially, the fervent devotion of one particular suitor—a young English nobleman who had come to the country and fallen victim to Adèle's charms only to find himself hounded from the district by the local swains jealous of his attentions to the village beauty whom they equally coveted. It was while visiting his grandparents that Fournier caught a glimpse of the abandoned château of Loroy—the ideal setting, in the fancy of Fournier and his sister, for the fairy tales of Perrault.

A third center of poignant memory was situated at Nançay where Fournier's Uncle Florent and Aunt Augustine with their eight daughters and one boy greeted the Fournier family at the threshold of their general store—a place of enticing smells, exhaustless wonder, and, as soon as the provisional formalities were exchanged, raucous with childhood laughter. The entire scene with its "big kitchen . . . next door to the shop," where "the little girls of the house . . . scurried about and chattered and filled the place with the faint scent of whatever it was they put on their glossy hair,"[13] would be painstakingly reproduced in the central chapters of *Le Grand Meaulnes*.

Fournier's cult of childhood reminiscences, though deeply personal and transparently sincere, was itself symptomatic of the age. As the century waned, the nostalgic celebration of childhood became all the more conspicuous. The emergence of a harsher universe, "adapted," as one critic puts it, "to the rhythm of the internal combustion engine,"[14] was threatening, through its contradictions, to erode all meaning and efface those moments of communion and grace that Fournier relished in his boyhood.

"My credo in art and literature," wrote Fournier in 1906, "is childhood: to render this state without puerility but with a profound sense of its mystery" (*Corr. R-F,* 1:323). Just two years earlier, "in 1904, an audience of adults in the Duke of York's theater in London responded to Peter Pan's appeal by thunderously assenting that, yes, they did believe in Fairies,"[15] while Kenneth Graham and Edith Nesbit were giving popular warrant to an attitude that may be traced back to Vaughan, Traherne, Blake, and Wordsworth.

Fournier's link with this peculiarly English tradition was, on the whole, unparalleled in his native France. It finds its artistic counterpart, as we have seen, in those impressionists who continued Blake's evangel to "cleanse the doors of perception," and see, "not with, but through the eye." As previously noted, the portraits of children by Renoir and Mary Cassatt are part and parcel of this romantic heritage, while Monet's claim that "every square inch of space is a miracle," bears similar witness to the spontaneous and unmediated vision of childhood. Then, too, there are the instrumental suites variously entitled "Dolly," "Children's Corner," and "Mother Goose," in which Fournier's favorite composers, Fauré, Debussy, and Ravel, demonstrate their penchant for the world of childhood magic.

Like the English romantics and the French impressionists, Fournier regarded the child as the most privileged of beings. In the first instance, the child enjoys a continuous imaginative transformation of reality; the boundaries between ego and world are nebulous and vague. Hence, the child becomes the type and emblem of the poet himself. Moreover, the sense of oneness with the whole of being is a state more readily available in childhood (before the process of ego building has begun) than it is at any other period. In consequence, the child's unconscious participation in the whole of reality is analogous to the conscious awareness of that wholeness deliberately cultivated by the mystic. It is for this reason that Fournier, like the English romantics before him, found childhood to be a source of inexhaustible inspiration. (Though it is only fair to add at this point that while Fournier was to claim that his hero Meaulnes was "the victim of too beautiful a childhood" [*Corr. R-F,* 1:323], in the final analysis, his novel dramatizes the besetting dangers and temptations that accompany a regressive yearning for childhood magic and belief when these vie with the grown-up's acceptance of the compromises inherent in growth and social adaptation. After all, it is one thing to be an adult and to cherish childhood as emblematic of the spiritually awakened conscience, but it is another thing altogether to be an adult and wish to return to a condition from which, by virtue of our temporality, we are debarred. Hence, *Le Grand Meaulnes* is informed by a growing awareness that the celebration of childhood, when protracted beyond its due limits, becomes demonic and obsessive.)

Notwithstanding the above qualification, we may safely accept the conclusion of one critic that Fournier "has left perhaps the last version of the world of childhood which can be compared with those of Wordsworth and Traherne."[16] In making this assertion, however, it is important to realize that the sources, influences, and affinities that helped Fournier to articulate his vision do not fully exhaust or explain the achievement of *Le Grand Meaulnes*. Whatever sources went into the shaping of this book were entirely subsumed by the author's poignant contact with his own childhood roots and his own creative destiny: like the music of Browning's "Abt Vogler," Fournier was able to create "out of three sounds" (in other words, that conscious sympathy of vision which he shared with his poetic forebears), "not a fourth sound, but a star."

If "Alain-Fournier is one among the very few of his countrymen who could have been perfectly at home in the worlds of innocence of Blake and Shakespeare, of Vaughan and Traherne,"[17] his peculiar vision of that world—trailing clouds of glory, "le vert paradis des amours enfantines"[18]—wells up from instinctual springs buried deep in the native soil of his own inimitable past.

As he wrote in a letter to Rivière apropos of his artistic intentions: "Perhaps my future book will be a continuous and unconscious coming and going between dream and reality,—'dream,' meaning the indefinite life of childhood, hovering above the other, and endlessly reverberating with echoes of the other" (*Corr. R-F,* 1:323).

Exile and Meeting with Rivière

At the age of twelve, Alain-Fournier entered into a period of exile from his native country which, with occasional intervals, extended throughout the rest of his life. His parents, ambitious for their son, overrode the boy's objections, and sent him to the Lycée Voltaire in Paris where they hoped he would soon demonstrate his abilities. Despite the disagreeable nature of his surroundings—he boarded in the house of Madame Bijard, a former friend of the family's, whose husband drank inveterately and was subject to protracted bouts of ill temper—Fournier was named "outstanding pupil" for two successive years and brought home, as a reward, several prize books including Scott's *Quentin Durward,* a novel of adolescent initiation into love and war. He won over fourteen prizes in his three-year tenure at Voltaire, and then transferred at the age of fifteen, to pursue a naval career at the military academy at Brest.

Fournier's fascination for the sea was something he inherited from his father—though neither of them was destined to pursue a naval life. Indeed, it was not long before the harsh routine, brutal society, and sneering incivility of the academy, his classmates, and teachers put a damper on his youthful expectations. Increasingly he turned to literature as an escape. At this period he discovered Fromentin's *Dominique*—"a long, fine needle," as he later wrote, "driven into my adolescent heart"[19]—which became one of his favorites. Moreover, he began to manifest a strong attachment to the rituals of the Catholic Church. The religious longings that possessed him at this time became, despite periodic lapses and bouts of skepticism, a permanent fixture of his mind: a source of agonized wrestlings, desires for renunciation, the pursuit of an impossible purity.

Fournier lasted only sixteen months at Brest, for him, a veritable hell—before he transferred to the lycée at Bourges, the famous cathedral town within close proximity to his beloved Cher valley. Though his parents had been recently reassigned to a small village within an hour's traveling time of Bourges, their move signaled a permanent break with Epineuil. To counteract the sometimes popular impression of Fournier as a pallid aesthete enamored of a chimerical symbolist purity, it is important to emphasize that not only did he excel at philosophy while at Bourges, he also won accolades from his fellow students for his astonishing performance at rugby. Throughout his life (and certainly during his two-year period of military service), Fournier was conspicuous for his hardy athleticism, sense of humor, and youthful high spirits. Though he chose, like Byron, to exclude these from his early work, one senses that had he lived, the ironic perspective—already evident in *Le Grand Meaulnes*—would have deepened into a more pervasive humor.

After a brief stay at Bourges, Fournier and his parents moved again: his parents, to their son's birthplace at La Chapelle; Fournier, to the Lycée Lakanal in Paris. He was accompanied this time by his sister, and it was here that one of the most singular and justly celebrated friendships in French literary history was to evolve—for it was here that Fournier met Jacques Rivière.

Rivière's relationship with Fournier can only be glossed here; though we shall have occasion to return to it in our discussion of Fournier's letters. Suffice it to say, that like the friendships of Wordsworth and Coleridge, or Amis and Amile, this friendship has acquired a mythic status in France: and no wonder, for it ripened on both a personal and literary level into one of the most profound, loyal, and sympathetic relationships in the history of letters.

When Fournier arrived at Lakanal, Jacques Rivière was alienated from his own family. Following the death of his mother, to whom Jacques was devotedly attached, Rivière's father—a somewhat cold and astringent professor of obstetrics—remarried and, out of deference to his new bride, did all he could to efface the memories of his former wife. To Rivière this was tantamount to sacrilege, the most heinous of betrayals, which permanently alienated him from his father. In consequence, he retreated into himself and cultivated his love for literature and the arts in the absence of friends, comrades, or close relations.

In some ways these friends were opposites: Rivière, shy, withdrawn, possessed of an analytical mind, though periodically swept away by a series of enthusiasms for Gide, Claudel, Debussy, Stravinsky, and, later, Proust; Fournier, increasingly obstreperous and assertive among his fellow students, prone to youthful high-jinks and grandly defiant of all academic rules based on injustice, exploitation, or comeuppance. In his introduction to a posthumous edition of Fournier's writings, Rivière describes the beginnings of that friendship: "He was fond of me and gradually the sincerity of his attachment became clear to me, won me over, wore down my resistance. Besides his insubordinate attitude, a completely different part of his character was slowly revealed to me, and I could not but love it. Beneath his untamed exterior, I found he was tender, innocent, filled with the stuff that dreams are made of, infinitely less equipped than I was in the face of life—which is saying a great deal."[20]

Together Rivière and Fournier discovered symbolist poetry, which, after a mutual adolescent crisis of faith, became for them a kind of surrogate religion—appealing all the more because of its vagueness and apparent impregnability to the assaults of materialism. Nevertheless, they would both return to the Catholic Church: Fournier, to linger at the threshold, with increasing though undeclared conviction, until his premature death in 1914; Rivière, to a formal reconciliation and in humble acceptance following his crucial correspondence with the Catholic playwright Paul Claudel. Rivière, incidentally, would go on to become one of the most influential and important critics of the first half of the twentieth century: editor of the prestigious *Nouvelle Revue française;* one of the first critics to apply Freudian psychology to the analysis of literary texts; author of the earliest and still among the most cogent commentaries on Proust; a writer equally at home in the criticism of music, art, and literature; a Catholic seer whose spiritual autobiography, *A La Trace de Dieu,* ranks among the most important religious testaments of the century.

Another schoolmate of Fournier's at Lakanal deserves mention: René Bichet, tender, effusive, slightly pathetic (one thinks of Watteau's clowns), in short, a far less resilient character than Jacques, though one to whom Fournier, in a number of highly personal letters, would describe the impact of a meeting to which Rivière, in his suspicion of all gushiness, would have responded less sympathetically.

Ascension Thursday, 1905

We now approach an event in Fournier's life that is quite without precedent in the annals of modern literature: perhaps the closest parallel would be Yeats's first meeting with Maud Gonne, though in Yeats's experience the nuances are more Shelleyan than Dantesque. With Fournier, however, as John Fowles comments, "one has almost to go back to Dante and Beatrice to find its equal."[21]

The whole experience, described by Fournier in a private journal, has been scrupulously preserved by Isabelle Rivière in her biographical study of her brother. When we add to this Fournier's subsequent confessions to Bichet, this epiphanic event emerges with unusal clarity and distinctness.

On 1 June 1905, Fournier, then eighteen years old, attended an exhibit of contemporary art at a Parisian gallery. As he was descending the steps and savoring the mild sunshine of an afternoon in spring, his attention was suddenly arrested by the image of a tall, blond girl in a brown cloak whose hair escaped in golden strands from beneath the rim of a straw hat wreathed in roses. Her eyes were of an intense cerulean blue. Her stately figure and poised carriage were further emphasized by the presence of an elderly woman who hobbled by her side. The young girl cast a furtive look in Fournier's direction. Instantly and irrevocably smitten by that glance, he followed her to the banks of the Seine where she and her companion boarded a steamer to the opposite side. Fournier unobtrusively followed.

As the ripples widened on either side of the trudging prow, the apparition of this fair young girl imperceptibly blended with memories of Fournier's youth. For some inscrutable reason she triggered an involuntary flood of recollections and seemed, though distinctly and uniquely herself, the breathing incarnation of a world of which she could know nothing, a world, as Fournier wrote, where "the cooing of [doves], filling each minute of the long, hot afternoon, is inexpressibly sad. I think of the corridors where the ladies who come to pay a call leave their sunshades, and of the conversation which will last until four or five o'clock, when the garden walks are cool, while the children are playing and the ladies pass as they leave for dinner."[22] This forsaken garden of an extinguished past, this laughter of children in the foliage (which T. S. Eliot would similarly associate with the paradisal world of inocence in *Four Quartets*) suddenly effloresced in the consciousness of Fournier, in all its original redolence at the sight of this young girl. Thenceforward she was inseparably associated with the irretrievable world of Epineuil.

The experience was not unlike that of Proust who, tasting a "petite madeleine" dipped in tea, suddenly felt raised above "the vicissitudes of life," and "hear[ing] the echo of great spaces traversed," was able to repossess "all the flowers [of his childhood] garden . . . and the water lilies on the Vivonne and the good folk of the village and their little dwellings and the parish church and the whole of Combray and its surroundings."[23] The difference is that while Fournier, too, felt translated beyond mortal contingency, beholding all time, as it were, like the Deity—that is to say, as an eternal and unchanging present—for him, this moment had not merely a subjective significance, but became a symbol and a token of humanity's supernatural destiny, an epiphany that enabled him to experience once again "the other mystrious landscape" of his own childhood, and also to find therein, as he later confessed, the suggestion of a nameless land that belonged not to him alone but to the entire human race.

After disembarking on the other side of the Seine, Fournier followed the girl to a fashionable townhouse which she entered, apparently oblivious of his presence. He returned obsessively for a succession of days, sitting on a bench beneath the drawing-room windows. Once the curtain was momentarily lifted by a delicate hand—again he saw the stately figure, dressed in black and holding a book—but the curtains fell, almost instantly, back to their accustomed folds. Presently, a fine but steady rain forced the young vigilant to retire.

The next day he was finally granted a brief interview. Towards evening, the door opened and the girl descended "in a cloud of lace." Fournier managed to catch up with her as she walked in short, quick steps toward the Church of Saint Germain-des-Près for evening vespers. "You are beautiful," he whispered almost inaudibly as she hurried on without response.

Fournier stopped, hesitated, then boldly pursued her into the church which he was almost prevented from entering because he lacked money for a seat. Nevertheless, the sacristan allowed him to pass into the hushed enclosure.

As the service drew to its close, Fournier, surrounded by the departing worshipers, almost missed her; but luck was on his side and she appeared again, but a few feet in the distance. He approached with resolution and murmured a breathless apology: "Tell me you forgive me for saying you were so beautiful."

Startled by his presence, the young girl uttered an icy disclaimer, but gradually the attentions of this ardent and handsome youth melted her reserve and she condescended to hear his entreaties. Fournier spoke of his ambitions as a writer, but the gulf between them remained unbridgeable. She belonged to a wealthy family, her father was a naval officer, she thanked the boy for his attentions but it was really quite useless. She uttered the same phrase over and over, "a quoi bon? a quoi bon?" (What's the use?), emphasizing the "b" with an almost childish pout.

"We are two children. We have acted foolishly," she said at last. Forbidding Fournier to attend upon her further, she walked slowly but decisively forward. Presently, she paused, turned around, and cast a last backward glance in Fournier's direction. Then she disappeared among the populous thoroughfares of the Parisian twilight.

What shall we make of this chance meeting? Is it nothing more than an adolescent vagary, psychologically quite normal, a matter of passing importance? Were it not for the intensity, duration, and final effect of this experience, the previous formula would be quite adequate to explain it. Yet John Fowles describes it as "one of the most famous private thunderbolts in the history of love,"[24] and it is not too difficult to see why.

Fournier finally reached a point where he accepted the loss of this lady, whose name was Yvonne de Quiévrecourt, as necessary and, indeed, indispensible for his further growth. Nevertheless, the significance he attached to this encounter, the conviction, which lasted so long, that no further experience of compensating intensity would ever replace or rival this one, the belief that only the renunciation of all earthly happiness would enable him to attain the perfect felicity prefigured in that moment, the desire to seek in another dimension of existence the consummation of the joy implicit in this chance encounter, endows this fairly typical event in the life of an adolescent with an almost mythopoeic radiance, of which *Le Grand Meaulnes* is, in part, the final expression.

To be sure, Fournier, in the aftermath of this meeting, proved no Galahad; on the contrary, as Fowles again asserts with understated irony, "his own chastity was certainly more theoretical than literal." Fournier did try, in a number of disillusioning affairs, to replicate the rarity of that moment. Like Shelley, "in many mortal forms [he] rashly sought / A shadow of that idol of [his] thought." And his hero Meaulnes shares this tendency to confuse the possession of a finite woman with that inestimable and infinite boon of which she is the involuntary symbol. But Fournier was capable of secondary reflection on these matters, and, in the final analysis, both his life and his novel grope toward the enlightened expression of love best described by Simone Weil: "To love purely is to consent to distance, it is to adore the distance between ourselves and that which we love." Or again: "All that man vainly desires here below is perfectly realized in God. We have all those impossible desires within us as a mark of our destination, and they are good provided we no longer hope to fulfill them."[25]

Fournier did not come to this insight easily. Indeed, T. S. Eliot's critique of Baudelaire is equally apposite to the case of Fournier. "In the adjustment of the natural to the spiritual, of the bestial to the human and the human to the supernatural, Baudelaire is a bungler compared to Dante." Very true. But, then, as Jacques Maritain remarks—and his words have a similar pertinence to Fournier—"Baudelaire, in the place where he was, and from which he looked at things, was precisely required not to perceive the adjustment [between Eliot's categories], but to feel the split and derangement."[26]

Yet when Fournier, in a letter of 1909, confessed, "I am looking for the key of escape to the land of heart's desire, and perhaps it is death, after all" (*Corr. R-F,* 2:303), he appears, strangely, as something of a Christian troubadour, lost in an alien age, the last exponent in western letters of a tradition that reaches back to Dante's *New Life.*

Like Rossetti, whose portrait of *Beata Beatrix* impressed Fournier as the closest equivalent, in art, to the image of Yvonne de Quiévrecourt, Fournier did not unequivocally follow the stages of spiritual illumination recorded in Dante's *New Life:* the movement from personal dissatisfaction and longing, to joy in the sight of the beloved, and from that joy to an experience of love that transcends desire and finds its fulfillment in the hereafter. Still if love, as Dante understood it, is not to be sought in its causes—an unresolved Oedipal attachment, the projection of a Jungian anima, an insatiable instinct forcibly repressed by social convention—but in its effects (namely, the orientation of the soul towards grace and the apotheosis of desire beyond "those false images," as Dante wrote, "which never keep their promises"), then Fournier, though in an age of materialism and disbelief and in a manner far more ambiguous than Dante, bears at least partial witness to that process. We may choose, if we wish, to regard the whole affair in the same light as one of C. S. Lewis's students who reportedly said of courtly love that it was nothing more than "a vast medieval erection," but then we would have forgotten, momentarily, what Dr. Johnson spoke of as "the attribute of soul." It is, perhaps, more correct to say of Fournier's hero Meaulnes and of Fournier himself what Robert Liddel says of Marcel Proust and his "hero" Charles Swann: though they remain unclear in their commitment to a "supernatural principle," they at least "desire what [Christianity] promises, and this is perhaps an even rarer sign of grace in the twentieth century. They not only have immortal longings, but they recognize that they have them."[27]

England, Paris, and Academic Failure

For the disciple of courtly love, it is necessary that the object of his affection remain virginal, veiled, and forever chaste if she is to retain her semblance of stainless purity. Fournier's trip to England, for the ostensible purpose of perfecting his English, and, hence, standing a better chance of passing the difficult national teacher's examination, occurred so soon after his meeting with Yvonne that it is difficult not to believe, that at the very least, it coincided with a subconscious need to refine his passion by keeping its desired object at a safe and inaccessible distance.

In any event, Fournier's travels to England in 1905—where he worked for the summer as a clerk in a wallpaper firm—enabled him to satisfy the love of things English that was first stimulated by his childhood enthusiasm for Dickens. The famous correspondence with Rivière begins at this time, and as we shall see in our subsequent discussion of those letters, Fournier's first tentative attempts to define his intentions as an artist, to see himself in relation to his contemporaries, and to understand the nature of his own sensibility, become matters of pressing and continuous concern.

Though he complained much at the absence of French cooking, he love the Dickensian atmosphere of London, visited all the art galleries where he stood hours before his beloved Pre-Raphaelites, and sketched the first inchoate scenes of the novel that would occupy him for the next eight years. He also began to write poetry in the style of Francis Jammes and Henri de Regnier.

His increasing proficiency in English enabled him to expand his knowledge of the British novelists, to add to the loves of his childhood—Dickens and Defoe—a knowledge of Victorian and early Edwardian masters: the Brontës, Stevenson, Wells, Kipling, and, above all, Thomas Hardy. From these writers he would pick up the distinctly British trait of using the seasons and associated meteorological phenomena as a sounding board, as it were, to the emotional life of his characters. He also steeped himself in the British romantics and Pre-Raphaelites. Fournier left England in September 1905 and returned home in the hopes of successfully passing the national teacher's examination and following in the footsteps of his parents.

If Fournier's putative purpose in going to England was to enable him to pass his examination, his behavior on returning to France seems strikingly inconsistent. Instead of applying himself to the study of history and literature germane to the exams, he spent virtually the whole of his time reading those works best calculated, by example and technique, to foster his own emerging powers as an artist. The demands of worldly self-adjustment were clearly in conflict with a more imperious obligation: namely, fidelity to the unconscious process of creative genius that requires the subordination of all knowledge and all experience to the necessities of poetic utterance. How far this subordination would take him and into what byways he would travel as a result, were not as yet apparent.

In any case, he neglected Molière and Racine for Gide and Claudel and instead of cracking the books, spent nights at the ballet and opera and his days at exhibitions of contemporary art. And, inevitably, mingled with all this, were memories of Yvonne: "One wears a hat like hers," he wrote to Rivière, "another has her way of bowing her head slightly forward, another a light brown dress like hers, another the blue of her eyes—but not one of them, however far I look, however long they take to pass by, not one of them is she" (*Corr. R-F*, 1:148). The entire passage would be transcribed with only slight variation into the texture of *Le Grand Meaulnes*.

Not surprisingly, Fournier flunked his exam in the summer of 1906, returned to La Chapelle to ready himself for a second try, spent most of his time writing poems, stories, and preliminary sketches for his novel, and, on returning to Paris (this time with his sister where they lived with Grandmother Adèle, recently moved from the provinces), failed a second time, after coming excruciatingly close, in July 1907.

In the meantime, Fournier had introduced his sister to Jacques Rivière. This would have important consequences for all three. Jacques and Isabelle spent most of their time together, while Fournier, stung by his recent failure and obsessed with memories of Yvonne, felt neglected and behaved peevishly. (This rather unpleasant side of Fournier's character would later be given autonomous expression in the character of Frantz de Galais, who similarly whines over his sister's "neglect.") Fournier would soon outgrow this rather callow phase, though not before it reached its apogee at a gathering where one of his friends sang Debussy's setting of Verlaine's "Mandoline," and Fournier collapsed in tears.

After this, he learned that Yvonne had married and his thoughts increasingly turned to religion. As he wrote to Jacques: "while you feel the insufficiency of everything in an abstract way, and say from the outset that you are unsatisfied and without hope, I, for my part, go eagerly towards everything until its mirage fades away in my grasp, then I am offered the perfect satisfacion, the pure, the beautiful, the everlasting which I seek. I am offered God" (*Corr. R-F*, 2:135).

Army Life and Religious Crisis

Rivière had been inducted in 1906, and Fournier, feeling within himself so many conflicts and antagonistic impulses, almost relished the idea of his imminent compulsory stint in the army as an anodyne to the vagaries of his own consciousness. The reality, of course, proved less tonic than he had supposed.

His first months in the army, between October 1908 and April 1909, were unremittingly harsh and, to one as fastidious and in many ways formal as Fournier, unrelievedly noxious. Having to share facilities and even drinking mugs with men suffering from who knows what varieties of venereal infections, not to mention the ceaseless bullying of superiors, the numbing effect of forced drills, and the virtual impossibility of achieving a moment of reflection— all doubtless contributed to the religious crisis of May 1909. The only consolation of this period was the recent appearance of his first published work, an essay on the image of woman in French culture, which had come out late in 1907 in *La Grande Revue*. Moreover, his last tie to his country home was irretrievably severed when his parents were transferred to a school in Paris. Then, too, in the same year his sister, whose unqualified attentions he formerly enjoyed, became engaged to Jacques. No wonder that in the midst of enervating drills and nightlong marches, he wrote to his friend, "I should like there to be in my works a book or chapter entitled: The End of Youth" (*Corr. R-F*, 2:194).

During breaks, at Christmas—where he saw a clown in Paris enact the perpetual fall of the hapless Pierrot ("it was like a sketch of a falling animal, a subconscious part of the self suddenly made visible," he later wrote[28] with an as yet unformulated notion of how this would later be reproduced by Ganache, the "Pierrot" of his novel)—and, again, during intermittent leaves, he would work assiduously on prose poems and stories: perfecting his art, preparing himself for that book on "the end of youth."

Somehow, after an initial period of resentment, he managed to establish some sort of rapprochement between his inner life and the world of the military. By the time he was discharged, around 1910, he had risen to the rank of lieutenant, apparently commanding the respect and loyalty of his men. Clearly, he was capable of greater fortitude than he had at first thought possible.

In the midst of all this, however, and under the influence of Paul Claudel (the Catholic poet and literary evangelist who, in response to a letter of Jacques's, engaged in a correspondence that would eventually lead Fournier's friend, after years of defection, to the eucharistic table), Fournier became possessed of irrepressible longings for religioius guidance and consolation.

The Bible and the *Imitation of Christ* were studied with daily assiduity. After concluding Huysmans's novel on the life of Bernadette, he traveled to Lourdes and, overwhelmed by the image of suffering humanity, prayed to the virgin and drank of the waters, though without the clear sense of absolution he sought.

These scruples finally reached a climax in a series of letters written on the eve of Rivière's marriage to Isabelle: "If . . . you have not seen that for three years the problem of Christianity was forever torturing me, then you have been deceived, you have misjudged me." And again: "It is only at the hour of the sweating of blood that the soul has been able to make itself heard, and it was then that Christ obtained an answer" (*Corr. R-F,* 2:295). He finally wrote of his intention to become a monk, precipitating something of a crisis in his parents' household, though this proved to be a passing vagary never fully entertained. But, above all, it was the need for purity, associated with childhood, with Yvonne, with the other mysterious landscape, the desire for which he spoke of as his "marvellous weakness," that continued to haunt him.

Whence this preoccupation with purity? Why these desperate outcries for an unmolested innocence? The answer comes with startling and somewhat bizarre suddeness in what is perhaps the most singular letter ever written to a betrothed couple on the eve of their marriage. "Certainly," wrote Fournier to Jacques and Isabelle, "I have known girls and women . . . and amongst these women, there were some who, for the space of a moment, suspected what I was offering to them, and they were afraid to accept it." Thence follows a long litany of betrayals and seductions, of furtive pleasures purchased at the price of irremissive remorse, voluptuous encounters entirely contrary to the ideals that he presumably cherished. "There was one," he writes, "who came into my house one night in the small hours, quite naked, and she offered me her poor body, with the voice of someone who has lost his way, and is offering all he has to rediscover it" (*Corr. R-F*, 2:320). The indescribable feud between these scruples of conscience and sins of the flesh was especially conspicuous in his affair with Jeanne Bruneau—the real-life model of Meaulnes's mistress, Valentine Blondeau.

The Affair with Jeanne

On his discharge from the army in 1910, Fournier moved in with the Rivières. The contrast with his former life in the army gave his spirits an unaccustomed ebullience, which displayed itself in verbal quips and puns, practical jokes (such as scribbling hearts with the names of "Jacques" and "Isabelle" inscribed in the middle all over the mirrors with toothpaste), and unbounded good humor. He took to tutoring to earn some money and, as previously noted, became the private instructor of T. S. Eliot. He found a job as a journalist for the *Paris-Journal*, reviewing books, plays, and concerts. And all the while, he was steadily working on *Le Grand Meaulnes*—a work initially intended to express his perception of the insufficiency of all earthly paradises and the search for an ideal of fadeless beauty and unfailing comfort. This theme became considerably complicated, however, by the effects of his affair with Jeanne Bruneau. If Meaulnes was designed at first as a kind of visionary who "sees right through all the mini-paradises that are offered him and recognized them for the fraud they are," he later develops into a "great, cruel angel," (*Corr. R-F*, 2:338, 340) unable to reconcile his conflicting impulses and, in consequence, all the more savage both to himself and to those around him who fail to maintain his ideals.

This change in Fournier's conception of Meaulnes is directly traceable to his affair with Jeanne Bruneau. Fournier apparently met her at Bourges where she worked as a seamstress. He tried, unavailingly, to make her into a incarnation of his ideal, but his conception of love was too august for her (and probably for any woman) to live up to. The liaison, based largely on physical attraction, came to an end during a weekend where they joined some of Fournier's friends

for an interlude in the country. During a solitary walk with Fournier,
Jeanne confessed to an affair with a man who had killed himself out
of love for her. She gave Fournier a packet of blood-stained letters
written to her by her former lover. Appalled by this revelation,
Fournier denounced and accused the flustered and browbeaten girl.
That night she was taken ill. After a series of tenuous reunions and
predictable break-ups, they were permanently estranged. "Only the
women who loved me can know how cruel I can be," observed
Fournier in a letter to Rivière, "because I want everything. I do
not even want people to live this human life. You can see this in
Meaulnes, the hero of my book" (*Corr. R-F,* 2:374).

Fournier's treatment of Jeanne enabled him to experience on his
pulses the "dialectic of desire" that would later become the fundamental theme of *Le Grand Meaulnes.* As he later wrote to Rivière,
"You understand my book is the story of Keats," (a slip of the
memory by Fournier, for the quote that follows is found in a letter
of Shelley's), " 'Certain of them met Antigone in another existence,
and no human love will be able to satisfy them' " (*Corr. R-F,* 2:373).
A discussion of this theme must be reserved for a later chapter, but
we may note here that Fournier's moral dilemma is not simply the
result of an ineffectual longing for the lost and, hence, untarnished
Yvonne and an insensate demand that the actual women who came
into his life should live up to that ideal. It is also attributable to a
fundamental tension that Fournier's contemporary, the Catholic philosopher Jacques Maritain, discerned between artistic creation and
ethical imperatives. If the saint, according to Maritain, is called
upon to suffer divine things by giving himself over to the contemplation of eternal wisdom, the poet is called upon to suffer "the
things of the temporal world," in order to render them permeable
to the light of creative intuition. The lives of both poet and saint
are characterized by a vertical, in-depth movement; but whereas the
saint is oriented toward the transcendence of this world, the poet
is obliged to descend into the vertiginous depths of the human
heart—not that he might aspire through that knowledge to the
state of perfection, but rather that he might use that knowledge to
deepen poetic expression. The danger lies in making life itself a
means to an aesthetic end. Hence, in order to be a poet, the artist
will often arrange the incidents in his life in such a way that certain
conditions arise that are best calculated to enhance his art—moreover, he will exploit those conditions to the detriment of his own

well-being. Fournier's attachment to Yvonne, treatment of Jeanne, and petulance with the Rivières, were in part, calculated to sharpen his sense of remorse for a lost ideal that he was best qualified to express. There is a certain degree of inauthenticity in all this—and it was from this that Fournier suffered (and made others suffer) as much as anything else. In the final analysis, our estimate of his behavior must take into account the words of Rimbaud that Maritain cites as the only legitimate response to this virtually irresolvable conundrum: "Charity is the key."[29]

The French Lieutenant

The last three years of Fournier's life were crowded with a series of events that he exploited to the full in bringing his novel to completion, and that anticipate a possible change of direction in his subsequent development as a writer—had he lived.

He continued to attend the premieres of important works in Paris: he witnessed a performance of Fokine's ballet after Schumann's *Carnaval,* gathering material for his dramatization of the "fête étrange" in *Le Grand Meaulnes,* and was present with Jacques at the notorious premiere of Stravinsky's *Rite of Spring,* which triggered a riot in the audience and a distinguished essay by Rivière in defense of the composer. He was overjoyed at the birth of his niece Jacqueline Rivière on 23 August 1911, struck up an important friendship with the Catholic poet Charles Péguy, and, through the efforts of his new friend, secured a position as personal secretary to Claude Casimir-Périer, the rich son of a former French president.

Of more interest to Fournier was Périer's wife: Simone Casimir-Périer, an actress of Jewish descent, nine years Fournier's senior; a star of international reputation who immediately responded to this "slim young man," as she described Fournier, "with warm brown hair . . . [gray] eyes with long lashes . . . and the bearing of a prince."[30]

There are those who accept Simone's claim, that had Fournier lived, she would have become his wife and stimulated him to expand and deepen his powers as an artist. Others, like Isabelle, look upon her memoirs with lackluster eye, arguing, in the last resort, that her wordly temperament would eventually have grated on Fournier's idealism, precipitating a crisis akin to the affair with Jeanne. That Fournier still remained attached to the memory of Yvonne, even as he courted Simone, is without dispute.

One day, without warning or anticipation, Fournier was given the opportunity for a second interview with Yvonne—now married and the mother of two children. It was Marc Rivière, Jacques's brother, who fortuitiously discovered her whereabouts and arranged the second meeting. Fournier spoke with her and learned that several years earlier, when her marriage was not going well, she had thought often and remorsefully of the ardent young man who had courted her by the quais of the Seine. She was happy now, however, glad to hear of his success and looking forward to a copy of *Le Grand Meaulnes*, which Fournier, accordingly, sent. After the interview with Yvonne, Fournier would write to his mistress: "as soon as we move on to serious ground, we're no longer united"[31]—hardly a ringing prescription for future bliss.

In any event, both bliss and bane were not to last much longer. There was, however, an unexpected shock in December of 1912: the death of his friend Bichet from an overdose of drugs. "I had imagined," wrote Fournier with unknowing prescience, "that after Bichet, the next one to go would be me" (*Corr. R-F*, 2:421). *Le Grand Meaulnes* was published in 1913, and though Fournier failed to win the *Prix Goncourt*, the reviews were generally favorable. One critic compared him with Dickens and praised the book's combination of symbolist depth and straightforward narrative, concluding that it was "a story . . . that touched the imagination as deeply as it touches the heart."[32] Fournier, moreover, received warm compliments from Valéry Larbaud, Charles Péguy, and, in England, from Joseph Conrad. The intervention of the war initially prevented the book from receiving the critical consideration it deserved. After the war, of course, it rose steadily in critical estimation to the point of becoming a celebrated and indisputed classic of French fiction. It would be the subject of critical encomiums by Jean Giraudoux, Julien Benda, Jacques Rivière, André Billy, Maurice Ruff, and Edmond Jaloux, while, in England, its devotees would include Harold Nicholson, Cyril Connolly, Edward Sackville-West, and John Fowles.

But the supervention of a less savory reality curtailed the preliminary show of enthusiasm. The last months of Fournier's life were characterized by a flurry of literary projects: a new novel, *Colombe Blanchet*, and a play for Simone entitled *La Maison dans la forêt*. As the summer of 1914 came to its close, France along with the whole of western Europe was poised for war. Fournier was called up and assumed the duties of his regiment with alacrity. Like the young men of his generation, unravished as yet by the horrors of trench warfare, Fournier's initial response was one of unbounded afflatus at the prospect of fighting for the French homeland. The first systematic use of technology for wholesale killings with no redeeming trace of chivalry and the cynical exploitation of human folly by entrepreneurs with a vested interest in keeping the war alive were still unapparent. Hence the famous words of Péguy may be applied, with few exceptions, to the generation of 1914:

> Heureux ceux qui sont morts pour la terre charnelle,
> Mais pourvu que ce fut dans une juste guerre.
> Heureux ceux qui sont morts pour quatre coins de terre.
> Heureux ceux qui sont morts d'une mort solennelle.
>
> (Happy are those who died for this carnel earth
> But provided that it was in a just war.
> Happy are those who died for four corners of the earth.
> Happy are those who died a solemn death.)[33]

And yet, as George A. Panichas accurately observes, "not a transfiguring nobility but a sense of disgust beyond despair marked the temper of Europe by November 11, 1918."[34] This disgust Fournier never lived to experience. He was one of the first casualties of the war, and his death, seen in the light of his life's work, strikes us as something almost sought after and courted, like Shelley's in that fatal shipwreck off the Italian coast, uncannily prefigured in the last lines of *Adonais*. Indeed, one critic, Robert Champigny, goes so far as to say that Fournier deliberately tempted God on that battlefield. Dissatisfied by the ambiguities of ordinary faith, disgusted with the compromises inherent in life's dome of many-colored glass, disappointed by the "error of seeking in a mortal image the likeness of what is perhaps eternal,"[35] Fournier may have sought to force God's hand and achieve, at once, unqualified access to the white radiance of eternity. As Champigny observes: "Fournier will accept religion if he is granted the grace of seeing eternity. He is willing to be a mystic, but he cannot be an average believer."[36] Did Fournier really commit the sin of "angelism" as it is denominated by certain theologians: namely, the insensate desire to aggressively attain occult knowledge independently of the divine will? Who, in the final analysis, can say? Fournier's last recorded words, spoken to a skeptical and mocking soldier on the front line, would seem to imply otherwise: "I don't know where God is in this war, but I know well that I shall be struck down when he wishes, how he wishes, and where he wishes."[37]

On 22 September, Second Lieutenant Henri Alain-Fournier was assigned to lead his troups into a debatable area of Eparges between the French and German lines. Approaching the outskirts of a wood, they were suddenly greeted by a hail of bullets. With his pistol raised in a gesture of command, Fournier endeavored to strike forward but was abruptly arrested by a wound in the arm. He slumped to one knee and, in the ensuing chaos and confusion, disappeared— never to be recovered.

Aftermath

The fate of Fournier's family and friends, following the novelist's death, epitomizes the new spirit of disintegration and breakdown ignited by the gunfire of that opprobrious August. Jacques Rivière was captured in the first weeks of the war. He wore out the remaining three years of the conflict as a prisoner of war subject to unspeakable privations and tortured by the thought of lost opportunities and wasted powers. He managed, however, to write a spiritual autobiography of great distinction and on his release resumed his duties as editor of the *Nouvelle Revue française.* His constitution, however, enfeebled by the war experience, was unable to survive an attack of typhoid fever. He died on 14 February 1925—in his dying words calling on his departed friend. Following her husband's death, Isabelle devoted herself to preserving the heritage of both Jacques and Henri, writing essays and books on their lives and achievements. She died in 1971. The Rivière children, Jacqueline and Alain (born in 1920), both entered religious orders. Jacqueline died in her thirty-third year at the Benedictine convent in Dourgne. In 1968, Alain Rivière left the monastery in Dourgne where he was former choir-master. He has written many articles on both his father and uncle.

After Fournier's death, his parents spent an anxious, long, and fruitless period in Paris, hoping for news of their missing son. Monsieur Fournier, demoralized and despairing, abandoned his home for several years, only to come back and find his wife ill and near death. Among the papers of her mother preserved by Isabelle, we find the following words: "Since I've lost Henri, I'm resigned to everything. I know that whatever I do, ill fortune will always make a point of conspiring against me."[38]

After the war, Simone Casimer-Périer attempted, through the courts, to claim Fournier's papers from Isabelle. She was unsuccessful and, thereafter, maintained a hostile public debate in the Parisian press with Isabelle over Fournier's memory. Yvonne de Quiévre-court, following the death of her husband in 1953, entered a convent in Italy. Taken ill shortly afterward, she spent the remaining years of her life in a state of semiconsciousness.

Frederick W. Locke observes that "as soon as one does read the life of Alain-Fournier, he receives a strange shock. Coming from the novel to the life one gets the shock of recognition that one ordinarily receives in going from one work of art to another. One is tempted to ask which is the fiction."[39] And for another critic, David Paul, "his early death seems not so much a literary loss as a personal one."[40] Each of these quotes epitomizes the extraordinary tenacity of Fournier's hold upon the imagination of those for whom his life and work are, in John Fowles's words, "like a secret garden . . . one never quite forgets."[41] After World War I, this feeling became ubiquitous in France. And it is in part attributable to Alain-Fournier's representative role as the last artist of what many survivors would regard as an Arcadian age of gold. Moreover, as Edmond Jaloux observes, Fournier's "is the only novel of truely classic stand-ing among the men of his generation"[42]—a generation, we might add, that seemed to inhabit a privileged universe, historically un-tainted by the encroaching nihilism of the postwar years. As Leonard Woolf wrote: "In 1914 in the background of one's life and mind there was light and hope, by 1918 one had unconsciously accepted a perpetual public menace and darkness and had admitted into the privacy of one's mind and soul an iron fatalistic acquiescence in insecurity and barbarism."[43] At the very least, Alain-Fournier's life and work give us unique access to an outlook and sensibility that seem to have vanished irrevocably with the First World War. To state the matter more positively, however, Fournier's oeuvre not only "springs from," but in the words of one critic, "appeals to, a fundamental religious instinct"[44]—an "instinct" potentially rich enough to counterbalance and offset that "iron and fatalistic acqui-escence in insecurity and barbarism" of which we are still the dis-illusioned heirs.

Chapter Two

Correspondence with Rivière

The Epistolary Art

There are few epistolary exchanges as intrinsically fascinating as the justly celebrated correspondence of Alain-Fournier and Jacques Rivière. In conveying the excitement of intellectual discovery, the freshness of awakening sensibilities, the rich diversity of minds keenly responsive to the creative vibrations of the modernist epoch, these letters are without compare. Considerations of space and emphasis compel us to focus principally on the contributions of Fournier, though we may briefly note that Rivière was precisely suited by temperament and ability, to be an ideal collaborator, disputant, or foil (as the occasion demanded) to the epistolary overflowings of his friend. They were close enough in sensibility and outlook to respond with uncommon sympathy to one another's intellectual enthusiasms, and yet divergent enough in orientation and taste to provide the perfect complement and, at times, corrective, to one another's ideas. Rivière was preeminently suited to be a critic; he lived almost exclusively in the realm of art and thought, passing from Barrès to Gide to Claudel in alternations of breathless impetuosity and dispassionate critical analysis. In each encounter with genius he was threatened with the loss of his own identity, but he was always capable of critical rebound and personal reintegration on a higher level—absorbing his influences and, in turn, preparing himself, in the breadth of his sympathies and the probity of his judgments, for his future career as a critic. As Rivière wrote to Fournier: "True reality for me is general. . . . I formulate general ideas while endowing them with a certain color, a certain precise beauty" (*Corr. R-F*, 1:131). Fournier, no less discriminating than his friend, responded, above all, to life. The arts—literature, music, and painting—remained ancillary to his principal concern: the fostering and understanding of his own singular vision as an artist. The letters—alternately chafing, sportive, commiserating, or effusive—are entirely without pretense and may be savored for the glimpse they give us into the lives of two energetic and exceptional young men on the threshold of their respective vocations, as a moving and panoramic account of the process of artistic and intellectual self-dedication, and as an accurate and firsthand reflection of an age of cultural innovation, complex sensibility, spiritual disquiet, and critical reevaluation.

Indeed, from a critical point-of-view, these letters are especially significant. Each of these correspondents was fully engaged and committed to the process of critical discovery—not for the sake of flattering a fashionable trend, or for reasons of promotion and tenure, or in order to appear clever among their colleagues—but out of a deep conviction of the value and purpose of art as, in the words of Jacques Maritain, "the most natural power of healing and agent of spiritualization needed by the human community." Unlike many contemporary critics who place all sorts of obstacles between the reader and the text, Rivière and Fournier honed their critical judgments out of a respect for the artist they celebrated, a need to deepen and enlarge their own sensibilities, and with a view to contributing something of value to the artistic exploration of the human predicament. It is hard to imagine an exchange of this kind transpiring in the contemporary world of letters. The attrition of the word, the absence of a common cultural heritage, the decline of a sense of beauty, the rise of a lubricious mass culture, the narrow-minded emphasis on specialization, in short, the general decay of those loyalties and values upon which such a friendship could repose, militate too strongly against it. In this regard, the historic worth of these letters is all the more precious and meaningful.

In France, the *Correspondance* has been the subject of critical commentary by Gabriel Marcel and Jacques Maritain, while, in England, Fournier's letters have been singled out by David Paul for possessing "the leisured penetration, the wisdom and the charity of Keats."[1] John Fowles goes so far as to say that "I would make them compulsory reading for would-be writers," and confesses that, in order to remind himself of certain stylistic essentials, he has adorned the walls of his study with excerpts from Fournier's missives.[2] Moreover, in the same way that the notions expressed in Keats's letters of "negative capability," "beauty" and "truth," or the "egotistical sublime," have entered into and assumed the quality of touchstones in the critical discourse of England and America, so certain locutions of Fournier's have become indispensable in the discussion of aesthetic

principles in France. "To insert the marvelous into reality," "the
other mysterious landscape," "to render childhood without childishness," "an image that can hold a world for the perceptive"—
these and many other phrases of equal felicity from Fournier's letters
have become a permanent part of the French critical vocabulary.

On one level, both Fournier and Rivière regarded each other as
ideal foils against which they could file and hone their respective
critical standards. Yet, in so doing, they became an index and a
touchstone of the French cognoscenti immediately before the First
World War, and prefigured the upsurge of cosmopolitanism that
characterized the twenties and early thirties in Paris. In painting
and music, literature and philosophy, their tastes were distinctly
avant-garde. The names of Bergson, Schopenhauer, Nietzsche, Stravinsky, Cézanne, Gaugin, Rouault, Bonnard, Gide, Ibsen, Mauriac,
Péguy, and Dostoevsky pass across these pages with an impact all
the more compelling by virtue of the authenticity with which Fournier and Rivière responded to these names long before they had
become fashionable. As discriminating advocates of the avant-garde,
they made contributions to the modernist era that are eloquently
acknowledged by T. S. Eliot, who confessed that "The Love Song
of J. Alfred Prufrock" was directly inspired by his parleys with
Alain-Fournier. "It was my friend and tutor, Alain-Fournier," writes
Eliot, "who introduced me to [Dostoevsky]. Under his instigation,
I read *Crime and Punishment, The Idiot,* and *The Brothers Karamazov*
in French translation during the course of that winter [1910–11].
These three novels made a profound impression upon me and I had
read them all before 'Prufrock' was completed."[3]

In addition, these letters reveal a constant and unappeasable thirst
for the absolute—a thirst more often sustained through a sense of
loss rather than gain, through the experience of acedia rather than
joy, by dwelling on the narrow ridge of an open abyss rather than
participating in the ecstatic certitude of divine grace. It is this that
makes these letters, on one level, a symptom and a portent of that
spiritual disquietude that would soon be felt and suffered, in the
postwar years, on a universal scale.

Finally, the appeal of these letters is traceable to their unstructured
spontaneity and the unprejudiced disposition of the correspondents
to life and art. The insights, the moments of change or crises, the
sudden enlargements of vision or revelations of creative power, when
they come, arise in the midst of anecdote or gossip—and appear

all the more impressive in this unpretentious context. Accordingly, an examination of the *Correspondance* will enable us to appreciate the ways in which the growth of a novel, an awareness of the contemporary arts, and the development of a critical sense coalesce in the maturing consciousness of a young artist.

Music and the Novel

Fournier's correspondence with Rivière was decisively initiated during the summer of 1905 when Fournier had come to London to improve his English by working as a translater for a wallpaper firm. Henceforward, both correspondents regarded this exchange as an indispensible exercise in mutual self-understanding.

One of the most arresting traits of Fournier's early letters is the wiry but atmospheric descriptions that characterize his renderings of London life—a combination of the indefinite and the precise that later emerges in his handling of "la fête étrange" in *Le Grand Meaulnes*. A London villa, for example, is "like a miniature chateau . . . with grainy doors of polished oak, mullioned windows and carven stonework, delicate curtains of diaphonous lace, and everywhere the sound of a piano or flute, heard but never seen" (*Corr. R-F*, 1:171). His descriptions of English garden parties are similarly invested with a Cytherean grace—the clerks and shop girls transformed into a body of amorous courtiers grouped on dappled lawns of unchanging verdure and surrounded by a pervasive musicality of uncertain origin. One thinks of Watteau or Monet. Though not entirely free, as yet, from a certain adolescent excess, Fournier is already using one of those devices—namely, unseen music from an indeterminate source—that he will later refine into a means of endowing tangible settings and palpable objects with an aura of inexplicable significance and nuance. Indeed, for Fournier as for Proust (whose hero, Charles Swann, finds spiritual renewal and rekindled purpose in a phrase from a sonata for violin and piano), distant or remembered music is one of the means through which access to a deeper dimension of existence is made available. This device is used again and again in *Le Grand Meaulnes*, while Fournier's preoccupation with his musical contemporaries remains a permanent feature of his letters.

Of more pressing and immediate significance, however, is Fournier's preoccupation with the theory and structure of the novel. In

a letter written on 13 August 1905, Fournier speaks of his intentions—already forecast in childhood—to become a writer. Even as
a child he had recognized that his peculiar abilities were those of a
storyteller rather than a poet. In his letters, however, his conception
of the novel is at first romantic and subjective—his work will be
a thinly veiled expression of his own inner life. Something of this
quality clings to be sure, to *Le Grand Meaulnes*. But we must avert
here the danger of interpreting the novel, as so many biographers
have done, exclusively in terms of the author's life. In this regard,
it is especially important to attend to the words that follow Fournier's
initial declaration to Rivière of his novelistic ambitions: "The novel
that I have carried in my head for three years was at first only me,
me, and me, but it has gradually been depersonalized and enlarged
and is no longer the novel which everbody plans at eighteen" (*Corr.
R-F*, 1:31). This is the first discrete allusion to the as yet untitled
Le Grand Meaulnes and the words deserve repetition: for they underscore the extent to which the novel, in its archetypal patterns
and paradigmatic motifs, grew increasingly beyond the subjective
experience of its author to become a story of universal import and
meaning.

Fournier continues with a long and lucid exposition—twenty-
three pages in the original, handwritten version—on the various
options and modes open to the practicing novelist. Three prototypical figures merge at this point—Dickens, the Goncourts, and,
surprisingly, the poet LaForgue—each of them offering a viable
alternative in terms of style and structure. Fournier dwells at length
on *David Copperfield,* one of his childhood favorites in which we see
the relationship of François Seurel and Augustin Meaulnes prefigured
in David's infatuation with Steerforth. Dickens's method, according
to Fournier, is, on the whole, episodic—individual scenes and situations being held together by the all-pervading consciousness of
the narrator. (Similarly, the tone and atmosphere of *Le Grand Meaulnes*
depends largely on the sensibility of François Seurel whose delicate
and subtly cadenced prose envelopes the characters, scenes, and
dramatic events with a profound and poignant sense of nostalgia.)
Moreover, in a response to Rivière's denigration of Dickens as a
sentimentalist too easily given to moving his readers by appealing
to stock emotions, Fournier claims that Dickens is not merely a
master of the bathetic, writing in a superannuated style: on the
contrary, he is above all an artist, one of the first to consciously use

the leitmotiv as a means of creating pattern and order and as a mode of adumbrating philosophical themes and highlighting certain aspects of his characters. "Sentimentality," writes Fournier, "is above all sloppy writing—doing things too fast in the easy way" (*Corr. R-F*, 1:52). Accordingly, Fournier's emphasis on Dickens's use of the leitmotiv gives unmistakable evidence, as one critic notes, of his "delicate but strong foundation of ordered and conscious purpose, of self-critical shrewdness in his work."[4] This shrewdness, especially in the use of leitmotivs, became an informing principle of *Le Grand Meaulnes*—a device he learned to deploy with the delicacy and skill of an accomplished craftsman.

If Dickens represents a rather straightforward approach to narration with the emphasis on a controlling sensibility, then the Goncourts with their naturalistic eye for detail, microscopic dissection of human motives, and explicit moral purpose, provide a complementary strategy to Dickens's more freewheeling and picaresque mode. Then, curiously, there is LaForgue: not a novelist at all, but a poet enamored of nebulous ideals though distrustful of his own idealism, sadly mocking and ingenuously aspiring all in the same moment. Fournier, however, sees LaForgue as having attained in poetry the immediate expression of feeling, alternately lyrical or tormented, that he would like to attain in his novel. Fournier wishes to blend these disparate modes—the realistic and the lyrical—into an organic whole without self-conscious seams. But at this point in Fournier's development, it is LaForgue who provides the greatest stimulus, for it is he who is able to project a sense of "dream-life." As Fournier writes: "I should prefer to adapt LaForgue's method, but for the writing of a novel. . . . What I mean by 'dream' is a vision of the past, hopes, reveries of long ago coming into contact with a departing vision"—in short, an experience like that of his recent encounter with Yvonne de Quiévrecourt. Significantly, Fournier concludes by stating his aesthetic ideal: "to be a story teller, but, above all, to be a poet" (*Corr. R-F*, 1:34). His first attempts to put this ideal into practice resulted in some rather inchoate material—prose poems of negligible value in themselves, though important as preliminary exercises in the art of fiction.

Over the next few months, Fournier gives details of his reading and concert going, commenting critically and cogently on Rimbaud (by whom he is first repulsed though later mesmerized), *Hamlet*, *Oedipus*, the Pre-Raphaelites, and Debussy. In a letter of 17 October

1905, after returning to Lycée Lakanal, he expatiates on the premiere performance of Debussy's *La Mer* by the Lamoureaux orchestra. His comments are astonishingly acute for someone without any formal training in music. He is especially struck by the similarity between the new symphonic poem and the orchestral interludes between scenes 2 and 3 of Debussy's opera *Pelléas et Mélisande*. Of *Pelléas* itself he speaks with equal discernment, realizing its imperfect effect as a verse drama when divested of Debussy's orchestral garb. To be sure, Fournier argues, the play itself has lyrical moments of exquisite and irresistible poignancy, but, on the whole, its effects are monotonous—the studied indirectness of the character's speeches, the portentous silences that Maeterlinck contrived presumably to suggest the ineffable, simply wilt the action and retard the progress of the drama. Surrounded by the haunting and elastic textures of Debussy's score, however, the drama is reborn, the characters live, the imagery effloresces, and the themes are driven home.

And among all those devices by which Debussy animates the play, the most ubiquitous and poetic is the evocation of the sea, a symbol of far-reaching significance for Fournier, as it was for Debussy and Maeterlinck. As Maeterlinck wrote: "Beneath all human thoughts, volitions, passions, actions, there lies the vast ocean of the Unconscious, the unknown source of all that is good, true and beautiful. All that we know, think, feel, see, and will are but bubbles on the surface of that vast sea." Maeterlinck seems to posit, here, the notion of a spiritual unconscious anterior to, though consubstantial with, that more personal and limited unconscious explored by Freud.

For Fournier, too, as Stephen Ullmann avers, the sea "was the embodiment and symbol of his profoundest aspirations—a fascination with immensity, purity, an unattainable ideal, a lure of the unknown, of adventure, of mystery."[5] Throughout *Le Grand Meaulnes* repeated and strategic references to the sea enable Fournier to telescope two landscapes: the fluvial fenlands of the Sologne and that vast symbolist beyond which, in the words of François Mauriac, is as an "unknown sea . . . the last dune of an infinite passion [which] lashes [us] with salt and spray."

It is not surprising, then, that Fournier should turn to this subject again in 1907, following a performance of Ravel's "Un Barque sur l'ocean." Here, too, Fournier displays considerable penetration as a critic; for Ravel's piece in his estimation is but a faint and derivative echo of Debussy's majestic oceanic soundscape. The devices are the same—the sinuous bass line, the shimmering violins, the discrete taps on the cymbal—but the sense of passion and conviction are all with Debussy. (Significantly, like Fournier, Debussy had hoped at one time to pursue a naval career.) Still, Fournier was impressed enough with Ravel to later allude to the title of his orchestral piece in a description of the schoolhouse at Sainte-Agathe: "At one o'clock on the following afternoon the classroom of the upper form stands out clearly in a frozen landscape like *a vessel at sea*" (*LGM*, 23). It may be parenthetically observed that Ravel, toward the end of his career, had hoped to return the compliment. Among his unfinished sketches are the plans for an orchestral suite entitled *Le Grand Meaulnes*.

Yet Fournier was no mere "Pelléaster"—a derisive term coined by one critic to describe the emotionally self-intoxicated youth of *le belle époque* who made a cult of Debussy's opera. On the contrary, in a letter of 1906 to Rivière, Fournier claims that Debussy's is primarily an art that captures the subliminal undercurrents that weave in and out of human relationships; his opera expresses, as it were, a musical stream of consciousness that fills the interstices of the words actually spoken or sung with a greater significance than the words themselves. These musical interludes and interweavings reveal, in their almost liturgical intonations, an unexpected depth and inscrutable power at work in human affairs: they express, "the ineffable harmonies of which human speech is but a faint and distorted echo." Moreover, Debussy achieves all this not only by abandoning himself to auricular sensations, but through the exercise of an unerring musical instinct "of such logic and subtlety that, in its final effects, we become oblivious of his technique" and totally absorbed in the contemplation of those "interior melodies" of which his genius has made us aware (*Corr. R-F*, 1:400–1).[6] Of special pertinence here for Fournier is Debussy's use of the leitmotiv— namely, the repetition of certain chordal patterns or melodic intervals that in their various permutations, attune us subconsciously to the inner life of his characters, the symbolic value of Maeterlinck's poetic images, or the omnipresence of recurring themes. This realization of Fournier's helps to explain the peculiar effects he attains in *Le Grand Meaulnes*—a work constructed, in part, on musical principles. Fournier's use of the leitmotiv is the most subtle in French, perhaps indeed, in European literature. It never calls attention to itself as in Ibsen (whom Fournier castigates for his heavy-handed effects), nor does it seem formulaic and contrived as so often in Dickens or Mann. Fournier's image-clusters with their mnemonic overtones and symbolic resonances are as constrained and instinctive as those of Debussy. As one critic observes, "for the novelist in general, symbolism either does not exist, or else it possesses a fascination which dominates his work, reducing every other element to a mechanism which will serve its ends—it becomes as deadly as a didactic purpose. Between the two extremes *Le Grand Meaulnes* seems almost to stand alone."[7] And it was the influence and example of Debussy that enabled Fournier, through cunning and recurring references to the sea, windows, roads, thresholds, hats, nests, baskets, indefinite sounds, and crepuscular light—in short, through talismanic images embedded naturally in the flow of the narrative—to attune his reader, in an almost clairvoyant way, to the underlying themes of his book and the undeclared motives of his characters. "My prose and perhaps my poetry," writes Fournier, "will be to the written word what the music of Debussy is to the human voice" (*Corr. R-F,* 1:382).

Before we examine other aspects of the correspondence, a final word remains to be said about the metaphysical dimension of music in Fournier's world. Next to literature, Fournier was most preoccupied by music. To be sure, his observations on modern art—on Cézanne, Vuillard, Maurice Denis, Bonnard—are uncommonly perceptive: but, in the final analysis, he was most arrested by the art of music. It is no accident that Meaulnes should discover Yvonne by following the aural thread of her distant piano through the labyrinthine corridors of the château at Les Sablonnières, nor that Seurel should hear the same music emerging from the depths of the newlywed's cottage, like "an entreaty asking fate not to be too cruel, a salutation to happiness and at the same time a genuflection" (*LGM,* 163), as he stands sentinel on the eve of Meaulnes's marriage to Yvonne. In his remarkable study *Music and the Novel* Alex Aronson observes that in modern fiction

the musical experience, insofar as it forms an integral part of the novelist's portrayal of . . . life, modifies the tangible reality of everday existence into something remote yet familiar, open to sense perception yet impenetrable to reason. . . . Music itself appears to originate in a psychologically and aesthetically more satisfying context of reality than the one the listener is condemned to share with his contemporaries. The musical experience claims from him responsiveness to metaphysical ideas and a closer attention to spiritual significance of a nonconceptual nature. . . . It engages the whole of his psyche in a manner comparable to the self-absorption induced by the discipline of meditation and the fulfillment consequent upon it.[8]

This is unmistakably true of Fournier and underscores, perhaps, those larger implications that Erich Heller speaks of when observing that the rise of music as the preponderant form of artistic utterance in the latter nineteenth and early twentieth centuries coincided significantly with the decline of architecture as a viable expression of the human spirit. "The symbol," writes Heller, "was made homeless in the real world and the real world made itself a stranger to the symbol. Architecture, the most 'real' of all the arts, steadily declined. The human spirit was most at home where there was least 'reality'—in music . . . it is the speechless triumph of the spirit in a world without deeds and deeds without words."[9] Heller's formulation is applicable, with some qualifications, to Fournier. As the inheritor of that "dissociated sensibility" that Eliot traces to the seventeenth century—the opposition, namely, between reason and intuition, logic and emotion, spiritual aspiration and dogmatic theology, poetry and science, life and art—Fournier, to be sure, did seek in music and in symbolist poetry an anodyne to the agony of that split. But it is important to note that his whole aesthetic is directed toward a reconciliation of "dream" and "reality," an attempt to invest homely details, everyday occurrences, and human relationships with a sacramental value increasingly alien to the spirit of the modern age. As he wrote to Rivière, "I like the marvellous only when it is strictly enveloped in reality, not when it overwhelms or surpasses it" (*Corr. R-F,* 2:395).

Aestheticism and Asceticism

Much of Fournier's correspondence is taken up with a discussion of two paradigmatic figures, each of whom resolved the conflicting demands of obedience and spontaneity, self-actualization and spiritual transcendence, sensuality and divine love, asceticism and aestheticism, in a diametrically opposed manner. These two figures were Paul Claudel and André Gide, and they became to Fournier and Rivière, the twin opposing points of their own spiritual conflicts and divided loyalties. It must be stated at the outset that Fournier

himself was never as fully carried away by either of these mentors
as was his friend—nevertheless, the conflict they expressed in their
works was central to Fournier's own character and it is the presence
or resolution of that conflict that drew him equally to the novels
of Thomas Hardy and the paintings of Maurice Denis. It brought
him on the one hand, to the grotto of Lourdes, the novels of Dostoevsky, and the desire for self-mortification; on the other hand, it
troubled and complicated his relations with women and led him at
times into the error of confusing romantic love with spiritual salvation. Moreover, it became a major theme in the development of
his novel.

A lead-in to this conflict between "Hebraism" and "Hellenism,"
(that is to say, "strictness of conscience" as opposed to "spontaneity
of consciousness," to use here, the helpful terms of Matthew Arnold)
was provided, at first, in the works of Maurice Barrès—a turn-of-
the-century French novelist who appealed especially to adolescents
by virtue of his introspective brooding on the interior self. Barrès's
cult of sincerity, his welcome acceptance of all moods, desires,
feelings, and vagaries irrespective of convention and regardless of a
moral system, appealed strongly to Rivière who, in the early stages
of the correspondence, valued sincerity and personal honesty above
all. We see here of course, a prefiguration of André Gide with his
emphasis on the "gratuitous act" (that is to say, giving oneself with
unpremeditated abandon to a momentary impulse), his embrace of
the sensuous flux of existence, and his insistence on fidelity to one's
urges and appetites. Unlike Rivière, Fournier was far more circumspect about all this and not as easily taken in (at least on a philosophical level).

In the first place, Fournier was instinctively antagonistic to the
elaborate self-consciousness of Barrès. His own peasant simplicity
remained an adamant part of his character, notwithstanding his
increasing erudition as a man of letters. Moreover, he remained
suspicious of Barrès's abstractive tendencies, his proclivity to reduce
human emotions and relationships to formal and isolated experiences, categorized by the intellect, and numbered among the possible sensations available to the sophisticated connoisseur of human
feeling. This was wholly repugnant to Fournier; for, in the final
analysis, it reduces other human beings to mere ciphers in the
individual's quest for self-realization: women become disincarnate
abstractions, embodiments of a male ego dissociated from instincts

of a less noble character. Now there are those who accuse Fournier of doing precisely the same thing with the women in his life, and the fact is that Fournier was canny enough to recognize his own idealizing tendencies and yet weak enough to go on nourishing them. Fournier never fully achieves the dispassionate understanding of his situation that Dante did in relation to Beatrice. The courtly lover continues to cling to and partially obscure the would-be mystic. Thus, in this regard, *Le Grand Meaulnes,* is clearly homeopathic; Fournier's dramatization of Meaulnes's insensate nympholepsy must be construed as a cautionary warning, and an exorcism of his own peculiar infirmity. Moreover, Fournier's heroine Yvonne is anything but a Pre-Raphaelite abstraction. She takes her stand against her brother and husband whose images of women are colored too strongly by unrecognized elements deep in the subconscious.

Fournier repeated his condemnation of Barrès's treatment of women in a later letter where he speaks of a category of women in modern literature who are involuntarily victims of the symbolist poets in the same way that Madame Bovary is a victim of romanticism. But for Fournier, "women are not literary creations"; they are as complex and independent as life itself: to reduce them to a mere role in the individuation of the male ego is to subvert their integrity and wholeness (*Corr. R-F,* 2:101–2, 363). Hence, just as Browning who in "My Last Duchess" wins our partisanship for the deceased lady of the jealous duke by enabling us to pierce beyond the duke's words and grasp the essential nature of his former wife's goodness, charity, and instinctive joy, so Fournier in *Le Grand Meaulnes* allows us, through oblique moments in the narrative of François where the character of Yvonne emerges with startling clarity, to grasp the fundamental quality of his heroine's existence apart from her role as chatelaine and sometime redemptress to Augustin Meaulnes.

In any case, it is the search for earthly happiness with a woman who complements and fulfills the yearnings of her male counterpart, and the realization that such a happiness is illusive and must be renounced to secure the imperishable and everlasting joy that the seeker desires, that informed certain dramas of Paul Claudel and became the basis of their attraction to Alain-Fournier. If Fournier had sometimes muddied the boundaries between emotional self-intoxication and fidelity to an ideal independent of the self, then Claudel, in his early dramas, may be said to have equally done so. The difference is that Claudel at least consciously knew the difference between the two and in his fervent adherence to a militant and sometimes unbending Catholicism had no doubts as to the ultimate end and aim of human existence. It was some time, however, before either Fournier or Rivière realized that Claudel was a Catholic, though when the revelation finally came, Fournier, already suspecting the trend and direction of Claudel's works, was not wholly surprised.

What attracted Fournier above all to Claudel was his sacramentalism. He was, for Fournier, "a man of the middle ages: a primitive man for whom the world exists as a text, a typological book of symbols." He did not share in the mistake of the symbolists: namely, of manufacturing a chimerical and nebulous never-land to stand over against and rival the created universe of God. There is nothing "arbitrary" in his symbolism; it is rooted inescapably in centuries of consecrated tradition and it is this that appeals to Fournier's "need of truth, of realism, of naturalism." His works "are true like the earth and yet also divine" (*Corr. R-F,* 1:36).

Claudel had initially come to the Catholic faith in 1886 when, after a reading of Rimbaud's *Illuminations,* he fell on his knees and remained, in a figurative sense, in that same posture for the rest of his life. After he passed an unsuccessful novitiate in the Benedictine order, his faith underwent a temporary eclipse. On a sea voyage to China (where he served as a French diplomat), he met and fell in love with a married woman with four children. Under Claudel's persuasion she abandoned her family and lived with her apostate lover for four years, bearing him a child. Continual upsurges of faith troubled Claudel's happiness. Seeing him torn and tormented for so long, his mistress finally left him, believing that this would allow Claudel to recover the peace and sanctity whose loss had never ceased to trouble him even in the days of their ecstasy. And this, as well, is pretty much the plot of Claudel's play *Partage du midi* (*Break of Day*). The only difference is that at the end of the play, the mystical lover Mesa is finally reunited with his mistress, Ysé. They expire in the midst of a local political rebellion, believing, as the walls of their dwelling collapse from a terrorist explosion, that God has accepted their love and will unite them forever. There is certainly a good deal of casuistry in all this: Claudel has his cake and eats it too. We can see, moreover, that this attempt to divinize romantic love in violation of, or perhaps, as Claudel would have it, in strange complicity with, the tenets of Christian orthodoxy, is startlingly reminiscent of Alain-Fournier who often wondered whether his own longings were actually for a fair-haired girl with a white sunshade, the marvelous landscape concentered in a child's eyes, or the light that never was on land or sea.

Yet Fournier's admiration of Claudel was not exclusively a matter of temperamental affinity. In his prose poems, odes, and subsequent plays, there is a sense of benediction and yea-saying to the whole of life, a rapturous embrace of experience in its manifold dimensions and contradictory occurrences, a tonic and resolute affirmation of the human predicament in the fascination of its horror and the resplendence of its glory. As Fournier wrote to Rivière: "I think Claudel's moral influence over me is enormous. . . . He has taught me the austere grandeur of that severity in the face of life which I have achieved since last summer. He has multiplied a hundred-fold my courage for accepting passionately all that is rough, harsh, unclean . . ." (*Corr. R-F*, 1:205–6).

And yet he would never follow Claudel in his unequivocal embrace of the Catholic Church. In the first place, Claudel's Catholicism was militantly nationalistic, dogmatically unbending, and politically far to the right. Fournier's politics, if he ever bothered to formulate them, were vaguely liberal. He became, moreover, the close friend of Charles Péguy—another militant Catholic, to be sure—but one who championed the cause of Dreyfus against the conservative pundits and right-wing nationalists. But this is more or less incidental. The real reason that Fournier failed to follow Claudel's lead derives from a fundamental difference in their respective views of the Christian religion. Fournier's Christianity was, if more troubled and problematic, of a more generous and, one might say, unassuming temper. He would have responded favorably to those often quoted words of Simone Weil that "Christianity is Catholic by right but not in fact. So many things are outside it, so many things that I love and do not want to give up, so many things that God loves, otherwise they would not be in existence." Notwithstanding that "eternal wound in our hearts," as Fournier wrote, "which Catholicism would heal" (*Corr. R-F*, 2:17), he confesses to Jacques that the Deity cannot be circumscribed by a particular creed; then, sounding very much like Simone Weil, he goes on to claim that "in each of our affections we desire God. In each thing that attracts us we may find God and the ardent desire for God. In each of our cravings it is God who lies beyond the object of our quest,

it is He and no other. For all things are in God and there is nothing
that exists outside of him" (*Corr. R-F,* 2:19). Still in all humility,
he is not sure if he is capable of desiring God with purity of heart
or of committing himself, after all, to the agonizing process of
Christian transformation.

In this regard, it was Dostoevsky who provided Fournier with
"the bridge I have sought so long," as he wrote to Rivière, "between
the Christian world and mine" (*Corr. R-F,* 2:296). In another letter
to his friend, Fournier praises Dostoevsky for the elasticity and
comprehensiveness of his Christian vision and for a quality indig-
enous to the Russian author that Fournier designates as "the tact
of the soul." He expatiates further on this quality as it informs and
shapes Dostoevsky's novel *The Idiot:* "That apperception of the soul,
very sudden, has something, at times, frightening and repulsive.
But then that infinite delicacy with which it is approached draws
tears of blood. To that gift Myshkin owes his secret, not for ex-
plaining *everything,* for he explains nothing, but for making *everything*
explicable through his sole presence" (*Corr. R-F,* 2:271). (We may
also note, parenthetically, that his reading of *The Brothers Karamazov*
provided him, in part, with a paradigm for the strategy of dividing
the conflicting parts of a single ego among three distinct and yet
interrelated characters.)

Given his preoccupation with the elements of faith, it is not
surprising that *Le Grand Meaulnes* should reflect Fournier's dilemma
in the same way (though it must be admitted, on a less exalted
plane) that *The Brothers Karamazov* is a working out of Dostoevsky's
own "burning furnace of doubt." There are those critics, especially
in France, who read *Le Grand Meaulnes* exclusively as a religious
quest for God. There are others, however—most notably, Robert
Gibson—who observe quite rightly that the work has hardly anything to do with the explicit requirements of the faith. Gibson,
however, while chiding other critics for the error of using Fournier's
letters as a means of diagnosing the novel, falls himself into the
opposite error of assuming that the lack of an explicit preoccupation
with the appurtenances of Christianity necessarily absolves the book
of all religious meaning. The fact is that Fournier adroitly contra-
venes the opposing pitfalls to which the artists of his generation
were peculiarly liable: namely, turning literature itself into a religion
(which is a form of idolatry); or using literature as a vehicle for the

preaching of doctrine (which, to paraphrase Proust, is like giving a present without removing the price tag).

Fournier's art, as he himself defined it, is an elaborate gesture of longing toward the land of heart's desire. In consequence, it cannot in itself be the object of that longing. Hence, Fournier is never in danger of deifying his artistic faculties or genuflecting before his own aesthetic designs as so many of his contemporaries. On the other hand, he realized that any attempt to give an overt and conspicuous meaning to his work would vitiate his effectiveness as an artist. Moreover, it would efface those frontiers that divide the felt rendering of human experience from the expression of religious faith. Still, as the word "frontiers" implies, there is a kind of art (and Fournier's would certainly be included, here) that brings us to the threshold of religious experience. All great art may be said to do this—though it preserves its greatness in proportion as it recognizes its limits and does not attempt to do more (or less) than it can. Hence, Fournier's observation to Rivière apropos of *Le Grand Meaulnes*, "I continue to think of my book as a most marvellous and discrete story for those readers capable of a modest and child-like wisdom—but there will be moments, in my book, of mortal fear and trembling; a foreboding calm and silence like that of a man suddenly dispossessed of all landmarks on the borders of a mysterious world" (*Corr. R-F* 2:304).

By the same token Fournier, in a letter of 1912, repudiates Mauriac's overt Catholicism: it not only inhibits the artist's presentation of human experience, but also undermines the suspension of disbelief required for all renderings of the numinous in that experience (*Corr. R-F,* 2:413–14). For Fournier, those who try to find themselves as Christian writers will be lost, whereas those who humbly lose themselves in the complex depth of their dramatic material will be found. Still, he was not without scruples when reflecting on his own aesthetic enterprise. He worries, in one letter, if his book will be "unChristian . . . since, doubtless, it will be an attempt without Faith to set up the world in wonder and in mystery" (*Corr. R-F,* 2:108). And yet Fournier's version of romantic *Sehnsucht*—namely, a state of intense longing for a nameless and seemingly irreclaimable joy—is more than just another example of what T. E. Hulme, in his general condemnation of romanticism, speaks of as "spilt religion." C. S. Lewis's understanding of this state is more generous and penetrating than Hulme's and, when applied to *Le Grand Meaulnes*, better enables us to appreciate the peculiar ethos or atmosphere of Fournier's novel: "I am quite ready," writes Lewis, "to describe *Sehnsucht* as 'spilled religion,' provided it is not forgotten that the spilled drops may be full of blessing to the unconverted man who licks them up and therefore begins to search for the cup whence they were spilled. For the drops will be taken by some whose standards are not yet sound enough for the full draught."[10]

In any event, given his strong, though sometimes nebulous, spiritual orientation, we are not startled to discover that Fournier's response to Claudel's opposite number—André Gide—is, on the whole, extremely reserved and hedged round with qualifications. He admires, of course, the classical lucidity of Gide's prose; he has cautious words of praise for the dithyrambic passages in *Les Nourritures terrestres (Fruits of the Earth)*; but he senses something pathological and unbalanced in the erratic swings of Gide's temperament, his oscillations between an aberrant form of self-mortification and an even more aberrant sensualism. The book of Gide's that appeals to him most is *La Porte Etroite (Strait Is the Gate)*—but even here he is quick to see that Alissa's renunciation of Jerome is the expression of an idiosyncratic psychological conflict in Alissa herself. Hence, her sacrifice—for the putative purpose of securing an everlasting happiness for herself, her sister, and Jerome—lacks universality and seems to be not so much a response to a clear religious imperative or ethical demand, but rather a rationalization of unresolved psychic stresses within Alissa herself. Like Gide, Fournier will employ the device of a diary to reveal his protagonist's central conflict; but when he formulates the intentions behind Meaulnes's renunciation of earthly happiness, Fournier places the complex motives of Meaulnes in contradistinction to the perverse motives of Alissa: "There will be a renunciation," he writes to Rivière, "which I want to make more beautiful than that in *La Porte Etroite*. Because it will not be without a reason. Because behind this gesture of human renunciation, it will be felt that the whole kingdom of joy has been conquered" (*Corr. R-F*, 2:373). This is Fournier in 1910. Within two years his conception of Meaulnes will gain in complexity, and his hero's actions will appear in a far more ambiguous light. Still, there is no question that Meaulnes's problems are more universal than Alissa's. Significantly, when Fournier delineates his intention to transcribe the mystery of his own intuited paradise, he places himself in conscious contrast with the "sensuality" of André Gide: "I shan't find, like Gide, words which suggest the mystery, instead I'll describe the other mysterious landscape" (*Corr. R-F*, 1:415).

And it is this feeling for landscape, this ability to transform the vast rolling heathlands of his fictional Wessex into the brooding natural counterpart of his own irremediable melancholy, that attracted Fournier to the novels of Thomas Hardy. He was especially overwhelmed by *Tess of the D'Urbervilles* and *Jude the Obscure*, for in addition to that endemically English trait of endowing landscapes with poetic resonances of far-reaching significance, these works were also, in their way, thematically engaged in the conflict between aestheticism and asceticism. Both novels throb with an almost pre-Christian sensitivity to the manifold moods and irresistible rhythms of the natural order, and yet both feature protagonists caught between a sensuous abandonment to those rhythms and an exacting conscience enamored of lofty ideals. Angel Clare abandons Tess when he discovers the secret of her past indiscretions, and yet pridefully forgets his own carnal lapses. Jude oscillates between two women of opposing temperaments: the dark-haired, fleshy, and unsophisticated Arabella, who slaughters pigs with alacrity and finds Jude's religious scruples a matter for mockery; and Sue Bridehead, a pre-Raphaelite wraith, blond, fragile, a confused worshiper of Swinburne's dark gods who shudders at her own apostasy and allows herself to be enjoyed by a man she despises at the same time that her affections remain coldly contracted in an icy circle of frigid and unfeeling chastity. Writing to Rivière about his enthusiasm for *Tess*, Fournier declares that "in the plot of this irresistible novel, and, above all, in the character of Tess, we are swept, in a dramatic crescendo, from the anguish to the inexhaustible joy of love—when suddenly, on the very brink of married bliss, without warning, and when the last doubts and uncertainties are seemingly past . . . suddenly, without warning, all is destroyed, and a great sadness begins" (*Corr. R-F*, 1:142). We see here a clear prefiguration of Meaulnes's behavior on the night of his wedding; moreover, like Angel Clare in relation to Tess, Meaulnes violates the "radiant wholeness" of his own beloved in the pursuit of a quixotic and chimerical ideal.

Throughout the correspondence Fournier remains preoccupied with his feelings toward the real-life Yvonne and his perpetual failings

as a suitor in the ordinary sense of the word. At times he doubts
if he is capable of achieving spiritual and physical equipoise with
any woman, his aspirations being too far above the state of average
wedded contentment. Conversely, he celebrates the pursuit of domestic happiness, only to reverse himself and wonder if his true
vocation does not lie elsewhere: as a monk or missionary. He passes
from a panegyric on the world of Mallarmé's *Faune* to a declaration,
in the next instant, of world-weariness and divine discontent. He
expatiates on a sermon he heard at Notre Dame during passion
week—"I am quite aware that it is above all the human drama that
moves me so. But what leaves me overwhelmed with dread, delight,
and wonderment is the thought that God was there perhaps, like
the most human, the most man-like of men"—and he avers, on
learning of Yvonne's marriage, that "it is terrible to admit that I
am not completely desperate all the same. I cannot believe that God
has shown me so much, promised me so much and will grant me
nothing—in this world, or the next, it's true" (*Corr. R-F*, 2:332,
431).

This last observation is especially important, for it reveals an
implicit avowal, veiled at times by the ardor and inexperience of
Fournier's youth, but nonetheless imperious and real. It also explains
the nature and direction of Fournier's Beatrician experiences. Like
Charles Williams, Fournier was a "romantic theologian." C. S. Lewis
defines the term as follows: "a romantic theologian does not mean
one who is romantic about theology but one who is theological
about romance, one who considers the theological implications of
those experiences which are called romantic . . . who believes that
the most serious and ecstatic experiences . . . of human love . . .
have theological implications, and that they can be healthy and
fruitful only if the implications are diligently thought out and
severely lived."[11]

No one has written more cogently on this subject than C. S.
Lewis, and it is by attending to Lewis's notion of the "dialectic of
desire" that we are given exceptional insight into one aspect of
Fournier's character and correspondence and provided with a discursive understanding of the central theme of *Le Grand Meaulnes*.
In his preface to *The Pilgrim's Regress*, Lewis distinguishes among a
number of different "romanticisms." He goes on to posit an enlightened romanticism that, born on the tide of its own excess,
implicitly recognizes (with the aid of reason) that its original desires

are a confused attempt to secure possession of the absolute by wrongly identifying it with some relative object or pleasure. This does not mean, for Lewis, that this romanticism is to be renounced wholly and irretrievably; on the contrary, by accepting these original longings as symbolic warrants of humanity's higher destiny, the romantic is able to heal the split between the subjective ego and the objective world by contemplating both as subject to a destiny that embraces but transcends temporal ambitions or goals. Lewis recognizes that romanticism in this context presents a path girded with dangers, but these dangers—notably, the confusion of the finite with the infinite, of the transitory with the eternal—arise as a consequence of taking necessary risks, without which humanity remains on an impoverished level. Fear or inability to experience the disappointment arising from the quest for the ideal—an inevitable circumstance since the ideal, for Lewis, may not be located within the framework of spatio-temporal human experience—is a necessary stage in the clarification of human destiny. But at the price of not facing down the "false Florimells" that beset us on such a quest, that safety easily translates into an iron and inflexible morality as threatening to man's spiritual life as the more dithyramic excesses to which the unenlightened romantic is prone. For Lewis, romanticism remains compatible with both reason and Christianity when our indefinable longings make us conscious

> that if a man diligently followed his desire, pursuing the false objects until their falsity appeared and then resolutely abandoning them, he must come at last into the clear knowledge that the human soul was made to enjoy some object that is never fully given—nay, cannot even be imagined as given—in our present mode of subjective . . . experience. The only fatal error is to pretend that you have passed from desire to fruition, when, in reality, you had found either nothing, or desire itself, or the satisfaction of some different Desire. The dialectic of Desire, faithfully followed would retrieve all mistakes, head you off from all false paths, and force you not to propound, but to live through, a sort of ontological proof. [12]

As Lewis observes, followed to its logical conclusion, the "dialectic of desire" imposes on the romantic aspirant two choices: either to expend his spirit in the lure of factitious thrills increasingly devoid of inner substance, or to transcend the finite round of desire and frustration by recognizing that the objects of his quest—whether they be the lost enchantments of childhood, the nympholepsy of some fond despair, or, in Fournier's case, a girl with a white sunshade who actuates a remembrance of things past—are intended to awaken in him a spiritual craving that these objects, in themselves, can never fulfill.

The letter of Fournier's quoted above where he confesses to Rivière that he is not "completely desperate," because he "cannot believe that God has shown me so much, promised me so much and will grant me nothing," is one among several instances in the correspondence that illustrate Lewis's "dialectic" in its psychological and spiritual ramifications. The *Correspondance* no less than *Le Grand Meaulnes* contains passages that echo Lewis's "news from a country we have never visited" and gives credence to those critics who discern in Fournier's oeuvre the longing for an "unnameable something, desire for which pierces us like a rapier."[13] Fournier's confession, "I would not love the land without a name so much—so that I feel faint at the mere thought of it—if I did not believe that it actually exists somewhere in the Universe," is, as Simone Weil would say, a form of the implicit love of God that exemplifies Lewis's interpretation of "a desire which no experience in the world can satisfy."[14] Moreover, like his protagonist Meaulnes, Fournier cultivated precisely that psychological condition of "extreme longing," which is, paradoxically, more cherished than the fulfillment of any real or imagined desire. Distinguishing between needs that are susceptible of fulfillment and the nameless desire that is itself an inestimable boon, Lewis observes: "other desires are felt as pleasures only if satisfaction is expected in the near future. . . . But this desire, even when there is no hope of possible satisfaction, continues to be prized, and even to be preferred to anything else in the world, by those who have felt it. This hunger is better than any other fulness, this poverty better than all wealth."[15]

A parallel expression of this psychological state—a state that Fournier will express consummately in *Le Grand Meaulnes*—may again be found in Fournier's letters: "Ah! if I wanted to, what couldn't I do. If I were to give up everything, what could I not overcome, if I could cure myself of my wonderful and delectable weakness" (*Corr. R-F*, 2:314). As Robert Gibson has observed apropos of this confession: "He was perceptive enough to diagnose his own malady, and, at the same time, honest enough to concede that he did not really want to be cured."[16]

In sum, Fournier's correspondence bears vital and dramatic witness to that lived dialectic that enabled him to transcend the first callow phase of his infatuation and acquire the discriminating distance of the mature novelist.

The Artist as Critic

The aspect of the correspondence that is perhaps most interesting to the student of literature is the process it presents of a young aspirant to the realms of fiction gradually acquiring and painstakingly building a sense of critical tact which would stand him in good stead when pen was finally placed to paper and the quality of his vision would be put to the test. At first, as might be expected, there is a good deal of groping. As we shall see when we turn to the volume *Miracles,* there are a number of false starts, a stubborn clinging to obsolescent modes—such as the prose poem—before that unique blending of poetry and realism, which is Fournier's peculiar hallmark, is finally achieved. It would be several years before Fournier was sufficiently equipped to write that book that one critic describes as follows: "Poetry and reality walk side by side throughout *Le Grand Meaulnes,* but neither one ever submerges the other. It is a delicate equilibrium maintained delicately by a man who knows how to write. And there is nothing quite like it in all the centuries of French literature."[17]

One of the things that enabled Fournier to make *Le Grand Meaulnes* like nothing else in French literature was his study of the English novelists and poets. We have mentioned his love of Hardy, Dickens, and Defoe. Another equally important example was provided by Robert Lewis Stevenson, whose novels of adventure, swiftly moving, suspenseful, pellucidly clear, gave Fournier the impetus to develop his own brisk and tightly wrought prose. We can add to this the example of the English poets. "For a long time," he writes to Rivière, "I had been meaning to speak to you of the English poets. But it's very difficult to begin. Their poetry is so pure and organic, that it resists paraphrase. Nature, for them, is an emblem of the Divine Life: Coleridge, Wordsworth, Shelley, Rossetti, Morris" (*Corr. R-F,* 2:23). Here we find that Fournier is a unique phenomenon in his country: a writer who responds to the French countryside in a manner characteristically English and whose concept of an accomplished novel derives more perhaps from English than from French example.

In a recent article, Q. D. Leavis argues that the English novel is more vitally conceived than those on the continent. "English novelists," she submits, "do not reduce life in the interests of an aesthetic concept of the novel." Nor are they obsessed as Flaubert or Mann with "a craving for logic in aesthetic form." In consequence, they are better able to "convey the whole experience of living."[18] There is no doubt that Fournier learned a good deal about conveying "the whole experience of living" from English mentors—but it fuses, of course, in a peculiar way, with the legacy of French symbolism, and the result is an original and unexampled work like nothing else in either England or France.

Moreover, Fournier's response to literary texts reveals a vigorous critical intelligence. One of the finest examples of this may be found in a letter to Rivière in which he calls attention to certain shortcomings in Ibsen's use of symbolism in the play *The Master Builder*. What he says is worth quoting in full:

Do you not find this symbolism rather facile, a thing of words and no more?—I build my tower, I climb to the summit, I lose myself in the clouds, my tower crumbles, and so on. It is all of the kind that becomes so tiresome in such expressions as "you are my princess" or "Building castles in Spain." I feel it is profoundly unsatisfactory when one can indicate precisely the symbolic meaning of all the characters: *He* stands for the sociological poet, *she* stands for the imagination, *she* stands for the past. I could wish simply that the lives of the characters and the existence of the symbols were so mingled that they could not be distinguished. I feel that their lives should be the symbol, and not themselves. Otherwise it becomes childishly easy to solve the equation A = Imagination, B = Routine and so on (*Corr. R-F,* 1:170)

"That the lives of the characters and the existence of the symbols were so mingled that they could not be distinguished"—this is the goal that Fournier will achieve in the writing of *Le Grand Meaulnes,* as contradistinguished from the meretricious effects of a dot-to-dot symbolism that he wisely eschews. Moreover, his comments here are revealing. Their critical cogency demonstrates the extent to which Fournier had developed, or was in the process of developing, those reflective faculties that would enable him to master his materials with a self-corrective tact. Indeed, as David Paul observes, "the letters show how constantly, how critically and how consciously

. . . this quality [of critical equipoise] was sensed and searched for by Alain-Fournier for years before [his] novel was written."[19]

The point of Fournier's comments on Ibsen is strikingly modernist in emphasis and orientation. In the first place, like the New Critics he condemns the aesthetic heresy of paraphrasable meaning—the notion namely, that a symbol has no intrinsic relation to the value it symbolizes and, therefore, the "meaning" of that symbol may be abstracted from its verbal context and elucidated in accordance with the requirements of discursive thought. For Fournier, as we have seen, the texture of the work—the characters, images, plot line, and prose rhythms—is consubstantial with and inseparable from the themes it enunciates. It is not a question of "A" (namely, the concrete image, character, or event embedded in the plot) equals "B" (namely, the so-called "meaning" or "message" that radiates outward from the artist's materials): for this would make "A" of subordinate and dispensable importance once the "message" is grasped. It is not a matter of "saying one thing and meaning another," in the words of Owen Barfield. On the contrary, for Fournier it is truer and more accurate to say that whatever "B" means or is cannot be discerned or understood in isolation from the artist's overall aesthetic design: in other words, precisely those encountered constitutents—words, dramatic relationships, naturalistic details— of which the work is made.

Furthermore, Fournier was very much concerned with the question of style. He wished to avoid, at all costs, the elaborate self-conscious syntax of the symbolists and strove, instead, to write a prose of transparent purity that called attention not to itself but to its subject. As he wrote to Rivière: "For a fortnight I forced myself artificially to construct this book. . . . Nothing much of it was coming. In the end, I scrapped everything . . . and began to write simply and directly, like one of my letters, a fairly straightforward story which could be mine" (*Corr. R-F,* 2:371). The result, as John Fowles observes, was a crisp and expressive style that has no exact counterpart in English. To come up with its equal one would have to imagine a "composite being: A Sherwood Anderson who happens also to be William Carlos Willaims, an Edith Wharton who was also Scott Fitzgerald."[20] We would be justified in adding to this composite author the name of Willa Cather. For it is she, especially in novels like *My Ántonia* and *A Lost Lady,* who attains that "idealizing pathos of distance and lost beauty," characteristic of Fournier.

One writer from whom Fournier acquired this knack of pellucid expression was Jules LaForgue, the ironic lyricist, who also had a decisive impact on T. S. Eliot. In his conversations with Eliot, "Fournier maintained," according to Herbert Howarth in his book *Notes on Some Figures behind T. S. Eliot,* "that the writer's aim should be to show the object as if the words were not there." This stipulation of Fournier's, Howarth further asserts, was responsible, in part, for those hard-edged images in Eliot's early poems: "Prufrock," the "Preludes," and "The Wasteland." Similarly, the hard-edged images in *Le Grand Meaulnes,* though softened somewhat by Fournier's tenderness and sympathy, derive from an enthusiasm that Fournier first communicated to Rivière in a letter of 1906: "There is no one in the world I know as well as [Jules LaForgue] and yet no one I like so much." According to Howarth, "the effect of this experience of LaForgue, and of his skill . . . was that he now had an objective to pursue in his writings: to describe whatever he described so precisely, and, strictly speaking, *sensationally,* that the reader would experience it without the intervention of words and page."[21]

Paradoxically, this goal of which LaForgue had given him a glimpse, would only be attained by Fournier when, abandoning all literary artifice and disclaiming all direct influence, he set out, as it were, to explore the unchartered regions of his own sensibility. As he wrote Rivière, with a premonitory sense of his future success: "I must forget for a time the verses I have written, and work at some job or other which will allow me to find in tranquillity what is myself." And then, a month later: "I shall not be myself as long as I retain in my head one sentence from a book. . . . Classical or modern literature has nothing to do with what I am and what I have been. Any attempt to turn my thought to that is pernicious. Perhaps it will take a long time, and need firm efforts before I discover deep down, under the literary and philosophical veils where I have hidden them, my own thoughts. Then, I shall kneel down before them and transcribe them word by word" (*Corr. R-F,* 1:164, 206).

In order to gain access to that secret something he alone knew how to tell, Fournier recognized that he would have to steep himself, as it were, in the pristine depths of his own creative unconscious and, thus, maintain a certain naiveté in his response to things and the world: to divest himself of all adventitious influences and attune his consciousness, as Jacques Maritain would have it, to those silent vibrations that extend from the inner self of the artist to the inner being of things. In so doing, Fournier would remain traditional in the sense that Eliot gives to that word—his work consciously reflecting the idealized conventions of quest romance as these exist in classical myth, Arthurian legend, and even *The Wasteland*—but fusing these with the low mimetic style of realistic fiction and hard-hitting perceptions felt at firsthand and expressed in an unrepeatable style of his own.

One critic, coming to the *Correspondence* after being swept off his feet by reading *Le Grand Meaulnes*, remarked that "reading the four thick volumes of *Correspondance between Jacques Rivière and Alain Fournier*, I was startled by the inordinate space given over to literature, criticism, textual analysis, style, and ideas. What a miracle that *Le Grand Meaulnes* could have been created under such conditions!"[22] But as the preceding quotes have demonstrated, Fournier was no epigone, beholden to his sources and without an original vision of his own. Like Eliot, he absorbed these sources, not that he might imitate them slavishly, but in order to enhance his personal vision by seeing it in relation to the collective literary voice of humanity. And, after all, he was never so far from the true source of his greatness. As another critic observes: "whatever his delight in Paris, in its art and music and theatre, he always was . . . 'substantiate with his darling plains,' a boy of the Berry, who always longed to return to his own little corner of earth."[23] In an extended passage, which reveals Fournier's ability to translate ideas into sensations (to paraphrase Eliot) and sensations into a state of mind, Fournier claims that he was never tempted by other people's books or the contemporary fashions of his day to wander from his true self:

If I have suffered rather less than other young people from the difficulties of adolescence, from anguished doubts about the Self and the trauma of being transplanted, it's because I've always been sure that I could find myself and my youth again here against the gate, in the corner of a field where they're harnessing two horses to a harrow. . . . And it's never been more friendly and compassionate than this year of pain and aridity. It cools down my fever, it seeks out the sources of my pain like lavender soothing a wound, and we each seem earthily accustomed to the other's company. . . . There's nothing to touch the joy of being alive which fills you as you sweep downhill on a bicycle, over a carpet of fir needles, or when you go to the fair, and for a moment, feel all forlorn amidst the bustling peasants and the girls in their red dresses, and then your pretty

girl cousin comes across you and invites you to the ball. And there's that
sudden joy of living (at the fair where you've met your male cousins in
their smocks and a humble old carpenter uncle in his black jacket), living
again for minutes on end, that unknown fair of long ago to which they
used to come in their sober costumes riding on the "white mare." When
I take my leave of them, I just have time to look back and see that the
wall opposite and the crowds of coaches parked in the yard are all bathed
in the dim light of that vanished gaiety—a gaiety which I experienced
there, once and for all, and now the sound of the shouting and the cracking
of whips have been muffled by time, just as my footsteps are muffled by
the grass in the cemetary I visit in September. That's what life's all about
and "your books are merely paper" (*Corr. R-F*, 1:338).

The final simile, which compares the distant sound of departed
joys with footsteps muffled by the mosses of a graveyard, is a mas-
terful piece of telescopic concision. The added tactile sensation enables us to experience Fournier's thought "as immediately as the
odor of a rose."

In any event, it was deep in the significant soil of his native
province that Fournier would find his creative roots. "We are plants,"
observes the German philosopher Martin Heidegger, "which—
whether we like to admit it to ourselves or not—must with our
roots rise out of the earth in order to bloom in the ether and bear
fruit." Like Thomas Hardy, Fournier was one of the last writers
whose inspiration is traceable to a sense of place, a feeling of hab-
itation, of "dwelling" in the poetic sense that Heidegger ascribes
to that word (a condition, that is to say, of consecration within the
encompassing context of seasonal change, earth and sky, the patterns
of growth and decline that attain the quality of a sacrament by virtue
of the intimacy of their bond). "On every page of *Le Grand Meaulnes,*"
writes one critic, "there slips and trembles the light that never was
on sea or land,"[24] But, all the same, it is a light that radiates out
of a world intimately known, freshly observed, and deeply loved.

The later portions of the *Correspondance* reveal Fournier reaching
his goal with increasing celerity. But the sources of this burgeoning
authority lie not in the realm of arts and letters but in the writer's
patient cultivation of his own perceptive powers. Foremost among
these powers is a capacity for self-identification with scenic tableaus,
obscure personalities, and private destinies customarily glossed over
by those who think in terms of large events or philosophical abstractions. This, of course, is an indispensible prerequisite for any

artist who would attain authenticity in his work and escape from the narrow circle of a personal and idiosyncratic lyricism. Fournier died too early for this power to reach its fullest proportions, but, as certain stories in *Miracles* illustrate (not to mention the intensity with which he has grasped certain minor characters in *Le Grand Meaulnes*), this power allowed him to move from the lyric to dramatic modes with increasing authority and determination. There are several instances throughout the letters of this power of abandonment to visual sensations and this capacity "to become," in the words of the Nobel laureate Elias Canetti, "anybody and everybody, even the smallest, the most naive, the most powerless." Many instances are bound up with Fournier's increasing vigor in conveying visual impressions in deft but telling brushstrokes and an imagistic economy of detail. So much depends, to paraphrase William Carlos Williams, upon these imagistic moments that Fournier captures for their own sakes—not only in terms of the verisimilitude that they will give to the scenes and events in *Le Grand Meaulnes* but also in terms of their stereoscopic significance: their tendency, on the one hand, to resist intellectual schematization or any attempt to reduce them to ciphers or symbols less concrete than their tangible selves; and on the other hand to suggest unseen essences or values that never become explicit on a cognitive level.

A telling instance of this power of visual perception occurs in a letter written to Rivière while Fournier was on maneuvers. He had stumbled upon a caravan of gypsies, replete with a proverbial dancing bear:

Tied up short under the first caravan there was an old bald bear, who kept on trotting three little steps, and lifting one of his hind feet, and then beginning all over again and repeating the three steps, and so on, with a persistence that made one dizzy. . . . For a long time after I could still hear the thud of the bear against the caravan at every third step. Suddenly I understood that he must be dancing, practising, without pause or interruption, a polka or a mazurka. . . . I believe that only a sympathy without limits is capable of communicating the life of the past, and the thought which it produced and which is itself. One must learn to dance for a while with the silent bear (*Corr. R-F,* 1:206–7).

In this passage Fournier again achieves a unique fusion of thought and image. It is at once an ocular impression, an empathetic gesture, a symbol of retrospect, and a declaration of aesthetic intent.

In another letter composed after a day of military drills, Fournier describes a discrete episode at a country inn where he paused with his troops for a brief respite. He is sitting on a long table by the side of the bar in utter silence. Everyone is exhausted, saying nothing, staring into their glasses. Suddenly a child from the neighborhood appears at the door, walks in, and sits next to Fournier. She folds her hands on her knees and stares at the soldiers with a gravity that is almost doleful in its intensity. For her, this sudden intrusion of soldiers into the daily life of the village is an event of wondrous importance. "I have never had so intensely," writes Fournier, "the impression of two existences, one external and trivial, the other such as the serious little child must conceive it. How mysterious and bygone must all this seem to her, how impossible to recount, so simple it was. It seemed to me that I had paused for a moment in the deepest country of a living soul; or rather that I was instantaneously conducted by her into those original and mysterious regions of the imagination to which childhood has perfect access, but which, from that moment, I was able to relive—or, at least, to long for" (*Corr. R-F,* 2:251).

Again, the swift evocation of the setting—the bedraggled soldiers, the oppressive silence punctured by the crepitations of an antique wall clock—the juxtaposition of jaded maturity and starry-eyed youth, the contrast between the enervated troops and the dreaming eyes of the child, (the implied question "which is the most real?"), and the final act of self-identification, which turns the whole scene into a moment of retrospective pathos, a sense that lost possibilities and distant enchantments are yet within reach, is thoroughly characteristic of the style and procedures that Fournier will cultivate to consummate effect in *Le Grand Meaulnes:* a movement, namely, from the familiar, the humdrum, the near-at-hand to the remote, mysterious, and far away.

There are many more instances in the *Correspondance* of this peculiar quality, which one critic defines as follows: "[Fournier] was possessed of an interior passion, which after concentrating a moment on the objects and persons round him, shot past them into infinity." As the *Correspondance* reaches it end, Fournier moves with surer and surer step toward his artistic goals: to capture childhood without puerility, to insert the marvelous into reality, to comprehend "beneath every instant of my life . . . the greater Life that comprehends me," to seek out "behind every landscape . . . the fabulous landscape of the heart's desire" (*Corr. R-F*, 2:20).

His conception of his characters deepens in complexity and nuance. Meaulnes is no longer conceived as a Dostoevskian innocent moving forward with undeviating certitude, but a "great, cruel angel" who forfeits human happiness not out of any noble impulse but through a fundamental confusion as to the nature of his quest, and a chronic inability to adjudicate between conflicting loyalties and passions.

As we reach the end of the letters, there is a privileged sense of eavesdropping, as it were, on a process of rare and inestimable worth—a process that not only charts the painstaking acquisition of artistic judgment, but also discloses the incidents, to paraphrase Browning, that go into the development of a soul. As Havelock Ellis observes, these letters are "a real contribution to the psychology of art."[25] And, as Melvin Friedman reminds us, "the correspondence of Alain-Fournier and Jacques Rivière is as fine an example of the genre *initiation du poète* as we have: initiation in both the literary and spiritual sense."[26]

Chapter Three
Miracles

An Artist's Scrapbook

"The imagination of a boy," observes Keats, "is healthy, and the mature imagination of a man is healthy; but there is a space of life between, in which the soul is in ferment, the character undecided, the way of life uncertain, the ambition thick-sighted: thence proceeds mawkishness."[1] With few exceptions, Keats's words from the preface to *Endymion* may be applied to the posthumous collection of Fournier's youthful works brought together by Rivière under the title *Miracles*. The reference here to Keats is not entirely fortuitous. Fournier was thoroughly aware of his spiritual affinities with the English poet and on the occasion of being presented (by his mistress, Simone Casimer-Périer) with a volume of Keat's poems he could not forbear reflecting on the resemblance between himself and the portrait of the young English poet on the frontispiece. More important, however, Fournier was preoccupied throughout his career, as Keats, with the problem of adjusting or understanding the relations between imagination and reality, or "beauty" and "truth" in Keat's more familiar cognomens. And, like Keats, many of his early works may be construed as a literature of temptation: to linger in the "realms of Flora and old Pan"—the dreaming innocence of childhood—as opposed to confronting with fortitude and resolution "the agony and strife of human hearts."[2] Though negligible on the whole as artistic achievements, these early works are worth preserving for several reasons. In the first place, while exhibiting more often than not "every error denoting a feverish attempt, rather than a deed accomplished,"[3] even the earliest and crudest of these efforts are not entirely devoid of distinction. Though obscured by layers of symbolist fustian or patchworked from minor poets with whom Fournier shared a tender and temperamental melancholy, there are in this volume lines, phrases, images, rhythms, or, indeed, occasional whole pieces that reveal the happy coalescence between thought and expression that Fournier achieved with seeming effortlessness in *Le Grand Meaulnes*. If, with the exception of two or three stories, *Miracles* as a whole is not very edifying to contemplate, we must remember that the majority of these works virtually qualify as juvenilia.

Still, in the short stories there are abundant hints of things to come. Marked by an increasing sense of inevitability in both execution and design, the three principal "miracles" from which the volume takes its title, leave us with something more lasting than a sporadic phrase of arresting interest. To be sure, as one would expect in any scrapbook—for in a sense that is what *Miracles* is—there are pages of second-hand sentiment and unrefined pastiche. On the other hand, the volume displays a developing sense of workmanship that takes us, in its final stages, to the threshold of Fournier's masterpiece. In this regard, *Miracles* is not unlike the 1817 volume of Keat's poems—in itself a collection of modest value, though punctuated throughout with work of a more strenuous substance and, of course, for the discerning reader, already pregnant with premonitory signs of future greatness.

Rivière's ordering of the volume clearly adumbrates Fournier's development as an artist: from wistful poet of hesitant and broken rhythms to thoughtful wordsmith of precise and atmospheric prose, from fatuous adolescent of puerile fancies and febrile escapism to cunning observer of human experience and painstaking artificer of poetic narrative. Furthermore, at all stages of his development, Fournier delights us again and again with images of striking suggestivity wrought in a style of impeccable transparence and rich with a sense of unspoken significance.

The Poems

It must be admitted that with the exception perhaps of "A travers les étés" ("From across the Summers"), the poems are, on the whole, of ephemeral interest. As Robert Gibson observes of these efforts, "the qualities are not truly poetic qualities, one searches in vain for rhythm, melody, real imagery."[4] The subject matter is repetitive and obsessive, falling into one of two categories: rustic landscapes of Whistlerian nebulosity, or diaphanous maidens who seem to dissolve in proportion as one draws closer to the touch. Sometimes the elements are combined: damozels in the damp, one blur against another. In addition, Fournier has a penchant for transitional moments in the seasonal cycle—especially the end of summer or twilights that are to the day what autumn is to the year. The atmosphere, though occasionally bathed in meridian light, is generally sodden, heavy, and awash with vapors. More than anyone else, Fournier's poems remind us of those by Francis Jammes. The humble village piety; the peasant self-abnegation in the face of seasonal rhythms; the shy, adoring, and distant glance cast in the direction of a virginal young lady; and a certain irremediable sorrow, are part and parcel of both poets' thematic materials (though Fournier's conscious attempt to emulate Jammes prevents him from attaining that pristine note of naked authenticity which he revered in his mentor).

It is, in short, easy to assume supercilious airs towards Fournier's poetry—but we must not be too hasty. He was capable of abrupt about-face in the midst of this early pastiche and, as we have noted, scattered at intervals there are delicate foreshadowings of future dexterity. The earliest of the poems, "L'Ondée" or "Wave," is interesting for its synaesthetic effects—a device equally dear to Keats. The approach of spring is conceived as an inundation breaking across the landscape, scattering children, like pebbles, in its wake; and, in the aftermath of its passage, awakening the gardens and the hearts of those who have slumbered through winter. The sentiments are conventional; the similes often hackneyed; the images, vague and imprecise. An indiscriminate use of pathetic fallacy is rife: the lilacs heavy with moisture, incline their heads before the tread of an anonymous "She" who appears suddenly—a pubescent female bud—at the threshold of the garden railing and then enters to gather flowers. Landscape and girl mingle imperceptibly in a kind of pastel wash—there is, perhaps, a faint reminiscence of Shelley's visionary maiden who presides over the flowers in *The Sensitive Plant*. More obvious influences are Francis Jammes, Albert Samain, and Henri de Régnier—all minor, turn-of-the-century symbolists. Of chief interest here is the wave imagery—so important in *Le Grand Meaulnes*—though at this point its significance is merely virtual. We may be on the threshold of "imagist" poetry, but the effects are palely opalescent and devoid of conviction.

"Conte du soleil et de la route" ("Episode of the Sun and the Pathway") is more wiry in outline, for it derives from an actual event in Fournier's childhood. The pathos borders, perhaps, on the bathetic—but it is redeemed by the increasing deliberateness of the details and the sympathy with which Fournier has fathomed the seemingly small but profoundly felt disappointments of a boy. Fournier recounts a religious procession at a village church in which he took part as a child: "Je songe a l'Un, petit garçon, qui me ressemble / et, les matins légers de printemps, sous les trembles" (I dream of one, a small boy, whom I once resembled / and of mornings giddy with spring, when the aspens trembled).[5] As he joins the Sunday pageant on the way to church, he finds himself next to the village girl whom he secretly worships. As they walk next to one another in stately tread and solemn ritual, his fondest hopes seem realized. But suddenly a gust of wind makes sport of his new straw hat and he is obliged to run after it amid the laughter of onlookers. To his mortification, the girl, indifferent to his plight, steps in line with another boy. The rhyming couplets give a certain dignity to this apparently trivial sorrow and compel us to commiserate with the child in his ordeal. The catastrophic wind prefigures those episodes in *Le Grand Meaulnes* where a damp gust or freezing draft act as monitor or warning of imminent loss.

"A travers les étés" ("From across the Summers") is among the most successful of Fournier's works in this genre. A poetic transcription of Fournier's decisive encounter with Yvonne de Quièvrecourt, the poem endeavors to trace the speaker's progression from the histrionics of imagined love to the consciousness of a female Other. Though the poet admits, at the start, that he was psychologically primed for such an encounter, he protests that the actual presence of this hitherto disembodied ideal is of such imposing reality that it shatters his former dreams and replaces them with something greater than he could have possibly imagined. Thence follows a fairly literal description of Fournier's meeting with Yvonne. A gradual fade-out shifts the scene to the gardens of Epineuil-le-Fleuriel where the lovers pass through a gate and thread a narrow path strewn with the fallen petals of white roses—a portent perhaps of love's fragility or a reminder of mortal vicissitude. Did Eliot recall his friend's poem, when years later in *Four Quartets* he spoke of "the passage which we did not take / towards the door we never opened / into the rose garden?"[6] In any event, Fournier's "spot of time," like Eliot's garden echoing with the laughter of children, evokes a similar world of childhood immediacy, a paradisal innocence vaguely recovered only to be lost in the compromises of adult existence. The poem comes full circle toward its close, following the customary tripartite pattern of the romantic lyric—a movement from the actual to the ideal and from the ideal back to the actual. Reality, however, does not intrude too harshly on this gossamer dream. With the same imperceptible fade-out, which formerly signaled the poet's return to an idealized past, he is again brought back into the present; the retreating image of his imagined idyll merging insensibly with the monotonous punt of the steamboat and the deserted quais of the river Seine. For all the poet's insistence that this woman with the wealth of the world's summers in her hair is a person of independent substance, she remains little more than a poetic confabulation—a symbolist variation of a Victorian angel in the house who exists solely to placate the poet's unrest or attune him to a childhood vision. She is like Wordsworth's sister Dorothy; for through her he is able to attain what he once was—but what she is, apart from her passive role as a conduit of reverie, remains immaterial. In *Le Grand Meaulnes* Fournier will attain the wisdom and distance to "ironize" in the words of U. C. Knoepflmacher, "the act of projection by which a devouring male ego reduces this Female Other into nothingness." In this lyric, however, he continues to "distort the Other into what she is not."[7]

"Sous ce tiède restant . . .," "Premières Brumes de septembre," and "Et maintenant que c'est la pluie" are all poems in which atmospheric effects become counterparts of psychological states. Landscape is used here as a means of suggesting discrete equivalences between seasonal change and emotional yearning. T. S. Eliot once observed of the poetry of William Morris that it was like an aura without a center—the same may be said of Fournier's poetic landscapes. There are, however, moments of vision, poignant and memorable close-ups in which certain images become resonant with rich emotional overtones. In "Sous le tiède restant . . ." ("Under the Sun's Fading Warmth") it is the immemorial gesture of an old peasant woman hanging out her laundry or filling her apron with autumn windfalls; in "Premières Brumes de septembre," ("First Mists of September") it is the first lighting of the fires and the crunching wheels of a retreating coach that signal the end of the summer holidays; and in "Et maintenant que c'est la pluie" ("And Now Falls the Rain")—perhaps the most distinguished of these poems—it is the drumming of rain on the windows, a shutter swaying in the wind, the piecemeal decay of a sparrow's nest on a wooden rafter.

"Dans le chemin qui l'Enfonce . . ." ("In the Hollow Lane") is the last of his works in this idiom. Little more than a personal confession, the poem describes the sudden apparition of Yvonne de Quièvrecourt amid the wheatfields and poppies of a Monetesque landscape. It is a lyric of wish fulfillment in which the poet imagines himself traversing the countryside with his beloved in a farmer's cart. The whole thing is as incongruous as the placing of a Pre-Raphaelite "stunner" in the midst of a humble Breton cornfield by Gauguin. At all events, he makes a garland for her head (like Keat's knight in "La Belle Dame Sans Merci"); then, with his head in her lap, he is lulled to repose by the sound of a far-off threshing machine. This, as Robert Gibson observes, is "his last prose in the form of poetry before a period of writing poetry in the form of prose."[8] There is little as yet to prefigure the mature artist. Indeed, the only claim made on behalf of the verse is that of Herbert Howarth who tenders the suggestion that Fournier's use of elastic free-verse rhythms, his penchant for subordinate "if" clauses, and his favoring of irregular or internal rhyme, all contributed something to the shape of Eliot's later poetry, especially "Ash Wednesday." This may be the case, but it only serves to emphasize the discrepancy between the diffusive ramblings of Fournier's youthful verse and the vigorous workmanship and firm inner substance of Eliot's crafted poetry.

Prose Poems

Though not strictly speaking a prose poem, "Le Corps de la femme" ("The Body of Woman") is an impressionistic essay that has more to do with association and image than logic or argument. Though Fournier's first published work—it appeared in *La Grande Revue* in December 1907—it presents the author in a somewhat questionable light. From a psychological point of view, it possesses a certain interest. It reveals, for example, Fournier's ambivalence toward female sexuality; and, on another level, it expresses that tension between Hebraism and Hellenism that was germane to the period. Fournier's dialectical opponent is Pierre Louÿs whose recent novel *Aphrodite* extolled the august and compelling beauty of the female nude in imagery of seductive and suggestive boldness. In contrast, Fournier's rebuttal seems somewhat prurient—the female mystique being inextricably intertwined for the young author with the frills and adjuncts of a lady's wardrobe. To be sure, Renoir would be the poorer without the aesthetic opportunities provided by velvet gowns, feather boas, or lace shawls—but Fournier is not talking about painting and it is somewhat disturbing to find him as enamored, or perhaps more enamored, of the apparel than the person. It is notoriously and unconsciously like the raptures of Nijinsky's faun over the diaphanous gown of an absent nymph in the Debussy ballet. Not that this is what Fournier consciously intended: on the contrary, his tone throughout is very much compounded of what the French call *pudeur*—an expression of modesty, reserve, and courtesy in the presence of a woman. Taken at face value, there is something to be said for this. When contrasted with the shameless exploitation of the nude in an age of uninhibited and self-congratulatory concupiscence, Fournier's attitude has an appeal beyond its seeming quaintness. Like a medieval troubadour, his attitude is rife with Marian associations and cannot be dissevered from the notions of courtly love inherited from the Middle Ages.

Still, Fournier's musings on this subject are apt to strike us as naive or oversimplified—a telling indication, perhaps, of the vacillating extremes of his own consciousness. Moreover, in each of the brief vignettes, woman is seen in one of two roles: prudent mother or unselfconscious child. Whether we see her genuflecting before an altar, surrounded by children on a boating excursion, or conversely, Alice-like, in crisp frock and fresh corsage, she clearly poses no threat or challenge to the male ego.

The essay oscillates between patches of critical argument and episodes of lyrical celebration. For one critic, at least, "the tone is correct, the writing both limpid and precise in praise of woman's glory."[9] Gibson, on the other hand, finds the writing verbose and meretricious, observing that "two or more adjectives are used apparently to release vague waves of emotion, when a single adjective, carefully selected, would have increased clarity and precision and brought music into the lines."[10] Claudel, whom Rivière frequently solicited for a comment, maintained a studious and none-too-flattering silence. Fournier's own assessment of the piece in a letter to Rivière reveals a clear knowledge of its shortcomings: "I've come to the end of my essay on *Le corps de la femme* . . . I've had a lot of trouble bringing it together and have struggled hard against its apparent obscurity and arbitrariness. I'm doubtful of its success, though I'm glad it's over and done" (*Corr. R-F*, 2:162). Significantly, the essay is dedicated to Maurice Denis whose hieratic images of robed women stylized in a quasi-medieval manner are a pictorial counterpart of Fournier's ideal.

"Dans le tout petit jardin . . .," "La partie de plaisir . . .," and "Trois Proses" are all bona fide prose poems in the tradition of Baudelaire, Rimbaud, and Mallarmé. But unlike his forebears, for whom this idiom provided the occasion for strenuous psychological probing, Fournier creates an overripe confection in cadences of sumptuous self-indulgence. The harmonics are cloyingly rich, oozing with a honied sweetness. In the same way, similes abound with irrepressible prodigality—distracting the reader from the central action and adding little in the way of mood or atmosphere. And yet the first two of these pieces was originally part of the author's larger drafts for *Le Grand Meaulnes!* A comparison of these loquacious outpourings with the restrained austerity and tonic clearsightedness of Fournier's novel reveals a startling change. It is all the difference between Keat's *Endymion* and the five great odes.

"Dans le tout petit jardin . . ." ("In the Very Small Garden") is a prose recasting of the pastoral situations in Fournier's poetry: a blooming garden with prelapsarian Eve (dressed, however, in postlapsarian costume). The action is relatively static: a series of breathless similes describing the effect of the young lady on the poet's consciousness is followed by a brief notation of the couple entering the house at the end of the garden. The final apostrophe, however, carries us into the world of a Wagnerian liebstod: "Now come summer night of insupportable splendor. On the balcony, pendant above the tenebrous garden, the ivy-covered door has opened; and a scented lamp, like a flare at the prow of a sinking vessel, glows feverishly in the depths of the house" (*M*, 140). Perhaps the only thing that can be said about this verbose effusion is that its rather obvious sexual urgency is a complement to, if not an improvement upon, the prudish obliquities of "Le Corps de la femme."

"La partie de plaisir . . .," ("The Game of Pleasure") dedicated to Claude Debussy, evokes the atmosphere of that composer's "Petite Suite"—a limpid aquarelle wavering in the warmth of a summer's day. It is moreover, a first sketch of the boating sequence in "La Fête étrange," the chapter from Fournier's novel that recounts Meaulnes's first meeting with Yvonne. In florid prose and with unstinting ardor, Fournier describes a boating party consisting of Renoiresque ladies intoning part songs. One can almost hear the

female choristers in Debussy's cantata after Rossetti's "Blessed Da-
mozel." In far-ranging and irrelevant similes, they are compared to
everything from a golden palace surrounded by pines to the voices
of Martha and Magdalene in the presence of the Savior. The pertinence of these images remains to be established. There is, however,
a moment of true and compelling significance. One lady—it is
clearly the real-life Yvonne—looks with disdain on the merrymakers
and accuses them of childishness: "But there is one insistent voice,
grave and disdainful, that intones that all of this is vain, that all
of this must vanish" (M, 156). What is interesting here is Fournier's
implicit recognition, through the hostile voice of this lady, of his
own tendency to aestheticize human relations. She refuses to be a
part of it. A small thing, perhaps—but pregnant with implications.
For her refusal constitutes a tacit repudiation by Fournier of the
devout swoons that often characterized his celebration of the eternal
feminine. For what he is celebrating, more often than not, is a straw
figure, a projected embodiment of his own ideals. Yvonne refuses
to take part in this game and in so doing implicitly asserts her own
autonomy. A feminist critic would find in this a hint of moral and
intellectual awakening on the part of Fournier and a prefiguration
of his success in creating the Yvonne de Galais of his future novel.
We should not blame Fournier too harshly for this adolescent nympholepsy, his inability to render as yet a female figure of convincing
viability and independence. After all, it is only in his last novels,
in the characters of Bella Wilfer or Estella, that Dickens was able
to create female characters of recognizable integrity. At all events,
the scarcely disguised hostility of Yvonne to the antics of her female
companions reveals an authentic tension in Fournier's consciousness:
an atavistic clinging, on the one hand, to a fictitious feminine ideal;
and a recognition, on the other hand, that such an ideal is inimical
to his development as both man and artist. However that may be,
the piece failed to win much approval. Gide returned Fournier's
submission with a curt comment: "this is not the time for writing
prose poems."[11]

The "Trois Proses" belong to the period of Fournier's military
maneuvers. Perhaps because of the austerity of his daily regiment,
the writing has acquired a certain astringence. Like Yeats, who
deliberately slept on hard boards to purge his verse of its early
Shelleyan lushness, Fournier's prose seems similarly to have benefited
from the Spartan schedule he was forced to follow. The tonality has

become biblical as well as symbolist, and the images are parceled out with greater economy.

The first is a Proustian evocation of a bedchamber. Though drawn out to unnecessary lengths, the comparison between room and ship is a first tentative gesture in the direction of investing reality with the marvelous—a gesture to be fully realized in *Le Grand Meaulnes*. The room, like so many of the rooms in Fournier's later novel, is a place of refuge and retreat—a womb out of which a new and transfigured self may emerge, or a trap confining one to a sterile repetition of the past. Here, however, like Madeleine's bedchamber in Keat's "Eve of St. Agnes" it is a meeting place of the ideal and the real, a fusing together of opposites into harmonious equipoise. As such it constitutes both a temptation and a promise.

In the second piece, "Marche avant le jour" ("March before Dawn"), the room is juxtaposed with a road—a contrast consciously sustained in *Le Grand Meaulnes*. In this instance the opposition between an ideal bower of imaginative bliss and a strenuous road of pilgrim's progress occurs in the darkness of a midnight march where a soldier, drunk with fatigue, catches a glimpse of an isolated and abandoned hut, and begins to imagine that it is a retreat of two truant lovers holed up against the world.

The third piece, "L'amour cherche les lieux abandonnés" ("Love Searches for Lonely Retreats"), is a variation on the last section of Hardy's *Tess of the D'Urbervilles*. Like Tess and Angel Clare, two lovers driven by some inescapable destiny are forced to seek refuge for the last time in an isolated château. There they lie, mouth to mouth, in a passage surprisingly reminiscent of Fournier's old nemesis Pierre Louÿs. The descripion of their ecstasy owes much, it would seem, to the perfervid raptures of *Chansons de Bilitis*. Fournier's poetic bowers, however, have much more in common with those to be found in the early poems of Keats, where "in the bosom of a leafy world" the poet and his none too ethereal muse "rest in silence, like two gems upcurled / In the recesses of a pearly shell."[12] And, as in Keats, the bower or retreat signals a first and relatively crude stage in the intellectual awakening and spiritual pilgrimage of the artist. It is associated, of course, with the unselfconscious joys of a naive sensuality, but it leads towards and is already troubled by a dim presentiment of darker passages and more threatening realities that require notice and command exploration. In the short stories Fournier will increasingly step outside the fabricated havens

of his early poems and begin to explore those darker tracts of which
Keats spoke.

In "Madeleine," the longest and most complex of the prose poems,
the sheltered retreat is already about to buckle under the pressure
of a new realization and more exacting claim. By far the most
successful of Fournier's works in this genre, it verges on the surreal
in its blending of the commonplace and the incredible. There are,
moreover, numerous reminders of Rimbaud—an influence that off-
sets the enervating *longueurs* that Fournier distilled from his reading
of minor symbolists.

The principal characters are a pair of jaded lovers of less than
subtle name, Madeleine and Tristan, who have each passed through
a series of disillusioning affairs. Unenlightened romantics who have
yet to awaken to the end and aim of joy's visitations, they have
endeavored to protract or recapture the wonderment of that state
associated with youthful ecstasy and first love. Their efforts, however, have only succeeded in producing bitterness, disappointment,
and heartache. And yet notwithstanding the misdirection of their
impulses and the folly of their passions, they retain an unappeaseable
yearning for something that can never be possessed on this side of
paradise. It is a state very much like that described by Thomas
Traherne in his *Centuries of Meditation:*

> . . . an eager thirst, a burning ardent fire,
> A virgin infant flame
> A Love with which into the world I came,
> an inward hidden Heavenly love,
> Which in my soul did work and move,
> And ever ever me inflame
> With restless longing, Heavenly avarice,
> That never could be satisfied,
> That did incessantly a Paradise
> Unknown suggest, and something undescried
> Discern. . . .[13]

Madeleine's reminiscences adumbrate this theme with uncommon
clarity. She recalls an incident in her childhood where preparation
for an actual feast gave rise to expectations and longings which that
festivity in itself could never fulfill: "The servant kindles the wall-
lamps, one by one; the shadows loom down the distant passage; and
a nameless desire for some other neverending ceremony seizes you

with vertigo as you cross the threshold" (*M*, 147). Similarly, the distant sound of running water heard from the inside of a rumbling coach seems, to the ear of childhood, the murmurous intonation of a secret and mysterious wellspring heard in the depths of the forest. In response to Madeleine's recollections, Tristan recounts his own litany of lost and defiled loves—the passage is almost a literal transcription of Fournier's confession in the letter to the Rivières on the eve of their marriage. At all events, goaded by some inexplicable and imperious need, the two lovers enter the depths of a forest where, Hansel and Gretel–like, they discover an old farmstead glowing in the moonlight with unaccustomed radiance. The place is peopled with travelers—chiefly children and the elderly—who are preparing for a journey to an unknown destination. As they gather together in one of the rooms, the darkness is suddenly dispelled by an outpouring of light through windows and under doors. Standing at the threshold is the angel Gabriel.

For all the unexpectedness of its ending, Fournier almost convinces us to suspend disbelief. In any case, it is his most conscious and explicit expression thus far of that "dialectic of desire" that will later inform the structure of *Le Grand Meaulnes*. As Tristan and Madeleine recount their brushes with the absolute, glimmerings and guesses never quite followed up, though tantalizingly alive with a sense of something evermore about to be, we are again reminded of C. S. Lewis's formulation of this phenomenon and its indisputable relevance to Fournier's own mixture of romanticism and religious longing. For one thing of which Madeleine and Tristan are both aware is that neither their experiences of love nor their inklings of beatitude have ever satisfied their appetites for the uncreated essence that has haunted them all their lives. Indeed, all their attempts to correlate these "echoes [which have] died away just as they caught [their] ears," with a specific and attainable satisfaction has led to discontent and self-derogation. In "Madeleine" Fournier's "land without a name" is identified for the first, and perhaps most clearly for the last time, with the traditional Heaven of Christian theology.

The Short Stories

"Madeleine" marks the end of one phase of Fournier's development; it is succeeded by a series of short stories each of which demonstrates Fournier's increasingly firmer grasp of his materials and more resolute blending of the "marvelous" and "reality." The characters grow in complexity and roundness; the images shed their embarrassing opulence; the prose quickens in pace and vitality; and the themes emerge with sharpness and vigor. The author, in short, has gained distance from his materials and in consequence is able to arrange his work with a steadier hand and perceive it from a larger perspective.

The first story, "Le Miracle des trois dames du village" ("The Miracle of Three Village Women"), is clearly concerned with the opposition of innocence and experience: the disparity between the idealized image of femininity that a callow male in the delirium of youth will attribute to the effigy he worships and the subsequent disillusion that possesses him when he discovers the actual person behind the factitious portrait. What is interesting here, however, is that this situation is seen from a woman's perspective. Fournier's empathetic treatment of three ladies who have awakened, despite their desire to retain an exploded illusion, to the present inequalities and disagreeable tawdriness of their married lives, is almost feminist in its critique of male boorishness in the presence of a female Other. That Fournier was capable of such boorishness himself on occasion is without question. But as this story underlines he was more than commonly insightful in depicting the ways in which the idealization of a woman by a self-regarding male may itself give rise to a horrible reaction, which subjugates the woman to a mere role in the man's life and denies her existence as an independent equal who is sexually mature, intellectually alive, and emotionally complex.

This is an important step for Fournier, for it not only demonstrates the extent to which the fervors of an eighteen-year-old have given way to a more circumspect attitude towards romantic love; it also shows a new ambivalence toward the heuristic role assigned to woman in the life of the courtly lover. The problem, which shall be reexamined in the character of Yvonne de Galais, is as follows: on the one hand, a woman of aspiring spirituality, intellectually gifted and charitably disposed, may be admired as an authentic image of Love-in-itself—that ultimate reality by whom the courtly lover (or at least the Dantean version thereof) feels himself addressed. After all, the Bible abounds in feminine metaphors of the Deity—"As one whom his mother comforteth, so will I comfort you." (Isa. 66:13) and "how often would I have gathered thy children together, even as a hen gathereth *her* chickens under her wings, and ye would not"

(Matt. 23:37), to cite just two. And, as we shall see, Fournier will consciously apply these metaphors to the heroine of his novel. But Yvonne herself is but an instance of a tradition that goes back to Dante—for not only Beatrice, but Shakespeare's Cordelia and Desdemona, Brontë's Jane Eyre, Dickens's Agnes Wickfield, and George Eliot's Mirah Cohen all play a redemptive and quasi-theological function in the lives of their various men. Some, of course, are sacrificed like Yvonne de Galais (or the three women in Fournier's short story who endure a lifetime of martyrdom at the hands of their husbands). They become in consequence Christ figures—a role assumed more often it would seem by women characters in Western literature than by men. The problem for the feminist critic, or for a reader capable of identification with the plight of women in a patriarchal culture, is intensified. For while we may admire a Desdemona or Yvonne de Galais and see their sacrifices as a Christ-like giving of the self, we certainly cannot admire the men who, consciously or unconsciously, exact such a sacrifice: whether they be Shakespeare's Othello, Brontë's Rochester (before his purgation by fire), or Fournier's Augustin Meaulnes. The complications and distortions involved in the idealization of woman—the refusal to accept her creaturely status, which brings redoubled scorn for her necessary failings (for she is, after all, a human being) is of worrisome concern to Fournier in "Le Miracle des trois dames du village" and looks forward to Meaulnes's vilification of Valentine Blondeau and his betrayal of Yvonne de Galais. And, of course, behind this vilification lies the male's unwillingness to confront his own offenses, temptations, and faults—all of which he would prefer to project onto a female scapegoat.

In any case, Fournier's story is not set in the symbolist neverland of the prose poems, but in a French provincial village in his native Sologne. An air of mystery and foreboding is maintained with understated tact and a few cunningly chosen effects: the alteration of sound and silence, the scraping of a rose bush on a window, a landscape transformed by a fall of snow, the sound of a piano intoning a melody of naive charm. The opposition between wish fulfillment and reality is highlighted throughout by the use of windows which, depending on the context, connote entrapment and suffocation or security and withdrawal. Three women gather in the country drawing room of Madame Meilant to reminisce about the past and forget about the present. In the warmly lit interior, they indulge in il-

lusions that their lives are happier than they are willing to admit
to themselves or to one another. The impoverishment of their married lives is forgotten, however, as Madame Henry, whose younger
sister Marie is about to be married, sits at the piano and begins to
play a simple melody redolent of the past. For each of the women,
the music evokes memories of lost felicity. Madame Henry recalls
Sundays spent with her infant sister before attending church; Mes-
dames Defrance and Meillant dream of days prior to the present
torpor of their wedded lives. Notwithstanding the snug security of
this gathering, an undertone of anxiety continues to surface. As the
last chord of the piano dies away, the stentorious tickings of the
mantle clock become increasingly insistent; a sudden wind rattles
the windows and a shriveled branch brushes repeatedly against the
panes. As the daylight wanes, the women rise to leave. They are
met, at the threshold, by the apparition of a transformed countryside. The snowfall has softened the sharp outlines of a winter landscape and muffled the village in a robe of silence. The scene,
illuminated by a moon of dazzling splendor, protracts the dreamlike
atmosphere of the afternoon as each woman departs rapt in illusions
of dissembling fragility. To be sure, Madame Defrance and Madame
Meillant are greeted with unaccustomed grace by their husbands—
but they have just come from a tavern and their exaggerated civility
is ironically undercut by their conspicuous intoxication. Moreover,
they have just condoned a heinous act of misogynistic brutality.
While their wives have been the victims of dissimulating visions,
the husbands have participated as prearranged witnesses at the beat-
ing and humiliation of Madame Henry's sister. On the previous
day, Marie had disclosed to her fiancé the existence of a past lover
to whom she had formerly given herself. Following this confession,
her fiancé had exacted from her a promise to meet with him on the
next afternoon at a prearranged spot. There, in an isolated house,
she is betrayed, beaten, and disrobed. No longer figuring as his
exclusive "possession," her self-righteous suitor has redressed what
he regards as a personal injury. Paralyzed by this unspeakable betrayal, Marie slumps in utter dejection in the empty room, her face
vaguely discernible through the dusty window. At this moment
Madame Henry passes by. She looks up and observes, without recognition, her sister's face, partially obscured by shadows and rendered the more lovely in the faint half-light. Simultaneously, a

young man passes by and is equally arrested by the beauty of the young face at the lofty window. He feels, involuntarily, that "there at the window is the girl I searched for so long all over the earth" (*M*, 180). But the young man on the outside is the naive counterpart to Marie's brutish suitor—it is as if Fournier is saying that such idealization potentially ends in spiritual intransigence and moral inflexibility.

Moreover, Marie appears for all the world like a late oil painting of Rossetti: a woman's upper torso and haunted eyes peering out of a framelike prison; a beautiful but brutalized image of constriction and longing claustrophobically entrapped in the contours of a double standard that distorts the female Other into Blessed Damosels or Lady Liliths and denies the existence of anything in between. She is Tess, Mélisande, Shelley's "High born maiden in a palace tower," and Yvonne—at once a caricature of the symbolist ideal and a critique of a male ethos that prefers fiction to reality, a stylized image to a self-integrated personality. As she huddles, "like a mangy little cat felled by stones" (*M*, 175), she is both the woman taken in adultery abused by those who project their guilt and frustration onto a female double, and the first of the Christian martyrs stoned to death by the rabble of fears, repressions, and resentments that lurk beneath the defensive mask of the male psyche. The miracle of this story lies in the fact that these women, despite continual disappointments and psychological oppression, can still dream of a world in which they are respected as equals and loved for their own sake.

Fournier's ability to enter into and dramatize the dilemma of these women shows an unmistakable advance over the emotional gush of his early poetry. From a stylistic point of view, a new note of ironic disillusion has hardened the images without eradicating the sense of mystery that pervaded Fournier's vision of the world. Perhaps, too, there is a note of absolution, signaled in the light of a maternal moon that presides over the scene like a numinous female presence, giving assurance to these women that their dreams are not utterly to be destroyed. A romantic to the end of his life, Fournier was also skeptical of this very romanticism. If his tendency to regard women as mediating images of divine reality seems to contradict the self-critical irony in the stories and novel, it merely demonstrates that Fournier possessed that "first-rate intelligence" that F. Scott

Fitzgerald defined as an ability to hold antagonistic views with equal conviction without losing one's sense of balance or yielding to opposing pressures.

In "Le Miracle de la fermière" ("The Miracle of the Farm Wife") Fournier offers us another story from a woman's point of view. It cannot be insisted upon too often that as Fournier matures his work reveals an increasing dubiety toward those male conventions by which women are victimized. Of course he is an artist and any special pleading would vitiate the retrained eloquence with which he probes male-female relationships. Hence, it is surprising that *Le Grand Meaulnes* is often seen as a naive and unselfconscious expression of traditional male pretensions; as we shall discover, it is a lucid and discriminating study of the ways in which a romantic ethos is rationalistically used to extenuate the instabilities of the male ego.

"Le Miracle de la fermière" presents us with another instance of marital disharmony and maladjustment. Moreover, the situation is complicated by the existence of a child. Here the mother's perhaps overzealous affection for her son is seen as a compensatory response to the hostilities that obtain between husband and wife.

Though Fournier draws a delicate pathos from his observations of the wife's daily routine, his chief concern is with the world of childhood. Through Claude, the young son of Monsieur and Madame Beaulande, we enter the world of childhood in the manner prescribed by Fournier to Rivière—"to render this state without puerility, but with a profound sense of its mystery." Through Claude's eyes we gain access to a world similar to that which Dylan Thomas evokes in "Fern Hill." To some extent Claude is Fournier himself, while the parents are modeled on the unsophisticated peasant farmers of Epineuil.

Resenting, perhaps, the oversolicitousness of the mother towards her son, or using the boy as a means of getting back at his wife, Monsieur Beaulande insists that Claude be sent away to boarding school, notwithstanding the boy's love for the village and attachment to his mother. Fournier's own experience at Brest is adumbrated here; but from a textual point of view what is most marvelous is the manner in which the local townspeople, the farmyard and surrounding countryside, and the child's secret hiding places are endowed with the genuine radiance of childhood magic. In one scene, Claude plops in the snow to make a snow angel. The boy's reaction to his humble design is one of triumph and delight. He has impressed himself on the whole of nature, which has become a sounding board for his dreams, a mirror of his imaginings, and a reflection of his wonder. Like the boy in Wordsworth's *Prelude* who hears the sound of his hootings protracted in the distant reverberation of the hills, so, in this visual metaphor of the child's ability to magically transform his surroundings, is Claude given tangible confirmation of his imaginative powers and creative capacities.

But if Fournier has captured the unbounded wonder of childhood, he also understands its sorrows and despairs. The boy's privations at boarding school anticipate the sense of dreariness and ennui that Fournier will capture in the schoolroom scenes of *Le Grand Meaulnes*: "Certainly, little Beaulande thought with regret of those endless winter days at Chevrix. Daily stifled by the withering routines of the Paris schoolhouse, he would watch the wind-driven rains of December lash against the panes. Then he would strain his ears toward some voice lost in the distance of memory, only to find it obscured by the captive morning cries of hucksters and merchants rising from the street below" (*M,* 184–85).

As a counterpoise to the dreaming wonder of Claude's visions, we behold the mother, prematurely aged, contending with a drunken husband lacking in civility, chafing her child's limbs by the glowing hearth, feeding chickens in the raucous farmyard, moodily brushing back an escaped lock of grizzled hair as she endeavors to placate her spouse or soothe her child.

After Claude is sent away, Madame Beaulande defies her husband who has subsequently grown remorseful and sullen at his ungracious behavior. She flees into the night, becomes lost for two days, but is at length reunited with her son. They return to the village in the early hours of dawn and hear, on their arrival, the distant bells of the village church summoning the people to seven o'clock Mass.

The restraint of the prose, the concreteness of the details, the dramatization of family tensions and the authenticity of Claude's childlike visions, are all indications of the strides Fournier has made as an artist. It is no wonder that Rivière should have exclaimed on receiving a copy, "Your first great step forward. Go on in that direction" (*Corr. R-F,* 2:380), or that, more recently, a critic should observe that in this story "one begins to glimpse the stuff of which Fournier's novel will be made . . . the rural setting is there, the gift of observation, and a compact, nervous style."[14]

The last of Fournier's stories, "Un Portrait" ("A Portrait"), is an

implicit warning against the dangers inherent in an unbridled romanticism. Its motto might be appropriately taken from Maeterlinck's book of aphorisms *Sagesse et destinée (Wisdom and Destiny)*, to
which Fournier and Rivière frequently alluded: "The desire for the
extraordinary," writes Maeterlinck, "can often bring great harm to
ordinary souls."

The story draws heavily on Fournier's adolescent experience at
the naval academy at Brest, even down to the actual suicide of a
fellow student. We may safely assume that the narrator is a thinly
veiled persona of Fournier himself. He describes his meeting with
an awkward and gangly classmate by the name of François Davy.
Though unprepossessing in appearance and awkward in manner,
François is attracted to the narrator and wishes to acquire some of
his qualities—a certain refinement and reserve, a self-conscious
aloofness that derives in part from an adolescent attempt to emulate
the heroes of romance, specifically the protagonist of Fromentin's
romantic novel *Dominique* (1862). Unable to subdue the well-in-
tentioned importunities and fulsome hero worship of his classmate,
the narrator condescends to share with François some of his literary
enthusiasms. This works a transformation in the boy who henceforth
endeavors to emulate the narrator in every particular. But the result
is a laughable caricature, which earns him the contempt of his
classmates and exposes him to ridicule for his incongruous pretentions to refinement and taste.

Dwelling in a fool's paradise, however, the impressionable François, derisively referred to by his school fellows as "the skinned cat,"
is convinced that he is made for noble aspirations, lofty heroics, and
ideal love. Accompanied one day by the narrator to a local circus,
he beholds through an opening in the tent, a beautiful bareback
rider who becomes the embodiment of his ideal.

The narrator, embarrassed by the absurd histrionics of his friend,
endeavors to place some distance between them. This is facilitated
by graduation. Though he receives two postcards from François, he
fails to answer and hopes that that will end the matter. When he
subsequently learns of François Davy's suicide following an unsuccessful courtship, the narrator blames himself:

With a sudden shiver, he found himself to be obtuse and stupid and
despicable. He recalled *Dominique*. He recalled that morning when they
chanced upon the young American girl in the circus gardens. This time,

however, he was entirely alone, lost on that difficult path, that roman-
ticized world into which I inadvisedly led him. I was not there to console
him, to extend him my hand in his difficult strait. Doubtless he returned
home and thought of writing to me, but he remembered the number of
cards he had sent without response. Then he decided there was nothing
more to say to anyone. (*M*, 210).

The problems raised by Fournier's story are disturbing and far-
reaching, for it ultimately brings into question the efficacy of art
itself—or, at least, that art which lyrically articulates an intense
longing for a remote ideal. In *Adonais* Shelley lays bare his ensan-
guined brow, which, we are told, is like Cain's or Christ's—a
seemingly irresolvable contradiction that reflects the poet's doubts
about his calling. Fournier similarly wonders in "Un Portrait" whether
the poet is a benefactor to his fellows, awakening them to their true
potential by invoking a vision of surpassing loveliness; or, on the
contrary, is he a shaman and trickster, diverting human aspirations
from legitimate aims and realizable goals, by declaiming a deceptive
ideal never to be attained and always to be regretted? It is certainly
ironic that *Dominique* should be the catalyst behind François Davy's
suicide. For while the central sections of Fromentin's novel are
eloquent examples of romantic *Sehnsucht,* the work as a whole is
sharply critical of romantic misadventure. The emphasis is rather
upon the inherent dignity of the ordinary—a point of view later
endorsed by Fournier's heroine Yvonne de Galais. Accepting limitations, finding joy in the commonplace, meaning in quotidian
cares, and fulfillment in family relations, is the final word in Fromentin's book. Of course, on a more immediate level, "Un Portrait"
deals with the question of human responsibility. To what extent do
our foibles and idiosyncrasies exert a destabilizing influence on our
associates and friends? And do any of us have the right to consider
ourselves exempt from the universal guilt of the human condition?
It is in such a state of self-critical circumspection and chastened
probity of judgment that Fournier will bring to completion his
greatest and most enduring work—*Le Grand Meaulnes.*

Chapter Four
Le Grande Meaulnes, Part 1

Le Grande Meaulnes is one of those few, exceptionally rich novels that remain inexhaustible to meditation and analysis. Its multivalent textures, organic use of imagery, psychological depth, and contrapuntal themes disclose a structural integrity that is peculiarly modern. The counterpointing of themes and events is virtually fugal, while the working out of multiple quests that turn back upon themselves in complex variations, demonstrates an authorial control of commanding virtuosity. The descriptive details emerge with the luminosity and plein-air vividness of an impressionist painting; but, as one critic observes, they are "fragments of a whole suspended, like the points of a mobile, from a single string." The result is a kind of visual counterpoint that recalls the multiple perspectives of cubist art. Clearly, *Le Grand Meaulnes,* "signals a new direction in twentieth century French prose."[1]

At the same time, however, it summarizes and brings to consummate expression a variety of concerns, preoccupations, and attitudes germane to the French symbolists. It may be construed simply and straightforwardly as a novel of adventure; or, on another and complementary level, as a quest for the absolute that makes abundant though discrete reference to medieval legend, ancient myth, folk and fairy tale, and the symbols and procedures of religious initiation. It may be relished for the haunting, restrained lyricism of its prose, its delicate evocations of a landscape flickering with impressionist light and symbolist overtones, its unprecedented fusion of fantasy and factuality, its insights into adolescent psychology, and finally, as a mythopoeic search for salvation.

Moreover, through tacit allusions to fable and folklore, *Le Grand Meaulnes* implies, like *The Wasteland* of T. S. Eliot, that the healing myths and paradigmatic legends of our ancestors have been lost or corrupted. In consequence, Fournier's characters are no longer nurtured in their quests for meaning by those symbols, ceremonies, and sacramental situations, that "community of consent" which formerly gave direction and coherence to the human predicament.

The failure of François Seurel, Augustin Meaulnes, and Frantz de Galais to fulfill their respective quests, to accept life as a series of initiatory deaths and rebirths that culminate in an ultimate vision of reality, anticipates, in its intended ironies, the ways in which Eliot ironically exploits myth in *The Wasteland* as a means of obliquely commenting on the spiritual lostness of the modern age.

Vision and Technique

Le Grand Meaulnes is narrated by François Seurel, one of the three principal characters who command our interest. Seurel structures his story in such a way that it repeatedly turns back upon itself. For all the surface frenzy of the characters—their frenetic journeys, purblind collisions, and desperate flights—the overall effect is that of a spinning top that never leaves the point of origin. The reason for this is fairly conspicuous: it is part and parcel of Seurel's psychological disposition, his fear of the deleterious effects of time on youthful illusions and romantic dreams. To forestall the attenuation of those dreams, to create the mirage of continuous renewal, the novel has its tail in its month. But this renewal is purely aesthetic, a matter of fictional illusion. For, on another level, the circular structure underscores the futility of a quest that is never consummated. The characters return, empty-handed, to their original states of frustration and longing—but with the added burden of conscious failure. The only escape from this is aesthetic. In the formal contours of François's narrative, the steps are retraced and the paces repeated. But it is a sad compensation for the human loss and mortal error that form the burden of Seurel's theme. Still, the flux and reflux of human aspiration is not the only reality that Seurel—or perhaps we should say that Fournier, the narrator behind Seurel, ultimately discloses. The circular structure also manifests that "dialectic of desire" which leads us, as the novel progresses, to a perception of realities that transcend the limitations of the individual characters. To be sure, that reality beckons from afar and only serves to deepen the sense of loss. But that reality, of transcendent scope and numinous depth, is indisputably there, a genuine given that intersects the novel at crucial intervals with tidings of the "other mysterious landscape" that the characters seek in vain and lament in perpetuity. In this regard, there is something outside the formal contours of the novel's aesthetic boundaries (though consciously suggested by the techniques endemic to those boundaries) that the characters vaguely intuit. But their failures as human beings and their fear of a genuine commitment prevent those intuitions from transforming their lives or curbing their excesses. It is this that forms the chief interest of the narrative.

Since Le Grand Meaulnes is a work to which that well-worn epithet *organic* applies most emphatically, our discussion of the novel shall be determined by the shape of the plot. For, like a bass line of music, this plot sustains an intricate edifice of suggestive details, symbolic episodes, and allegorical events. We shall attempt to follow these events as they unfold, allowing the themes to emerge from their original context and adjusting our comments to the sequential flow of the narrative. In this way we hope to suggest the manner in which, as Jean-Paul Sartre reminds us, "the technique of the novel always refers us back to the metaphysics of the artist." In Le Grand Meaulnes these elements of vision and technique are so closely interfused that we become conscious throughout of a poetic structure that defies discursive analysis. As Frederick W. Locke observes, "for this novel of Alain-Fournier is that kind of writing which may be described in the broadest terms as a poem, as that concise structure of imagery whose object is to express the discursively ineffable."[2]

The Awakening of Françoise Seurel

When the novel begins, François Seurel is in his thirties. He is in the process of creating a distinguished work of art in which he figures as an essential element. For it is his story, the story of his youth, that fifteen years earlier had been forever and decisively transformed. His novel, especially in its circular structure, will enable him to escape from the linearity of time into the permanent stasis of an idealized past. This is Seurel's triumph. But it is a triumph qualified at the outset by the fact that Seurel never fully grows up. He looks out at us with the eyes of a bemused child. Like the figures on Keats's urn, he remains permanently arrested in a work that records his avoidance of the demanding exigencies of life. Though successful as an artist, he remains impoverished as an individual—though perhaps less so than either Augustin Meaulnes and Frantz de Galais, the companions and instigators of his youthful quest. Though he is able to create and, in that sense, to achieve self-actualization in a way that eludes both Meaulnes and Frantz, he fails to become, like David Copperfield (of whom he sometimes reminds us), the hero of his own life.

The novel's opening paragraph immediately enunciates the note of nostalgia that Seurel sustains in exquisite minor key throughout the narrative. After glossing a nameless "He" whose subsequent arrival will have such important consequences, Seurel switches focus to evoke the setting of his youthful adventure. The schoolroom, the family dwelling, the courtyard, and the countryside are magically summoned in a few deft strokes, preceded by the rueful reflection, "we shall not be going back to it" (*LGM*, 11). Though casually broached and tentatively suggested, the theme of lost illusions, squandered gifts, and failed opportunities continues to haunt the lives and attitudes of the chief characters. Lost angels of a ruined paradise, their attempts to recover an idealized childhood, an uncorrupted heart, or a state of pure and disinterested love, brings ruin and devastation to the one best calculated to ensure the preservation of these very things.

Several of the novel's themes and motifs are clustered tightly in this opening paragraph. From thence they explode outward into a constellated series of events and images all of which take us back to the novel's beginning—a strategy that, again, reflects Seurel's discomfort with linearity or closure, his need, even in the structure of his reminiscences, to escape from the remorselessness of time and mortality.

The story begins with Seurel's arrival at the school at Sainte-Agathe where his parents—Monsieur Seurel and Millie—are assigned to teach. A brief description of the school building discloses a number of significant details. It is a "red building" covered with "virginia creeper" (*LGM*, 11). Greens and reds dominate the novel's coloristic scheme and are associated with the opposing forces of innocence and experience. Reds frequently denote an imminent danger or signal the intrusion of explosive and irrational instincts. Greens, on the contrary, belong to the world of vernal promise and pristine innocence. Throughout, these colors highlight the conflict between the emotional and spiritual antinomies by which the characters are divided.

After a rather matter-of-fact itinerary of the household and schoolroom associated with his early adventures, Seurel suddenly introduces an image that has the effect of transposing us above the immediate scene into an atmosphere of haunting suggestivity and alien coldness: "This was the setting in which the most troubled and most precious days of my life were lived: an abode from which our adventurings flowed out, to flow back again like waves breaking on a lonely headland" (LGM, 11). The startling image of the "lonely headland" coupled with the fairy-tale superlatives, "most troubled" and "most precious," have the effects of jolting us out of the homely world of familiar objects and domestic routines into those ineffable regions that Fournier designates as the "other mysterious landscape."[3] Throughout the novel sea imagery suggests the ocean of Absolute Being, which is at once the source and the goal of all earthly quests. As the novel develops, however, this imagery darkens in tone, as connotations of shipwreck and loss supplant the first hopeful sense of youthful discovery. Yet even here Seurel's image with its emphasis on the twofold surge of the waves, anticipates the self-frustrating circularity of a quest that falls backward upon itself in shattered fragments—fragments, like those shored up in Eliot's *Waste Land* against the ruins of an increasingly desacralized world.

Another arresting detail arises when Millie, immediately after her family's arrival at Sainte-Agathe, complains of the numerous doors and windows "that would have to be blocked before the place was habitable" (LGM, 12). Doors and windows constitute a threat to Millie's domestic arrangements. Among these arrangements are those that involve her son François, who confesses that he was a timid, cautious, and sensitive child easily intimidated by convention and authority. The family dwelling is the outward and tangible emblem of Seurel's need for security and protection. Since windows and doors are threatening apertures through which the outside world can penetrate, his mother wishes to seal these off. From this point on, door and window images ramify in an exceedingly suggestive manner. They belong to that network of images in the novel that oppose interiors to exteriors, warmth to cold, and light to darkness. For Seurel the warmth and security of the maternal home is both a starting point and an orientation. Throughout the novel he persists in identifying happiness or fulfillment with the domestic hearth: a womb with a view. Meaulnes, on the other hand, is associated with both roads and cold. In fact his arrival occurs on a "cold Sunday in November" (LGM, 12), and it is he who, as Seurel later reflects, "extinguishes the lamp around which we had been a happy family group at night-time *when my father had closed all the wooden shutters*" (LGM, 18). Contrary to Seurel, however, Meaulnes is continually tempted by the allure of a ceaseless journey toward an indeterminate goal.

The Arrival of Meaulnes

On a Sunday, shortly after his arrival at Saint-Agathe, Seurel returns home from Mass. On the way, he is impeded by a crowd that has collected in front of the church for a christening. Suddenly, however, "the pealing of the baptismal bells left off—as though someone issuing a joyous summons to a fête had become aware of a mistake in the date, or the parish" (*LGM*, 13). This small detail is big with implications. *Le Grand Meaulnes* is fundamentally about the failure of three boys to successfully complete their rites of passage—to outgrow the vagaries of adolescence and embrace the demands of adult reality. The aborted baptism foreshadows this failure and epitomizes Seurel's fear of immersion in the quickening currents of life, his timorous recoil from the demanding process of death and renewal as the inescapable means, according to Mircea Eliade, through which "human existence is fulfilled." "Every human existence," writes Eliade, "is formed by a series of ordeals, by repeated experiences of death and resurrection. And that is why in a religious or mythopoeic perspective, existence is established by initiation."[4] Unlike Seurel, Meaulnes will endeavor to embrace this pattern of initiation; but he, too, will ultimately recoil from its severer implications. Hence, the sudden suspension of these baptismal bells in the novel's first pages also prefigures Meaulnes's canceled rite of passage, while the reference to a "fête" anticipates the broken-off wedding party at Les Sablonnières (another failed rite) where Meaulnes will remain, in an emotional sense, permanently arrested.

When Seurel returns home, he is confronted by an unexpected visitor. A lady dressed in black (she is presumably in mourning for the death of her youngest son), is administering a series of sharp taps to the glasspaned doors of the dining room. When Millie appears, at length, from the *red* room (the color is significant) where she has gone to work on a new hat, she is surprised to see François in the company of this unexpected guest. Instinctively, Millie clutches her hat (which is compared to a nest) close to her breast in a gesture with strong psychological overtones. In the meantime, the mysterious lady, who has introduced herself as "Madame Meaulnes," explains that she wishes to place her son Augustin *en pension* with the Seurel's. François describes her as having "the look of a hen whose wild changeling is missing from the brood" (*LGM*, 15). Presently, Madame Meaulnes relates stories—to Millie, unspeakably threatening and seditious stories—of Augustin's delight in trapping birds and searching for the eggs of wildfowl among the remote marshlands of the Sologne. On one of these excursions, Augustin bathed in a polluted pond with his younger brother who died shortly thereafter. All of these details, disclosed in the first moments of Madame Meaulnes's arrival, leave Millie wondering and incredulous. Apart from the tacit allusion to "The Ugly Duckling"—for Meaulnes, the "wild changeling," will prove to be something of a swan, albeit a stricken one (in good symbolist fashion), amid the farmyard fowl of the Sainte-Agathe schoolyard—the death by water of Augustin's younger brother (another failed baptism) already reveals a questionable element in the hero's character and a less than trustworthy soundness in his judgment. Moreover, the repeated references to hats, nests, eggs, baskets—all of which belong to the same cluster of images—take on, as the novel progresses, the quality of a leitmotiv that underlines one of Fournier's primary themes. The ravished or violated nest becomes associated with the premature decay of a creative potential, the loss of childhood magic and belief, the end of youthful innocence, the failure to develop emotionally and spiritually. Accordingly, Millie's instinctive gesture indicates a subconscious awareness that the domestic "nest" needs to be protected from an intruder like Meaulnes; and while it is true that Seurel needs to be pushed beyond the confines of the family "nest," his veneration of Meaulnes will paradoxically keep him in the safe and subordinate position of voyeur, forever paralyzed by his hero's shortcomings, incubating indefinitely in the protective circle of his parents' world. The frozen squirrel in a basket displayed by a schoolboy on the day of Meaulnes's disappearance, the fact that Frantz and Ganache take to poaching as a means of sustenance, that Seurel comes close to replicating Meaulnes's adventure on a day when his fellow students are pilfering the nests of wildfowl, or that in a later episode, Yvonne should succor a nest of overturned chicks some of which have perished, are all part of this single image-cluster, which extends throughout the novel.

Yet Meaulnes, on first appearance, has a largely positive appeal. Confident, imperious, and willful, he steals into the Seurel's attic, discovers a forgotten skyrocket, and beneath Millie's nose invites

Seurel into the courtyard where he ignites the fuse. The crepuscular glow, which illumines the humble village of Sainte-Agathe, bespeaks Meaulnes's ability to transfigure reality, to unearth magic, and to evoke wonder. It also introduces an image of recurring significance. This red burst against a night sky is the first of several related images: the sparks in the shadowed smithy where Meaulnes conceives his exploit, the blast of Frantz's pistol, the wavering candlelight by which Meaulnes discovers Frantz (and by which, in turn, Frantz discovers the map to the lost domain), the red light of Ganache's gypsy caravan, the red and black drapes in the room Meaulnes shares with Valentine, and finally, the black-frocked priest and the boy "wearing the red cap of an acolyte" (*LGM,* 184), both of whom confront Seurel as a portent of Yvonne's death. This configuration of images takes on increasingly sinister connotations and highlights the ways in which a creative potential, subverted by the hero's failure to develop, gradually changes into its destructive opposite.

But these menacing undertones remain in abeyance until much later. In part 1 Fournier largely stresses the imaginative capacities of starry-eyed youth—capacities unperplexed, as yet, by the moral dilemmas of Meaulnes's later career. And, of course, it is the imagery that contributes profoundly to the atmosphere of magic and wonder. One important device that enables Fournier to transform the commonplace and lend an air of ideality to normal occurrences is the artful use of sounds. Sounds of indeterminate or unknown origin become the means of concretely rendering a sense of the uncanny in everyday events or evoking the lure of the long ago and far away. Like the sea imagery, it is a means of "inserting the marvelous into reality." This is first instanced when, on the day of Meaulnes's arrival, François hears "an unknown footstep, very sure of itself . . . coming and going, shaking the ceiling" (*LGM,* 15). The sounds of these unknown steps, which hold François and Millie in suspense as they wait for the stranger to appear, makes Meaulnes's initial entry all the more mysterious.

This entry, too—which precedes the explosion of the skyrocket— is of great significance. François first glimpses Meaulnes as he stands in the shadowed contours of a doorway. If Meaulnes may be said to embody that puissant force that makes Seurel and the other schoolboys conscious of their limitations, if he initiates the transition to adulthood by compelling his schoolfellows to recognize impulses

that no longer appertain to the period of childhood, we must hasten
to add that he is able to carry the urge to self-actualization only so
far: he arrives at the threshold of adult reality but remains to the
last unable to pass through the door. Hence, the significance of the
literal threshold at which he first appears—the first of several that
not only make us conscious of the opposing worlds of security and
adventure but additionally highlight Meaulnes's tendency to vac-
illate between antagonistic impulses.

The Beginning of Meaulnes's Adventure

With the appearance of Meaulnes at Sainte-Agathe, Seurel's existence is entirely transformed. The limp from which he suffers gradually begins to heal, while his customary routine of sitting by the
window after school hours and reading, gives way to more extrovert
pursuits. But it is not Seurel alone who is stirred by Meaulnes's
spirit—the other schoolboys immediately acknowledge him as their
leader and implicitly respond to his creative energies. These energies
soon erupt in a bold and rebellious way.

One day, Monsieur Seurel announces that François's grandparents
are due in for the Christmas holidays. He asks for a volunteer to
accompany his son to the train station. A general clamor that arises
in favor of Meaulnes is suddenly silenced when Monsieur Seurel
chooses Moucheboeuf. (As his name implies, Moucheboeuf is at the
lowest end of the hierarchic ladder on which the chief male characters
of the novel are placed according to the level of their abilities and
aspirations.)

In any event, finding his hopes forestalled, Meaulnes contrives a
stratagem to circumvent Monsieur Seurel's authority. This becomes
apparent in the chapter significantly entitled "I used to take a great
delight in standing at the basket-makers . . ."—a quote from
Defoe's *Robinson Crusoe.* Just as Defoe's hero thinks of going to sea
(again the marine reference is significant), as he lingers outside the
shop of a basket maker, so Meaulnes conceives of his plan while
lingering at the threshold of a smithy, the sparks of which purposely
contrast "with the glacial blasts that found their way in" (*LGM,*
21). The basket, too, is another permutation of the nest image and,
hence, looks forward to the dramatic upset and subsequent failure
of an adventure into which Meaulnes, as it turns out, will be prematurely precipitated. It is at the forge that Meaulnes learns of the

local farmer Fromentin who can supply him with a cart and horse. And as Meaulnes presumably muses on this fact, Seurel concludes the chapter with another reference to Defoe: "I suddenly recollected a picture of Robinson Crusoe which portrayed him as a youth before his long voyage . . ." (*LGM*, 23). And, of course, Crusoe is another hero indifferent to prudent admonitions and destined for shipwreck.

Significantly, the sea motif returns in the very next chapter: "At one o'clock on the following afternoon the classroom of the upper form stands out clearly in a frozen landscape like a vessel at sea" (*LGM*, 23). We have noted that one of Fournier's signal achievements in the first part of *Le Grand Meaulnes* lies in his ability to awaken in us what Wordsworth calls "a dim and undetermined sense of unknown modes of being." This sense is largely actuated, as we have seen through the consistent use of marine imagery. Through repeated and strategic references to the sea, Fournier is able to achieve that sense of what the French call *dépaysement*—namely, the feeling of being transported out of one's present surroundings into another and more mysterious dimension of existence.[5] It is not surprising, therefore, that Meaulnes's disappearance should be preceded by a recurrence of this motif.

On the day when his grandparents are scheduled to arrive, Seurel is the first to become conscious of Meaulnes's absence from class. Gazing through the schoolroom window, Seurel is able to see Fromentin's farm—the so-called "Belle-Etoile"—in the distance. (We recall that Eugene Fromentin, one of Fournier's favorite writers, was the author of *Dominique*—another romantic novel with cautionary overtones.) And "Beautiful Star," recalling perhaps the soaring skyrocket of the first chapter, is indeed an appropriate starting point for Meaulnes's far-flung adventure. But Seurel supplies a further detail that gives us pause: "surrounded by high greyish walls whose buttresses rise up from a moat of manure, this relic of feudal days" (*LGM*, 24) is founded in a flimsy base of ordure. Nothwithstanding Meaulnes's aspirations, mud will cling to his adventure, as it does, quite literally, to the shoes of all the protagonists. "Les Sablonnière's" or "sand-pit," manorial home of Yvonne de Galais, will be pulled down and the river drained to a mudbank. The reference, moreover, to "feudal days" hints at the direction Meaulnes's quest will take—a fin-de-siècle adumbration of Perceval's search for the Holy Grail.

The discovery of Meaulnes's truancy occurs immediately after

Monsieur Seurel places a final problem on the blackboard. "This one," he remarks, "is mere child's play" (*LGM*, 25). But Meaulnes is gone; for his excursion will take him outside the circumscribed and unproblematic boundaries of a child's protected universe.

As Meaulnes directs his cart and horse to the boundaries of Fromentin's farm, the stable hands begin to have some misgivings as to whether this tall boy is acting under Monsieur Seurel's authority. They run after him, and at this point the students of Sainte-Agathe, apprised that something untoward is afoot, behold a marvelous apotheosis. "He is on his feet, like a Roman charioteer, one leg thrust forward," observed Seurel. "Shaking the reins with both hands, he urges the mare on at full speed, and at no time they are over the brow of the hill" (*LGM*, 25). Meaulnes is no longer a rural schoolboy playing hookey; he has become a local incarnation of what Joseph Campbell terms, "the hero with a thousand faces"—a particular instance of a character universal to Western myth. Meaulnes's journey will not only bear the earmarks of the grail legend but also replicate the customary rites and events associated with primitive initation rituals. Like an archetypal hero of medieval legend or ancient myth, Meaulnes will stray from the limited and myopic confines of Sainte-Agathe, engage in a quest for a nameless goal that transfigures his existence, and then return to his former state with the presumed intent of lifting his associates to an awareness of their own potentialities.[6] It is at this point, however, that the analogy between Meaulnes and the legendary hero of romance breaks down. Although Meaulnes's journey reflects that tripartite movement that Campbell sees as prototypical to the myth of the hero, Meaulnes fails to successfully complete the return journey. Instead of pointing the way to his fellow students, Meaulnes remains stuck in one phase of his development. Instead of accepting workaday existence and transforming it from the perspective of his adventure, he clings to the thrills and trappings of the mysterious fête, refusing to accept anything of less intensity or to prize any goal of slighter significance. In a word, Meaulnes's journey to the lost domain bears the earmarks of a rite that misses completion.

For three days the members of the Seurel household wait in anxious incertitude for the return of Meaulnes. We might parenthetically note here that Fournier has arranged his story in such a way that months, dates, and numbers assume a symbolic importance that contributes in part to the sense of repetition and circularity cognate

with the novel's overall theme. Even numbers are generally associated with the workaday realm of socially organized events; odd
numbers, on the contrary, point toward that which is mysterious,
remote, and incommensurable with the mundane world of ordered
activity—hence, Meaulnes's three-day absence.[7]

At length, an inauspicious token of Meaulnes's adventure arrives
to further disconcert the Seurels. The horse and buggy have returned,
but with no sign of the rider. Seurel speaks of it "as a piece of
wreckage brought in by the tide—the first, and for all I knew the
last debris of the adventure on which Meaulnes had lost himself"
(*LGM,* 29). The sea image, heavy with associations of disaster and
defeat, lashes across the narrative with a sudden tang of foreign
lands and coralled isles; but shaded, as it is, with connotations of
shipwreck and loss, the image already foreshadows a denouement
of dashed hopes and drowned ideals.

In the even-numbered sixth chapter, and on the morning of the
fourth day since his disappearance, Meaulnes returns. His appearance
is preceded by a brief but telling detail—namely, "a tap on the
window" (*LM,* 30). We have previously noted the opposition between exteriors and interiors, the static world of stable events and
the dynamic call to self-actualization. Windows obviously provide
a point of rapprochement between these polarized states and, hence,
Meaulnes's reentry into the dry-as-dust confines of the Sainte-Agathe
schoolroom is signaled by a tap at the window (just as his initial
arrival at Sainte-Agathe was presaged by the three resounding taps
of Madame Meaulnes). But the window motif is destined to undergo
a fundamental change during the course of the novel—Fournier's
images having, in general, an organic relation to the convolutions
of the drama, which gives them a compelling vitality. While windows repeatedly signal a flight from reality or a transposition to
another dimension of existence, they may also, as we see here,
configure the reverse of that process: namely, a descent from the
marvelous into reality. As the novel progresses, however, the window imagery loses its initial connotations of mystery, transcendence,
and wonder and devolves into a motif associated with an irresponsible
escapism.

In any case, the psychological tensions experienced by Seurel and
the other boys at the moment of Meaulnes's reinstatement into the
classroom, is graphically rendered in one of those impressionistic
bits of pure observation with which the novel so richly abounds.

After the truant returns to his seat, Seurel observes that "now and then le grand Meaulnes glanced towards me, or looked out of the window through which one could see the garden as white as cotton, all life arrested, and fields abandoned except for an occasional crow. In the class-room the red stove gave out an oppressive heat" (*LGM*, 31). The juxtaposition here between the lure of lonely distances and the mediocre confines of the schoolroom, the frigid fascination of the snowy fields and the suffocating warmth of the red stove, not only expresses the irrepressible yearnings that smoulder beneath the drab routines of the schoolroom, but the lingering enchantments of Meaulnes's unknown adventure, which is still apparent in the rapt gaze of the truant who appears as though "under a spell" (*LGM*, 30).

From this point on, Meaulnes, the former leader and acknowledged master of the schoolyard is slowly but steadily estranged from his peers, alienated by the experience he has undergone and resented by the companions he has outgrown. He becomes secretive and withdrawn—preoccupied with the construction of a map that he zealously protects from the eyes of his envious schoolmates. Only Seurel learns of the reasons for this change.

In an episode that significantly reverses the situation established at the beginning of the novel, Meaulnes locks himself in the classroom to work in unmolested concentration upon his map—and it is now the ordinary schoolboys of Sainte-Agathe who foil him by bursting through the window. Clearly, this reversal points to Meaulnes's need for a period of introspection in the wake of his adventure, an increase in self-understanding if the impulses there actuated are to reach fruition. But unfortunately this period of self-examination is suspended before Meaulnes achieves the maturity and equipose necessary for the fulfillment of his quest.

But what were the elements of Meaulnes's quest? Where has he gone? What has he seen? Whom has he spoken to? To build suspense, Seurel purposely keeps us in the dark. Significantly, it is in the odd-numbered chapter 7 that Meaulnes finally reveals the particulars of his pilgrimage.

Meaulnes's Rite of Passage

Chapter 7 takes us to the draughty attic bedroom of Fournier's childhood. Seurel shares this room with his mentor whom we observe pacing it "like those sailors who can never shake off the habit of keeping watch and in the heart of some Breton retreat get up and dress at regular intervals to inspect an earthly horizon" (*LGM*, 36). Again the note of *dépaysement* is delicately but tellingly struck. But a genuine shiver possesses Seurel and is communicated to the reader when Meaulnes, undressing for the night, reveals beneath his schoolboy smock, a glorious waistcoat of a bygone era, resplendent with silk and mother-of-pearl. We have apprehended something all along and the waistcoat, like a veritable talisman from the land of faerie, gives objective and tangible evidence of Meaulnes's having moved about in worlds not realized. But François's inquiries and solicitations go unheeded and the tall boy whose shadow looms prodigiously against the attic wall settles into bed without a murmur of response.

Two months pass; February arrives. Unable to suppress the memories by which he is haunted, Meaulnes attempts to reenact his former flight. But Seurel awakens and argues the futility of such a quest across a landscape buried in darkness and without guideposts. Meaulnes hesitates and at midnight on the second month of his return (all even numbers and, therefore, inappropriate for further adventures),[8] he reveals his secret.

The novel now turns backward on itself: two months and four chapters to be exact. We are in the ordinary world of Sainte-Agathe as Meaulnes, having stolen the cart and horse, strikes towards the train station to retrieve Seurel's grandparents. But gradually and imperceptibly Meaulnes's delinquent behavior assumes the status of a magical quest. Taking a wrong turn, Meaulnes becomes lost. The countryside is now "a vast frozen plain devoid of landmarks" (*LGM*, 40). Its desolation and haunting stillness are further accentuated by the sudden movement of a bird—"a magpie which rose in alarm and flapped away to perch on the stump of an elm" (*LGM*, 40). Presently Meaulnes falls asleep; and when he awakes, the scene is transformed. He arrives at a crossroads and injures both his head and knee as he stumbles from the cart to dislodge a stone from the mare's hoof. Of course, Meaulnes is now on the archetypal road of a fairy tale. The crossroads bear allegorical witness to a psychic quest that obliges Meaulnes to leave familiar guideposts and well-trodden thoroughfares behind. He has entered the enchanted forest of saga and legend, familiar to us from the Brothers Grimm, Charles Perrault, tales of chivalry, and the bucolic romances of Shakespeare. The image of a traveler, be it Dante, the Red Cross Knight, or

Hansel and Gretel, lost in the environing gloom of a thick forest invariably denotes that "psychic chaos" and disorientation that, according to Mircea Eliade, give imminent "sign that the profane man is undergoing dissolution and that a new personality is on the way of birth."[9]

But Meaulnes never achieves this final "birth." The cost of following a single road to its end—for the path is narrow and strait is the gate—is finally too much for him. And the many roads that traverse this novel—the map Meaulnes constructs with the presumed intent of completing his quest; the dead end where Meaulnes and Seurel are ambushed; the trail Seurel follows in an attempt to repeat Meaulnes's adventure; the road through Bourges "flanked by brothels, offering no remedy for the deep sorrows of a pure love" (*LGM,* 201)—are all reminders of the original road that Meaulnes fails to thread successfully. Because he mistakes the afflatus of departure with the shrine of his seeking, Meaulnes is forever fated to engage in a self-frustrating journey, a "dialectic of desire" in which he confuses a particular road with "the unnameable something it symbolizes" and toward which it points. To love only to seek, on condition of never finding, condemns Meaulnes to a perpetual disquietude.

But as Meaulnes awakens for the first time in this new and transfigured landscape, the quest is still pristine and the promise undefiled. The wounds Meaulnes sustains on getting down from the cart not only connect him symbolically with François and Frantz (and beyond that with Yvonne and her child), they are also equivalent to the symbolic wounds sustained in primitive cultures by young novitiates in preparation for adulthood. The wounds represent the death of the old unawakened self and signal the candidate's rebirth to a higher, more complex plane of existence.

Throughout these episodes that treat of Meaulnes's adventure, we become especially conscious of Fournier's ability to weave commonplace incidents into a highly wrought fabric that blends the marvelous with reality. But the marvelous here is not merely a matter of vague atmospherics (though Fournier is astonishingly adroit in creating the appropriate tonality for Meaulnes's adventure). While we remain in close and immediate contact with the topographical features of the Cher valley, we are gradually translated into a timeless domain in which two interdependent realities—the existence of the subconscious and the presence of the sacred—are simultaneously disclosed.

The fact that Meaulnes falls asleep immediately before his arrival and after his departure from the lost domain, adds, of course, to its dreamlike quality, but also underlines its significance as a symbolic projection of subconscious forces gathering to a crisis in the final stages of Meaulnes's adolescence.

In any event, roving about in a dark and silent landscape, the stillness of which is mysteriously heightened by Fournier through the use of contrast ("now and then a dead branch would catch the spokes of a wheel and break off with a snap") (*LGM,* 41), Meaulnes presently descries "through the branches a faint glimmer of light" (*LGM,* 42). This is the first temptation Meaulnes successfully overcomes: the temptation, namely, to retreat to an earlier, less complex phase of his existence, crystalized here in the maternal security of a farmhouse whose benevolent peasant owners entreat him to stay for the night. After trampling on the chrysanthemums outside the window, Meaulnes lingers characteristically at the threshold. (The trodden flower of gold signals, perhaps, the end of childhood's golden age or possibly points forward to the ruined paradise of the "fête étrange" whose promise is never fulfilled.)[10] Caught between conflicting impulses—the desire to stay and the longing to depart— Meaulnes ventures outside to blanket his horse only to find himself swallowed by the darkness and unable to find his way back.

After much wandering, he arrives at a sheepfold, draws up his knees in an embryonic pose and dreams of a "green apartment with curtains the color of foliage" where a girl sits sewing by the window. The next morning he trudges on (famished and limping from a swollen knee). Save for a shepherdess in the distance, he is utterly alone. (The shepherdess, of course is a plausible bucolic detail, but at the same time she subtly suggests a world as remote as Tempe or the dales of Arcady.) Meaulnes's isolation is broken, at length, as he approaches a colonnade of firs that echoes with the voices of approaching children. To avoid frightening them, he hides and overhears a strange conversation to the effect that these children have the run for a day of a remote manor where a wedding festivity is in preparation.

When seen in the light of primitive initiation rituals, the bewildering incidents surrounding Meaulnes's adventure take on a strange and compelling logic. As Mircea Eliade has demonstrated in his book *The Sacred and the Profane*, these primitive rites generally follow an established pattern, notwithstanding certain incidental variations.[11] And the whole of Meaulnes's adventure conforms remarkably to these patterns. The novice's confirmation generally begins with a period of separation from his family during which he is isolated in a remote wilderness, and cared for by a group of select elders as if he were an infant. This return to the primal virtuality of infancy (we recall Meaulnes's embryonic pose) precedes a series of ordeals (fasting, symbolic wounds) that signal the death of his former self, and prepare for his rebirth as an adult. The novice is then initiated into an awareness of those fundamental realities that undergird human existence. These realities involve a perception of and acquiescence in the generational cycles of death and birth—an understanding, in other words, of the interdependence of sexual procreation and human mortality. Finally, the novice is instructed in the mysteries of that ultimate, unsearchable Being through whom the patterns of human generation acquire the quality of a divine sacrament. Death, sexuality, and the sacred—these, then, are the three principal elements of human experience which Meaulnes will confront at the lost domain.

The sexual element in Meaulnes's initiation is already prefigured in the dream of the "green room." This is complemented by another dream that occurs on the following evening—a memory of his mother seated at the piano (which foreshadows, of course, the meeting with Yvonne). Interestingly, pianos and sewing machines function as symbolic counterparts throughout the novel and connect each of the female figures with Meaulnes's subconscious image of the eternal feminine. François's mother, as we have seen, is a seamstress who designs her own hats; Yvonne appears, like Meaulnes's mother in his dream, seated at the piano; and Valentine earns her living as a seamstress. Moreover, each of these women may be construed as variants of that buried feminine component that each man carries in his unconscious—what the Swiss psychologist Carl Gustav Jung refers to as the "anima" or feminine portion of the male ego. At the moment of "falling in love," according to Jung, this unconscious image—partly derived from ancestral memories, partly colored by a child's first contact with women—attaches itself to a particular woman: hence the coalescent images of femininity that cluster about Yvonne. (Significantly, both Meaulnes's mother and Yvonne are associated with mother hens whose fledglings are missing from their brood.) The homophonic resemblance between the French words *mère* (mother) and *mer* (sea) is surely no coincidence and underscores the relationship here between human sexual impulses and the great fertile womb of uncreated being. Meaulnes's courtship of Yvonne at the lost domain brings both of these realities to the fore.

It also involves them in a primitive reversion to childhood—a reversion that is not all that unusual when placed in the context of modern psychology. Scientists have observed that the mating calls of birds resemble the sounds of newborn fledglings and everyone is familiar with the endearing diminutives, the so-called "billing and cooing" that characterizes the first stages of the human "mating process." Meaulnes's failure, however, lies in his unwillingness to grow beyond the early courtship stages of sexual attraction. He remains infatuated with the image of himself as a hero of romance and, in consequence, fails to enter fully the world of adult responsibility. Similarly, he is unable to discriminate between the fairy-tale image he projects on Yvonne and the real flesh-and-blood woman who has distinct needs and perceptions of her own. Moreover, it is his failure to integrate his conception of woman into a composite whole that later divides him between Yvonne and Valentine. Each of these women is associated with a fragmentary portion of Meaulnes's anima. In consequence, Meaulnes remains divided between the chaste and disincarnate image of Yvonne and the seductive, potentially explosive image of Valentine.

But it would be a mistake to assume that the episode of the "fête étrange" is entirely reducible to clinical psychology. Meaulnes's initiation involves both a religious and ontological dimension, which Fournier has been at pains to suggest. The sleep with which Meaulnes's adventure is rounded not only connects the events at the lost domain with Meaulnes's subconscious but also hints of the atemporal nature of Meaulnes's experience. Commenting on that moment in the rite of passage where the initiate reverts to a childlike state, Eliade observes that "this state is meant not only in terms of human physiology but also in terms of regression to virtual, precosmic life"—to the womb, in short, of uncreated being. [12] The fête étrange involves, then, a recognition of that second component in the rite of passage: the reality of the sacred. Like the Gardens of Adonis in Spenser's *Faerie Queene*, the lost domain represents the original ground of being or precosmic womb out of which all life proceeds. Thus the revelers dress in period costumes, embracing and, hence, transcending the manifold changes of history. The party itself is a saturnalia and takes place during Christmas. Furthermore, although it is midwinter, a springlike warmth involves the season and adds to the sense of atemporality. "Mid-winter spring is its own season / Sempiternal though sodden towards sundown," writes Eliot on the moment of Pentecost in *Four Quartets*.[13] Here, too, "mid-winter" spring suggests the moment of the intersection of eternity with time, the sense of an infinite present, an eternal now, which both Fournier and Eliot associate with the immediacy of childhood. These larger archetypal concerns and mythic elements enable Fournier to sustain the atmosphere of ideality and the sense of mystery that inform Meaulnes's experience at the lost domain.

After entering the château *through a window*, Meaulnes finds himself in a room cluttered with miscellaneous objects. Among these are a lute with broken strings, a candlelabra, and a large oval mirror. The broken lute recalls the figure of Orpheus; the mirror, of Narcissus. Like the mythic poet Orpheus, Meaulnes fails to retrieve his lost Euridyce from the underworld (which must be construed as a failure to dissociate and, hence, liberate Yvonne from her status as an idealized projection of his own ego); and, like Narcissus, Meaulnes never outgrows the self-infatuation of adolscence. (The episode at the fête where Meaulnes admires himself in a standing pool is especially pertinent here.)

Moreover, the items that clutter Meaulnes's bed at Les Sablonnières (the candlelabra and broken lute) point to the sexual element in Meaulnes's rite of passage. They are symbolic descendents of the lance and cup sought after by the knights of the Holy Grail; and like the lance and cup, they may be construed on one level as emblems of sexual fertility. Meaulnes's polarized conception of femininity—Yvonne and Valentine, virgin and harlot—is never fully resolved. In consequence, he vacillates between opposing images of womanhood and fails to establish an authentic relationship with either his mistress or his wife.

But here, at the inception of Meaulnes's spiritual passage, these failures are not yet apparent. As he climbs into bed, the silence of the room is punctuated at intervals by the "muffled wailing of the December wind" (*LGM*, 51)—another instance of Fournier's use of contrast. Immediately before Meaulnes drifts into sleep, he is suddenly arrested by a distant music of indeterminate origin (just as

Millie and François in the first chapter are disoriented by the sound of footfalls from an attic presumably empty). The music is a prelude to Meaulnes's transfiguration over the next few days (it is, in fact, the piano of Yvonne de Galais), and, as we have formerly noted in our discussion of Fournier's letters, facilitates the isolation of "the individual from the society of his contemporaries, make[s] him aware of his separateness and, finally, provide[s] a personal significance to his life."[14]

And yet notwithstanding the many inexplicable occurrences that diversify Meaulnes's experience at the domain, we never lose touch with the matter-of-fact basis of this fête. When Meaulnes awakes several hours later, it is dark and the room is illumined by a *green* lantern hung at the window—Meaulnes's dream of the "green room" has become a reality. Gradually the mundane particulars of this strange celebration begin to emerge. Meaulnes's sleep is disturbed by the acerbic voices of two sceptical clowns who have been hired to entertain the guests. One of them is to have an important role in the events that follow. Ganache, or the Pierrot of the fête, may be taken, in Fournier's own words, as a "subconscious projection of the self."[15] He is described as having "the look of a drowned man stretched out on a slab" (*LGM*, 62)—again we recall the canceled baptism, the death of Meaulnes's younger brother, the sea imagery with its portent of shipwreck. Ganache (or "good-for-nothing" as his name indicates in French) is, indeed, the unexorcized, irrational side of Meaulnes's ego, which needs to be recognized, confronted, and subordinated through a conscious effort of the will. In the company of Frantz de Galais, he dogs Meaulnes's footsteps throughout the novel. And despite his redeeming fidelity to the mercurial Frantz, his appearance invariably portends a break-up of psychological balance and a disruption of emotional poise. Moreover, as Eliade observes, the rite of passage frequently entails the covering of the neophyte with a white powder that mimics the aspect of death. As the white-faced Pierrot, Ganache is the dead or dying portion of Meaulnes's psyche, which is undergoing the travails of rebirth. It is significant, therefore, that Ganache leads the other revelers in a wild dance through the labyrinthine corridors of the château—a tacit allusion, perhaps, to medieval images of the dance of death.

In any event, after Meaulnes awakens and regales himself like a costumed hero from the novels of George Sand, he enters the main building where the festivities are in progress. To create the sense

of timeless immediacy, the narrative switches to the present tense
as a pair of girls sweep by, their "wide skirts swirling, and billowing"
(*LGM,* 55), like two dancers caught in vibrant color and foreshort-
ened perspective by Degas. A group of children pass by speaking
in awed tones of Frantz's fiancée. "My mother," observes one, "said
she had a black dress and a muslin collar and looked like a pretty
pierrot" *LGM,* 56). (Though far more sympathetic than Ganache,
Valentine—a kind of female counterpart to the Pierrot of the fête—
will become in part 3 the poor scapegoat of Meaulnes's frustrations.)

As yet, however, Valentine is merely a nebulous figure, Frantz's
bride-to-be, the honorary beneficiary of this extravagant party for
whom everyone is waiting. As Meaulnes enters a long dining room,
he joins a group of garrulous peasants seated at a table and learns
more particulars of the wedding feast. The meal is interrupted by
the appearance of Pierrot. (The kaleidoscopic whirl with which
events succeed each other at the fête étrange contributes to the sense
that these episodes, though perfectly explicable, are somehow out
of space and out of time.)

It is interesting that during his meal Meaulnes is overcome by a
nameless sense of remorse. As he looks about at the kindly faces of
the elderly peasant guests (one of whom turns out to be none other
than Seurel's Aunt Moinel), he feels a sense of comfort and absolution
as if for some unspoken wrong or heinous action. What are we to
make of this? Does Meaulnes's guilt spring from a subconscious
recognition that he is unfit, as yet, for induction into that threefold
mystery that the fête discloses? Or does it anticipate, in some imponderable way, the callow behavior that later characterizes his
relations with both Yvonne and Valentine?

In any event, he is soon swept up into the train of revelers who
dance attendance upon the seductive Pierrot. Meaulnes, "losing all
sense of identity" (*LGM,* 59)—in other words, experiencing the
dissolution of the old prepubescent self as he confronts headlong
both the threatening realities and creative possibilities of conscious
adulthood—is, at length, separated from the other revelers and
finds himself alone, following the aural thread of a distant piano
(the same he had heard on his first night at the domain) to the
hushed enclosure and sovereign shrine of the lost domain.

This is the climactic moment of Meaulnes's rite—a moment
similar to that of Keats's knight-at-arms who enters the fairy grotto
of *la belle dame sans merci,* or, of Keats himself in *The Fall of Hyperion*

where he tastes the cordial profferred by the priestess Moneta and is inducted into the sacred mysteries of human existence. Like Keats, in the famous "Ode on Melancholy," Meaulnes has entered the "temple of delight" where under the aegis of a veiled priestess he will simultaneously taste the joy and sorrow, ecstasy and pain, delight and dole of human existence. His initiation, like Keats's in so many poems that enact this primitive and paradigmatic ritual, will involve a recognition that a total surrender to sensuous beauty and mortal fellowship invariably entails a recognition of the brevity of all beauty and the fragility of human love—that the sexual act carries consequences that last for the rest of our adult lives and exacts responsibilities to the sacred principle of life itself: in other words, to that unknowable essence through whom the singularly rare privilege of existence is conferred. In a word, Meaulnes becomes here a representative figure, an individual instance of a universal pattern endlessly repeated in myriad identities and through successive generations. When he returns from this initiatory fête, "he will no longer be the child he was . . . he will have undergone," in the words of Mircea Eliade, "a series of initiatory ordeals which compel him . . . to assume a new mode of being, that which is proper to an adult—namely that which is conditioned by the almost simultaneous revelation of the sacred, of death, and of sexuality."[16]

But Meaulnes's behavior at this point, as well as in subsequent episodes, reveals a timorousness of disposition beneath the schoolboy bravado he assumes so easily on the Sainte-Agathe playground. He will remain, to the end, unable to reconcile himself to the loss of childhood innocence and fearful in the face of life's inexorable demands.

This timorousness betrays itself at the moment of his meeting with Yvonne de Galais. He enters a room full of children quietly turning the pages of picture books. In the alcove a young girl in a brown cloak is playing the piano. But Meaulnes remains with the children, refusing to cross the threshold, or even to glimpse the young girl's face. "Meaulnes," we are told, "was now immersed in a deep and wonderfully peaceful enchantment" (*LGM*, 60). The verb "immersed" with its baptismal connotations and its association with the image of the sea—emblematic source of all life—brings us to the heart of Meaulnes's initiation. The fusion here of water imagery and music is a particular instance of a metaphorical motif which Alex Aronson in his book *Music and the Novel* repeatedly discerns in modern fiction. As Aronson observes, "implied in the metaphor is the image of the listener who by immersing himself in music, 'melts' into it, 'dissolves,' and finally, 'drowns' in it. Equally suggestive are images of transparency, of timelessness, of the regular coming and going of waves. The calm surface of the sea, the unruffled expanse of lakes . . . are associated in the writer's mind with . . . the return to some primordial element of being, the very essence of femininity, the cradle of all life."[17]

These words are singularly apposite to Meaulnes's situation, Fournier's imagery, and to that young girl, "the essence of femininity," whom we later discover to be Yvonne de Galais. We might parenthetically note here that in part 1 we see Yvonne largely through the haze of Meaulnes's awestruck eyes. In consequence, she has as yet little personality of her own. It is the levelheaded Seurel who in part 3 introduces us (despite his idealism) to a young lady with considerable independence of character. Still, she is a remarkable creation—at once a fair-haired girl of tender disposition and personal charm who strikes us, nonetheless, as an archetypal image of the feminine principle in creation, "the cradle of all life." There are few female characters in literature—Beatrice, Desdemona, and Cordelia are the only ones that come to mind—who strike us simultaneously as cosmic or spiritual symbols while retaining their individuality as distinct personalities. Somehow Fournier manages to create a woman who is at once domestic and familiar, very much "the girl next door," even as she adumbrates the *princesse lointaine* of symbolist poetry.

In any event, Meaulnes's fear of giving himself to the transforming power of this ultimate situation does not prevent him from "dreaming in a way that recalled his old dream" (*LGM*, 60). Seated among the children as Yvonne plays the piano, Meaulnes's dream is, of course, the universal dream of adolescence—a kind of imaginary playacting through which a youth projects himself into a role and situation that he is not yet ready to assume—the role, namely, of father and husband. Still Meaulnes refuses to cross the threshold, lingers with the other children, and prefers to contemplate the girl's back from a safe and undemanding distance.

The Meeting with Yvonne

Though it is the end of December, the following morning is like "one of the first days of April" (*LGM*, 61). We continue in an atemporal zone, the timeless world of mythic beginnings, as Meaulnes has yet another chance to consummate his ritual passage to maturity. Signs of his unfitness for this venture, however, begin to proliferate. First, in an obvious allusion to Narcissus, he pauses at the edge of a pond to admire himself with some complacency. Meaulnes has become infatuated with the medium rather than the content of his adventure. The genuine and unidirectional quest for self-actualization is turning here into a histrionic game that removes Meaulnes from the demands of an immediate personal encounter and allows him to become the spectator of his own existence.

At this point all is in readiness for a boating party. The girl in the brown cloak reappears accompanied by a decrepit woman, "old and bent" (*LGM*, 62)— a *memento mori* perhaps that tacitly underscores the fact that a senuous involvement in the whole of life (in other words, courtship and marriage) involves an acceptance of one's own mortality. Meaulnes follows the girl into the same vessel. When they arrive on the opposite shore, he contrives to speak to her alone and discovers that she is the daughter of the domain, sister to Frantz de Galais, for whom all these proceedings have been arranged.

Meaulnes's inability to break through into a personal and responsible directness is intimated several times in the dialogue. When he learns Yvonne's name, he responds by saying, "The name I gave you was a more beautiful one" (*LGM*, 66). In short, he prefers to think of her in the idealized light of his own imaginings, rather than admit her irreducible reality as a distinct female Other. Yvonne's misgivings are suggested in the telling imagery of birds and nests, the implications of which we have previously noted: "She was quivering at his side, like a swallow which had come to rest for an instant but was already trembling with the wish to resume its flight" (*LGM*, 66). After an awkward exchange, ominously punctuated by the recurrence of the words "grave" and "gravely," Yvonne stipulates that they not return together in the same boat.

Yvonne's injunction is remarkably similar to that of Gretel's in the initiatory fairy tale of the Brothers Grimm. We recall that in their last ordeal, Gretel admonishes Hansel that they cannot cross the river together. For their convoy—an accommodating duck— would collapse under their collected weight. The point is that if they are both to achieve full personal autonomy and self-determination, they can no longer depend upon each other as they have in the past. Instead, they must exercise their individual resources in-

dependently. Yvonne similarly recognizes Meaulnes's obvious need
to achieve personal autonomy before they enter the same boat together—in other words, mutually pledge themselves to a single
shared destiny. (As so often in *Le Grand Meaulnes* the discreet allusion
to fairy tales not only extends the range of meaning but sustains
the note of the marvelous.)

Afterward, Meaulnes returns to his room, feeling "the slight
depression which follows a day which has been almost too perfect"
(*LGM*, 67–68). Like Keats, he has come to recognize that "Aye,
in the very temple of delight / Veil'd Melancholy has her sovran
shrine."[18] The intimate relations between joy and sorrow, human
finitude and infinite being, sex and mortality, all of which he
confronts in his rite of passage impose a burden too hard for Meaulnes
to sustain. His fear of fully committing himself to the excruciating
pathos of the human condition will keep him in a state of perpetual
suspense: attracted toward the joy and beauty he wishes and yet
fears to embrace, and longing at the same time for an unalloyed
purity that will enable him to circumvent the contradictory elements
of human experience.

The Arrival of Frantz

Despite the positive elements, numinous aura, and magical connotations of the fête étrange, Meaulnes is permanently afflicted by
this experience. We have suggested that this affliction is traceable
to certain shortcomings and failures in Meaulnes's character. But to
understand the full reasons for his failure we must turn to Yvonne's
brother Frantz de Galais.

Throughout the novel, Meaulnes stands in symbolic relation to
both Frantz and François. The similarity in names is no coincidence,
nor is it merely fortuitous that Meaulnes has sustained injuries on
both head and knee—the exact respective locations of Frantz's scar
and François's affliction. While maintaining their autonomy as dramatic figures, these boys are to a certain extent psychological counterparts of one another. We need not go so far as to claim that they
are partial fragments of a single differentiated ego—but the secret
of their attraction to one another lies in the fact that they express
complementary aspects of one another's character. Seurel with his
sense of order, control and responsibility constitutes a kind of su-
perego for Meaulnes—a person through whom Meaulnes recognizes

the need to keep his own explosive energies in check. Frantz, on the contrary, may be taken as an embodiment of Meaulnes's id— that instant need for self-gratification and childish self-indulgence, regardless of consequences and irrespective of social demands. In Kierkegaardian terms, Frantz is the aesthetic man in search of artfully contrived pleasures. François is the man of ethics who bases his decisions upon the principles of loyalty and right action. Meaulnes is caught between the two. Still it is possible to discern a third element in Meaulnes's consciousness that potentially elevates him above either of his associates: namely his perception of the religious ground of human existence and his need to conform his life to an immutable ideal and an ultimate concern. Notwithstanding his many failures, Meaulnes is unmistakably driven by the search for absolutes.

But it is Frantz and his companion Ganache who frustrate this search. Indeed, Frantz's love for Valentine caricatures Meaulnes's love for Yvonne in the same way that Frantz's gypsylike wanderings are a distorted and counterfeit version of Meaulnes's quest for the ideal. Thus, while childhood and adolescence are celebrated in this novel as stages that must be assimilated rather than left behind in the development of the ego, Fournier demonstrates, in the character of Frantz, the fatal consequences that befall those who fail to integrate the freshness of childhood and the self-dedication of adolescence into the mature perspectives of adulthood. Frantz is the "spoilt child" unable to apply an inner check to his expansive impulses.

In accordance with the circular scheme of the novel's structure, Frantz's appearance takes us back to the novel's beginning. The characters simply change places. In chapter 1, Meaulnes had come to disrupt the domestic comfort of the Seurels; now Frantz has come to disturb Meaulnes's stability and threaten his comfort. Frantz enters through a *window* accompanied by "a rush of cold air" (*LGM*, 68). In a crepuscular light—like that in which Meaulnes made his first appearance—he paces back and forth, whistling "a ditty sung by sailors, and the girls they meet in their taverns, to cheer themselves up" (*LGM*, 68–69). With Frantz's arrival, the marine imagery has clearly taken on less savory and majestic connotations. He announces to Meaulnes that the party is suspended, that his fiancée, intimidated by the far-flung nature of his love, has broken the engagement and disappeared. He orders Meaulnes to communicate this news to the other guests.

As Meaulnes descends the staircase, he witnesses a sad spectacle. The revelers, grown restless and cynical at Frantz's protracted absence, have begun to indulge in immoderate draughts of wine and to entertain themselves with bawdy stories: "Meaulnes heard vulgar songs *desecrating* a park which for two days had harboured much grace . . ." (*LGM*, 71; emphasis added). The liturgical language underscores the failure of Meaulnes's initiation, his inability to balance or choose between the conflicting claims of spirit and sense, love and mortality, eros and agape, a life of spiritual devotion or domestic responsibility. In consequence, the sexual element in Meaulnes's rite takes on a daimonic and undisciplined independence signaled in the cacaphonous chorus of revelers who cynically intone a ballad of seduction and betrayal: "Dear little libertine, where have you been? / Your bonnet's awry, Your hair's coming down." The battered bonnet is a variant on the ravished nest, while the woman in the song gives us a prefigurative glimpse of the destinies awaiting both Yvonne and Valentine in the third part of the novel. A subsequent refrain consciously echoes the dove's song at the conclusion of *Cinderella*—a song that points again to Meaulnes's own sexual maladjustment: "I've got on red shoes . . . / Lover, good-bye! / I've got on red shoes . . . / Forever, good-bye!" (*LGM*, 71). This is not only a final farewell to a moment of peculiar and privileged grace, it also, with its reference to a vaginal slipper of blood red, reminds us of the ruse whereby Cinderella's sisters endeavored to fool the prince by cutting off one of their toes. As Bruno Bettleheim observes, the bloody slipper is associated in the prince's mind with menstruation, but "Cinderella is the virginal bride; in the unconscious, the girl who does not menstruate is more clearly virginal than one who already does."[19] Like the prince, Meaulnes cherishes a virginal image of femininity and clearly fears the demands of mature sexuality. When Cinderella's sister cuts off her big toe, she enacts perhaps a castration fear, which the prince overcomes by virtue of Cinderella's lack of sexual aggression. Like the prince, Meaulnes will initially place the slipper, as it were, upon the wrong foot—but, unlike in the fairy tale, he will be seized by a conviction that he has forever forfeited his claim to the true owner (namely, Yvonne de Galais). The reference, moreover, to the "red shoes" is a clear gloss on Andersen's fairy tale of the same name and provides a further ironic comment on Meaulnes's subsequent behavior. Like the child in Andersen's story who wishes her life to be a perpetual self-delighting dance unburdened by constraining obligations, so Meaulnes will desire to cling to the emotional thrills provided by the fête étrange, to denigrate his later experiences insofar as these fail to excite an equivalent kick, and to lament the necessity of returning to a lower, disenchanted plane of existence.

Hence, the progressive dissolution of the party looks ahead to Meaulnes's ultimate failure: "The park, the garden, the courtyard were now blotted out. And tonight there were no lanterns in the windows" (*LGM*, 70). Again, there is a sense of déjà vu, of an event repeating itself in a slightly altered context. For just as Meaulnes had figuratively blotted out the lamp around which "the happy family group" of the Seurels gathered at night, so here again Frantz has extinguished the last embers of Meaulnes's fading and unfinished rite. "It was a portent of disintegration" (*LGM*, 71), observes Fournier, glancing forward to the progressive fragmentation of Meaulnes's ego in parts 2 and 3 of the novel.

Though Meaulnes hopes that he will be able to return again, "without any false pretenses" (*LGM*, 70) (a tacit admission of his psychological unreadiness and present inability to confront the realities disclosed at the lost domain), he will remain to the end the victim of his own divided consciousness. Moreover, the collapse of the fête in a cacaphony of discordant and "rowdy" songs signals the breakdown of those musical images that have accompanied Meaulnes's initiatory adventure. Once again, the disruption of these images adumbrates the pattern Alex Aronson sees as endemic in the modern novel of initiation: when "the music is over, the memory [is] shattered, the dream dissolved. What remains is the non-musical reality of thought, of analytical introspection and, more often than not, of self-deprecating irony."[20] And, of course, in parts 2 and 3 of *Le Grand Meaulnes*, notwithstanding the periodic "music that comes to the hearer out of some obscure recess of remembered time,"[21] this irony deepens into a kind of religious and moral despair.

At all events, Meaulnes's behavior during his last frenzied moments at the domain is indicative of his present unfitness for the girl who has brought him to the threshold of adult consciousness. Racing back to his room, he discovers that Frantz has fled, leaving behind a suicide note, which contains an apology to his sister. But what does Meaulnes do? He thinks of the "unhappy girl sick with anxiety, spending a feverish night while these louts filled her house with their singing" (*LGM*, 73), but he makes no attempt to seek her out and commiserate in her misfortune. Instead, he accepts an invitation to join a carriage on the way to Sainte-Agathe where "he would be free to dream of the young lady of the chateau" (*LGM*, 73). His behavior speaks for itself.

A final important detail emerges as Meaulnes is hurried away in the rumbling coach. Through the *window* he sees "a flash" accompanied by a "detonation" (*LGM*, 74)—the brilliant skyrocket of youthful aspiration has become, by virtue of Meaulnes's failure, a fatal engine of destructive light. Moments later, he observes the grotesque spectacle of the costumed Pierrot toiling through the forest with the inert body of Frantz clasped to his breast (just as Millie had formerly clasped her hat, or as Seurel in part 3 will clasp the dead body of Yvonne, or as Meaulnes in the last pages will return to clasp his motherless daughter). After a hiatus in the narrative, during which Meaulnes falls asleep, he is awakened, six kilometers from Sainte-Agathe, by *a tap on the window.*

Meaulnes and Perceval

Part 1 of *Le Grand Meaulnes* not only blends the marvelous with reality, but fuses the idealized conventions of quest romance with the low mimetic style of realistic fiction. The archetypal significance of Meaulnes's adventure is not only enhanced by frequent allusions to fairy tale and folk lore, but, more specifically, to the Arthurian legend of Perceval. There are many interesting parallels between this legend and Meaulnes's ill-fated quest. Furthermore, just as Eliot alludes to this myth in *The Wasteland* as a means of highlighting the spiritual maladjustment and sexual lawlessness of the modern age, so Fournier similarly evokes the image of this questing knight to underline the failures, the conflicts, and the misadventures of his three hapless protagonists.

Of the many variants of this legend, Fournier's has most in common with the *Perceval* of Chrétien de Troyes. In this version, the knight similarly undergoes an aborted rite of passage. Arriving at a "Castle of Wonder," he fails to ask the appropriate questions concerning the grail and the lance (emblems, at once, of sexual fertility and tokens of supernatural order). Because of this failure, the king of the land succumbs to illness and impotence and his domains are laid waste. By the same token, in *Le Grand Meaulnes*, the château will be destroyed stone by stone, Monsieur de Galais will die of heartbreak following the death of Yvonne, and Seurel will be robbed of all human comfort. Chrétien comments on his hero's failure as follows, but the words have an equal pertinence to parts 2 and 3 of *Le Grand Meaulnes* where the consequences of Meaulnes's erratic behavior become manifest:

> Ladies sad will lose their mates,
> The land in desolation lie,
> Damsels unconsoled will sigh
> Widows and orphans, mournful all
> And many a knight in death will fall.[22]

Apart, however, from these general relations to the Perceval legend, there are many details that identify Meaulnes with the hapless knight of Chrétien's poem. Like Perceval, Meaulnes is fatherless and leads a peasant existence in a remote backwater. Both are skillful trappers and cunning in the ways of the hunt. When Perceval joins the Round Table, he engages in the quest for the Holy Grail after a flash of light bursting over Arthur's castle discloses a glimpse of the mystic cup and rouses the knights to commit themselves to its recovery. Similarly, Meaulnes's adventure begins shortly after the explosion of the Catherine-wheel above the Sainte-Agathe schoolyard. In the course of his search, Perceval loses his horse. Meaulnes's horse will return limping to Sainte-Agathe, while Yvonne's broken-down mare is presumably put to sleep after the outing arranged by François in part 3 of the novel.

Like Perceval, Meaulnes will rely upon a group of children to guide him through a grove of trees to the scene of his initiation. And like the knight of Arthurian legend, Meaulnes will remain hopelessly divided between two antipathetic desiderata: a life of spiritual devotion as opposed to a commitment to marriage and the family. Both heroes, moreover, betray both options when they yield to similar sexual temptations.

Furthermore, Fournier's telling of Meaulnes's adventure is shaded along the lines of Tennyson's version of the Perceval legend in the *Idylls of the King.* Tennyson, it may be recalled, chose to make the quest of the Holy Grail, "a mistaken and neurotic quest for certitude or mere excitement," as Douglas Bush observes, "an escape from the real righteousness and performance of duty exemplified by Arthur."[23] Though Meaulnes's quest is initially pregnant with the most wondrous possibilities, it too eventually takes on the quality of "mere excitement," losing its authenticity in the way that Tennyson's King Arthur ruefully prognostigates:

> . . . how often, O my knights,
> Your places being vacant at my side,
> The chance of noble deeds will come and go
> Unchallenged, while ye follow wandering fires
> Lost in the quagmire.[24]

Yet Meaulnes's failure is representative and prototypical—a particular instance of an affliction increasingly universal to the modern age. Like Eliot in *The Waste Land* Fournier has endeavoured to surround Meaulnes's adventure with the mythic rituals of humanity's spiritual past. But these allusions, severed as they are from any organic connection to the whole of human existence, remain, at best, but tantalizing glimpses of a lost unity and scattered sacrament that seem irretrievable. Like Eliot's *Waste Land* or Yeats's *A Vision, Le Grande Meaulnes* is a private mythology. "But," as Mircea Eliade observes, "modern man's 'private mythologies'—his dreams, reveries, fantasies and so on—never rise to the ontological status of myths, precisely because they are not experienced by the whole man, and therefore do not transform a particular situation into a situation that is paradigmatic."[25]

Still, it would be wrong to emphasize too strongly the futility and frustration hinted at in part 1 of Fournier's novel—it is only in retrospect that the relevance of Eliade's words become fully apparent. The distinctive element in Part 1, as enchanting today as it was for the novel's first readers, is the note of mystery, wonder, childlike credulity, and romantic illusion that Fournier has so cunningly fashioned. To paraphrase Rivière's remarks on Debussy's music, "our pleasure," in reading this novel, "lies precisely in our feeling ourselves directed toward an indistinct something that is palpitating nearby, half-concealed."[26] This is especially evident in part 1. For readers who genuinely dispose themselves to Meaulnes's adventure, their perceptions of reality will never be quite the same. As Kathleen Raine observes, henceforward, "a door in a wall, an empty house, a neglected garden, [are forever] fraught with the paradisal poignancy of Alain-Fournier's lost domain."[27]

Chapter Five
Le Grand Meaulnes,
Parts 2 and 3

Le Grand Meaulnes and the "Dialectic of Desire"

Notwithstanding the conscious interweavings, structural reverberations, and architectonic unity that bind the three parts of *Le Grand Meaulnes* into a single irreducible whole, critics have not infrequently opined that there is a general falling off in imaginative vitality and sustained inspiration after the episode of the fête étrange. "*Le Grand Meaulnes* has a grand start and then rather flounders to an unfortunate ending," observes Denis Saurat.[1] Leon Cellier virtually echoes this judgment in his book "*Le Grand Meaulnes" ou l'initiation manquée,*[2] and André Gide, in his diaries, complains that Fournier was unable to recapture the freshness, piquancy, and ingenuous emotion of the opening pages in his subsequent working out of the plot.[3]

But Alain-Fournier was extremely conscious of what he was doing. As his characters move from their middle teens to their early twenties, there is, to be sure, an increasing sense of disenchantment that possesses the narrative. As in Wordsworth's great ode, "the glory and the dream" become progressively threadbare: the tattered arras, as it were, of an unraveling romanticism. For Wordsworth, of course, this imaginative decline is compensated for by the "years which bring the philosophic mind." It is this which enables the poet to realize that a return to the lost enchantments of childhood would not dissipate his growing anxieties (for the child in Wordsworth's ode paradoxically exults in what appears to be the boundless future available to him as an adult). C. S. Lewis would interpret Wordsworth's desire for childhood as a mistaken attempt to secure an infinite boon, which appertains to no age in particular and no spot in especial (even though such a desire arises out of and manifests itself in the temporal exigencies of time, place, and circumstance).

Le Grand Meaulnes, too, quite consciously records the fading of a dream, though without the explicit compensations or consolations

provided by Wordsworth's somewhat didactic ode or Lewis's philosophical analysis of the "dialectic of desire." But then *Le Grand
Meaulnes* is all the more powerful by virtue of the fact that this
central theme remains implicit and virtual in the events of the book.
Critics who regret Fournier's "drop" in inspiration have miscon-
strued his intentions and limited the range of his achievement. *Le
Grand Meaulnes* is not a work of palsied or undisciplined fantasy, a
journey into the realms of romance for the sake of titillation or
escape. On the contrary, it is an earnest and far-seeing dramatization
of the struggle to grow up and, most especially, to incorporate the
indeterminate longings of adolescence into the conscious commitments of maturity. That the characters fail to achieve this integration
does not belie the fact that for Fournier, Meaulnes and Seurel (Frantz,
as we shall see, is another matter) have had, in their youth, a genuine
glimpse of a "far-off country . . . the inconsolable secret which
hurts so much that we take our revenge on it by calling it names
like Nostalgia and Romanticism and Adolescence."[4]

It is Meaulnes's failure to comport himself in an authentic manner
to that "far-off country"—transcendent, immutable, and everlasting—which breaks across the first part of the novel in recurring
waves and vital currents, that constitutes his spiritual undoing.
Fournier's novel, then, is a probing and insightful dramatization of
the spiritual law of cause and effect that operates in the life of a
gifted and sensitive individual who refuses to acquiesce in that
dialectic which time imposes upon all youthful ecstasies and moments of transfiguring grace. In a word, *Le Grand Meaulnes* may be
construed, on one level, as a work of religious psychology.

As we have noted in our discussion of Fournier's life and letters,
Le Grand Meaulnes is informed by a growing awareness that an
attempt to arrest the magical and animistic world of childhood leads
to regression, disappointment, irresponsibility, and despair. It leads,
in brief, to that "dialectic of desire" which C. S. Lewis, following
Pascal, Samuel Johnson, and other Christian writers, describes as a
state in which one mistakenly endows a finite and temporal blessing
with its infinite and unconditioned Source.

To recapitulate, this dialectic, as outlined by Lewis in his preface
to *The Pilgrim's Regress*, operates as follows: human beings are so
constituted that they perpetually feel the vacuity of present satisfactions (what Samuel Johnson would call "the hunger of imagination which preys upon life"). In order to hide this emptiness and

discontent they are perennially engaged in the search for some object able to fill the vacuum of their existence. Each object that they pursue inevitably disappoints precisely insofar as it falls short of their expectations or fails to secure an imperturbable contentment. In consequence, they scuttle from object to object, goal to goal, in the hopes of securing that indefinable something the lack of which makes them miserable. The fallacy inherent in this pursuit becomes evident, however, when the attainment of some cherished object does not produce the expected lasting effect. As present satisfactions fade, the error repeats itself: happiness becomes associated with a luminous moment in the past (as Meaulnes associates the "peak of perfection" with the fête étrange). But a return to the past would only reveal that that "luminous" moment similarly involved the pursuit of a distant goal or the longing for a vanished object. Paradoxically, it is the longing to long that is the very thing they long for, but it is precisely this that they fail, in their naive pursuit of power, luxury, or sensation, to recognize. For this longing, by its very nature, can never be fulfilled. Hence, human beings, according to Lewis, are given the option of resigning themselves to a moody cynicism or, through an act of secondary reflection, of arriving at a deeper understanding of their dilemma—an understanding, namely that they were created to enjoy a felicity not available to them in the world of spatio-temporal objects. Thus, the things Meaulnes seeks—the wonder of childhood, the purity of love, the brilliance and magic of the fête étrange—have an anagogical relation to the true object of his quest, but are unfortunately confused with it. This divine discontent is part and parcel of Meaulnes's romanticism, and genuinely points to a reality of ultimate and transcendent worth. It is his attraction toward this reality (or his recoiling from it) that is thematically central to parts 2 and 3 of the novel.

At the end of *The Pilgrim's Regress*, Lewis comments on the proclivity of his allegorical adventurer to cling ungenerously to the consolations of grace and the gifts of love—to lament their absence as a sign of an indifferent universe or a disapproving God. Unable to accept or abide in that spiritual dryness which is the counterpart to moments of inspiration or grace, Lewis's pilgrim reflects a condition which is similar to that of Meaulnes (for whom it is imperative that Yvonne remain poised on the lofty pinnacle of an imperishable dream). In response to the pilgrim's plight, however, a hermit appears who endeavors to console the pilgrim with the following reflection—its relevance to the case of Augustin Meaulnes should be readily apparent: "Do you not know how it is with Love? First comes delight, then pain; then fruit. And then there is joy of the fruit, but that is different again from the first delight. And mortal lovers must not try to remain at the first step. . . . You must not try to keep the raptures, they have done their work. Manna kept, is worms."[5]

But Meaulnes, having failed to complete his rite of passage, spiritually covets that first step and refuses to move beyond it. To be sure, he is possessed at intervals by an awareness that the delights of the fête were in fact the beginnings of a process that has a theocentric orientation. But he scurries insensibly between a finite manifestation of beauty, fellowship, and joy (first Yvonne, then Valentine, and then again Yvonne), without recognizing that for him, these women have become confused with the "transtemporal, transfinite good" that he indeterminately glimpses as his "real destiny."[6] This is not to say that marriage to Yvonne would not be a goal both legitimate and sacerdotal—but for Meaulnes, the restless wanderer, who refuses to admit limits or fix bounds, this blunder into marriage is the worst of his mistakes: a distraction from an understanding of the dialectical nature of his desires. For, as his behavior subsequently reveals, it is not Yvonne whom he desires. For him, she is "not the thing itself—but only the reminder of it. The things—the beauty, the memory of our own past—are good images of what we really desire," as C. S. Lewis observes. "But if they are mistaken," as in Meaulnes's case, "for the thing itself they turn into dumb idols, breaking the heart of their worshipers. For they are not the thing itself; they are only the scent of a flower we have not found, the echo of a tune we have not heard, news from a country we have not visited."[7] If Meaulnes were less of an idealist, marriage to Yvonne would be a legitimate consummation of his rite—but given his eternal restlessness (which recalls that of his namesake Saint Augustine), he personally reifies (though without fully knowing it) the fundamental tenet of Augustine's theology: "Our hearts are restless, oh Lord, until they rest in Thee."

It is not Meaulnes, but Seurel who would be the appropriate husband for Yvonne. Unfortunately though, through misunderstandings, scruples, a mistaken sense of loyalty, or misdirected passion, each of the characters seems bent, albeit unconsciously and with the best of purposes on ransacking and frustrating one another's lives. A note of fatality creeps in toward the end of *Le Grand Meaulnes*—at best, as in Debussy's *Pelléas*, there are broken portents of an unseen power toward which the characters stretch out their hands. But the spiritual condition reflected in this novel is best and almost quite literally summed up (if we recall Meaulnes's waiting outside the Galais's Parisian residence) in the words of Simone Weil: "God and humanity are like two lovers who have missed their rendezvous. Each is there before the time, but each at a different place, and they wait and wait and wait."[8] The ensuing tragedy, whether a result of human folly or providential design, leaves us finally face to face with that postulate which Fournier reiterated again and again in his letters to Rivière as forming the principal theme of *Le Grand Meaulnes*: namely, the impossibility of a purely temporal happiness, for, in the words of Pascal, "here is no real and lasting satisfaction."[9]

Before we proceed with our consecutive analysis of parts 2 and 3 of *Le Grand Meaulnes*, a few further reflections are in order. For these will enable us to grasp more fully the dramatic situations that unfold in the latter half of the novel and to appreciate more clearly the motivations behind the aberrant behavior of Meaulnes and Frantz. As we have seen, one of Meaulnes's problems (like that of Keats in the "Ode to a Nightingale") is his unwillingness to surrender a moment of illuminating grace. He clings to the fête étrange like a spiritual miser hoarding some sort of gratuitous indulgence, and loses the capacity to realize, as Meister Eckhart would exhort, "that we must look through every gift and every event to God and never be content with the thing itself. There is no stopping place in this life—, no, nor was there ever one for any man, no matter how far along his way he'd gone."[10]

This helps to explain certain events in part 2 that have bedeviled critics who see in them a lack of psychological verisimilitude. The first of these events is the construction of Meaulnes's map. Why doesn't he just inquire of one of the adults in the neighborhood, say Monsieur Seurel, as to the whereabouts of the eccentric family in the remote château with the pretty daughter? Second, why does it take him so long to identify Frantz de Galais when he shows up, of all places, at the Sainte-Agathe schoolyard? And, third, why does Frantz have such a keen interest in keeping Meaulnes in the dark with regard to Yvonne's location? The first two questions have a simple answer: given Meaulnes's peculiar psychology, his fear of consequences, his desire to linger forever in a state of chaste suspension on the point of but without reaching fulfillment, both the completion of his map and the identification of Frantz would entail conscious choices—such as returning to Yvonne—that he does not wish to make. It is all very fine and well for him to live in a quest untarnished by contact with base reality, but to bring things to a consummation, well, that is another and more delicate matter entirely—one he is not prepared as yet to deal with. By the same token, Frantz's deliberate misleading of Meaulnes is, in part, an expression of his own erratic and childish personality—it gives him the opportunity to indulge in a bit of gratuitous mystification, of playacting, if you will, that simply keeps the game of childhood afoot. On the other hand, it is purely selfish. We learn later of his dependence on Yvonne (who is more of a mother than a sister to him). Why should he enable Meaulnes to find her, and thereby divide her affections, which have hitherto centered on himself alone?

Finally, Meaulnes's dilemma following the experience of the fête is in part the dilemma of vocation. Having confronted the threefold reality of death, sexuality, and the sacred, Meaulnes begins to regress backward, fearing the demands that these impose on his growing consciousness. Moreover, though he seems to be genuinely in search of Yvonne, the question always remains for him as to whether the consummation of his rite should entail a commitment to domestic responsibility—to marriage and the family—or rather a dedication of his life to the ultimate reality disclosed in the "purity of that moment" (LGM, 148), which he associates with the lost domain. A life of lay or religious commitment is at the heart of Meaulnes's vacillation—it never enters his head for a moment to lead a life of casual sex or self-aggrandizement. The great dilemma of part 3 is that this is precisely what he finds himself doing (partly in compensation for the apparent loss of Yvonne, partly out of consolation for the conflicting forces by which he feels himself divided). Is Meaulnes overscrupulous, even neurotic, in his search for absolutes? In a sense he is a Dostoevskian character—a bit like Prince Myshkin on the one hand, and Dimitri Karamazov, on the other. He dramatizes a conflict in the human condition which from Saint Augustine through Dostoevsky was accepted as a spiritual given of human nature. For Meaulnes is a man troubled by conscience, in search of self-discipline, enamored of perfection, fastidiously aware of his own shortcomings. "Do you know what it is," asks the Abbé Lamennais, "which makes man the most suffering of all creatures? It is"—and his answer is certainly relevant to Meaulnes—"that he has one foot in the finite and the other in the infinite, and that he is torn asunder, not by four horses, as in the horrible old times, but between two worlds."[11]

In the context, then, of Lewis's dialectic, and with an awareness of the fundamental dilemma that divides Meaulnes's consciousness, we are now in a position to examine the dramatic convolutions of parts 2 and 3 of Fournier's novel. Instead of falling off in inspiration, the last two-thirds of *Le Grand Meaulnes* deal accurately and insightfully with the repercussions of Meaulnes's adventures. And, as Cyril Connolly observes, "the sequel is adult and exciting."[12]

The Arrival of Frantz

With part 2 of *Le Grand Meaulnes*, the novel makes a second turn backward on itself. This is not only true in terms of the narrative structure, but in terms of the characters' development as well. Abashed, perhaps, or baffled by the manifold experiences of the fête, Meaulnes seems to regress to the level of schoolboy existence. And, indeed, in part 2, the whole attempt by Meaulnes and Frantz to maintain the air of mystery characteristic of part 1 seems increasingly factitious. It is an attempt to prolong a spell that has reached the limit of its purpose (namely, the spiritual awakening of Meaulnes), but which now, being protracted, turns sour and increasingly unsavory.

In any event, just as in part 1, a stranger arrives at Sainte-Agathe on a Thursday (the same day on which Meaulnes's idyll at the lost domain was interrupted by the appearance of Frantz). His appearance is startling and unexpected, signaled (as was Meaulnes's) by a sound of indeterminate origin—"a whistle blew—a shrill, prolonged note that could have been heard as far away as the Church" (*LGM*, 80). Suddenly, while Meaulnes and the Seurels are at supper, the house is surrounded by the raucous cries of schoolboys, their faces hidden by mufflers, their voices discernible "just beyond the *window* sash" (*LGM*, 81). It is another "*wave* from the adventure," observes Seurel, "we no longer spoke of" (*LGM*, 80). The repetition of image-clusters, the recurrence of related events, the reenactment of the opening sequence, is a slight variation on the theme enunciated with Meaulnes's appearance in part 1. Indeed, the sense of a Sisy-

phean quest repeating itself in a series of endless and finally futile
endeavors is underscored even in the slightest of details and least
central of characters. When the fracas subsides outside the Seurels'
home, Monsieur Pasquier, the butcher, appears to relate the news
of two strangers in the village who have apparently "possessed" the
other schoolboys. His story, told between sips of liqueur, is a mi-
crocosm of the novel's structure—for he never finishes his tale, there
is no closure. Instead, he repeats the initial details over and over
again: "I happened to be out in my yard," then, a paragraph later,
"There I was, out in the yard," another sip of wine, and again, he
"resumed his story with more gestures than facts" (*LGM*, 82–83).

Frustrated by his garbled explanations, Meaulnes and François
dash outside in pursuit of the retreating schoolboys where they are
led down a "blind alley" (*LGM*, 84), surrounded, overpowered,
and, under the command of a stranger who shouts orders, thoroughly
searched, until Meaulnes's map is discovered and handed over to
the leader whose head is wreathed in bandages. (It is, of course,
Frantz.) The pursuit down the "blind alley" is a variation on the
corridors of the fête; the fact that Meaulnes and Seurel come to a
dead end prefigures their failure to reach full maturity. Moreover,
these alleys pass by a district of "weavers and dressmakers," one of
whom, "the dumb woman," sometimes works for the Seurels (*LGM*,
84). The weavers are connected with Millie, Yvonne, Meaulnes's
dream, and with Valentine—all images of the eternal feminine,
which, in Jungian terms, is associated in the male unconscious with
"a secret knowledge or hidden wisdom."[13] But as previously noted,
this wisdom will ultimately be obscured by virtue of the fact that
Meaulnes never distinguishes between this Jungian projection and
the real Yvonne. As the psychologist Frieda Fordham observes, "the
image is an archetype . . . and although many women will conform,
at least outwardly to this image, it in no way represents the real
character of individual woman."[14] If maturation consists in discriminating between image and reality, then Meaulnes never matures
and his image of femininity remains under the control of inner
unconscious compulsions. Hence, Meaulnes's anima — divided between the "good, the noble goddess-like figure," of Yvonne and
the "fairy-like or elfin" (a pierrot?) character of Valentine, "the
prostitute, the seductress, the witch,"[15]—obscures his understanding of the opposite sex and keeps him from achieving a balanced
relationship with a female Other. The "dumb woman" at the end

of the "blind alley" is a symbolic prefiguration of what Meaulnes, in his dichotomized consciousness, will do to the women from whom he expects, in romantic terms, his ultimate salvation. Both Valentine and Yvonne will never be more than stuffed dummies to him—the instabilities and unrecognized compulsions of his own ego preventing him, at all times and in all situations, from genuinely breaking through to authentic encounters with either Yvonne or Valentine. In any case, Meaulnes returns from this attack, "limping" like Seurel—it is the outward and tangible emblem of an emotional weakness and spiritual maladjustment that will have dire repercussions for those around him.

Frantz the Magician

The substitution of characters in part 2 continues as Frantz (still unrecognized) becomes a member of Monsieur Seurel's class (traveling or itinerant youngsters often being allowed to join a village school during the tenure of their visit). The loyalty formerly commanded by Meaulnes now passes to Frantz and, accordingly, there is a general deterioration in the order and stability of both the schoolroom and the youngsters of Sainte-Agathe.

If Meaulnes disclosed authentic tidings of a genuine mystery stretching beyond the warm circle of the maternal lamp illuminating the Seurel household, then Frantz is the bearer of a kind of ersatz and artificial magic, contrived, manipulative, and highly questionable. He too "inserts the marvelous into reality," but in a way that caricatures the procedures of Seurel (or Fournier) whose images genuinely bring us to the threshold of that which is numinous in human experience. In short, Frantz is the charlatan and trickster who delights in mystifying rather than illuminating his companions. This is epitomized in the schoolroom scene where he passes around items pulled from his knapsack or bag of tricks. One of these, "a picture penholder," discloses, when held up in the light, "a blurred view of the Basilica of Lourdes" (*LGM*, 88). It is significant that the view is "blurred," or that it again refers to a spot associated with sacramental waters. For here, although we move from the familiar to the faraway, the ordinary and near-at-hand to the marvelous and magically remote, the whole thing is achieved through a mechanical contrivance—it is the exact opposite, in fact, of Fournier's sense of "the other mysterious landscape" that can neither be

consciously willed into being nor artificially summoned from beyond. Frantz, in a sense, anticipates the self-conscious and contrived
experiments of the surrealists, whereas Meaulnes and especially Seurel remain rooted in a sense of nature that is sacramental and Words-
worthian in its fusion of the homely with "a sense sublime of
something far more deeply interfused."

Meaulnes endeavors to keep his distance from Frantz, but unfortunately Frantz's arrival signals a recrudescence of Meaulnes's own
childishness to which he finally and fatally capitulates. When Frantz
organizes a rather sadistic game in which the boys mount each other
in an attempt to throw their opponents onto the gravel (in another
ironic caricature of Arthurian knight-errantry), Meaulnes initially
refuses to participate. It is significant that when he finally joins in
and hoists Suerel up on his shoulders, he is unable to unseat his
enemy Frantz. For Frantz and Ganache remain ineradicable parts of
Meaulnes's ego: dangerous, pathetic, vulnerable, and explosive. It
is significant that even the other boys who feel charmed by the new
stranger listen to Frantz's exploits in a symbolic posture that denotes
their uneasiness in his presence. In one scene, where Frantz expatiates
on his itinerant life, the boys listen in fascinated attention, but are
careful, all the while, to "get warm by the stove . . . keeping one
foot on the fire-guard to make sure of not losing their place" (*LGM*,
91). In Frantz's presence, the boys gravitate towards this variant on
the secure domestic hearth out of an instinctive need to counterbalance his disruptive and irrational powers.

The Brotherhood of Three

Gradually, however, Frantz gains the confidence of Seurel and
Meaulnes. Realizing that his hold on the other boys is slipping, he
switches allegiance and coerces Meaulnes and François into a sort
of secret brotherhood in which each promises to respond to the call
of the other (it is important to remember that these boys are still
in their mid-teens). Frantz's chief antagonist is Jasmin Delouche,
Meaulnes's former rival, who has slipped again into resentful obscurity following the arrival of Frantz. (In a sense Delouche represents the pedestrian and ordinary side of François, in the same way
that Ganache embodies the irrational element in Frantz. It is not
surprising then that Frantz should consider Delouche his chief enemy, or that Seurel, following Meaulnes's departure at the end of

part 2, should naturally gravitate toward the quotidian and unexceptional world of Delouche.)

Be that as it may, following this schoolboy pledge of Meaulnes, Seurel, and Frantz (in which Frantz, who has not as yet revealed his true identity, disingenuously promises to put Meaulnes on the track to Yvonne), Frantz joins his partner Ganache and in a few days arranges a makeshift circus for the villagers of Sainte-Agathe.

This, of course, is a contrived and somewhat threadbare repetition of the original fête. As Seurel and Meaulnes anticipate the evening's entertainment, Seurel's prose vibrates poignantly with the quenchless hopes of aspiring youth: "Ah, brother, comrade, rover. How sure we were that felicity was within reach, that to attain it we had only to set our feet on the path" (*LGM*, 100).

But the lights outside the circus tent are *red* not green, underscoring the duplicitous, even devilish nature of Frantz's game—for it is a game with the lives of other people. The diabolic associations are reinforced by the performance of a goat—an animal traditionally related to Old Nick. Having lost his chance for happiness, Frantz has nothing better to do than frustrate the happiness of others.

Meaulnes and Seurel take their seats on the innermost circle of the arena where Frantz and Ganache (dressed again in the costume of Pierrot) are to perform. The conscious mind has, as it were, turned inward on itself, beholding in the center of the circular stage the embodiment of those unexorcized psychic elements that threaten its collapse. (Indeed, Jasmin announces to several of the company before the show begins, that a rash of stolen chickens has been reported in the neighborhood—an event dubiously coincident with the arrival of Frantz and Ganache. Again, the image of the ravished nest returns by way of an oblique commentary on the undisciplined and chaotic forces set loose by the arrival of these two.)

The climax of the performance occurs in a scene that epitomizes the role of Pierrot as an avatar of those subliminal forces that eventually destroy Meaulnes's chances for happiness. (We think, too, of the traditional image of Pierrot in the commedia dell'arte as the hapless and forlorn lover—an image reinforced in the contemporary ballet of Stravinsky, *Petrushka*, which Fournier witnessed in the company of Rivière.) In any event, the clown, climbing a stack of balanced chairs, reaches the top only to fall again and again in a series of hysterical contortions. The scene of climbing and falling, reaching a point from which one recoils in vertiginous descent, crystalizes the self-frustrating circularity of Meaulnes's continually crumbling quest. Moreover, the image of the falling Pierrot cannot help but remind us of two of the most famous archetypal falls in literature: the fall of Milton's Satan (with whom Frantz and Ganache are vaguely associated) and the seemingly endless fall of Alice into the frightening hinterland of the subconscious mind.

When, following this, Pierrot balances on the topmost chair and proceeds to stuff "a little doll . . . with bran," which is then forced to "vomit up the entire contents of her body" (*LGM*, 103), we get a grotesque and horrible adumbration of the way in which those living "dolls"—Valentine and Yvonne—are subsequently stuffed, as it were, "with the inherited collective image of woman" that exists in Meaulnes's unconscious and that he "projects on to the various women who attract him."[16] It also, of course, in a more harrowing way, anticipates the birth and perhaps the fate of both Meaulnes's little girl and her mother.

At this point Meaulnes recognizes both the Pierrot of the fête and the brother of Yvonne, as well he should. For they are more then reminders of the lost domain: as their carnival antics underscore, they are the doubles and alter egos of Meaulnes himself.

Though he searches for them the next day with Seurel, they are gone. The police, alerted by Jasmin, have come to investigate their whereabouts, and the spot at the four roads (we recall Meaulnes's crossroads in part 1) shows no traces of their former camp.

François's Adventure and the Departure of Meaulnes

Chapter 9 of part 2 is, in some ways, an exact replication of the same chapter in part 1. It is also one of the pedal points of the novel: again the shifting panorama of scenes and events is disrupted by a persistent and sustaining tone from beyond the dimensions of human experience.

On a day when the other boys are playing hookey to hunt for *nest eggs*, in a chapter significantly entitled "In Search of the Lost Trail," François finds himself separated from his companions, "like some patrol with whom the corporal has lost touch" (*LGM*, 110). (There is an almost eerie biographical resonance here, given our knowledge of Fournier's actual fate in the Battle of the Marne.) Like Meaulnes, who in the parallel chapter of the first part "descried through the branches a faint glimmer of light," so Seurel in this significant interlude comes close to recreating and defining Meaulnes's original experience:

For the first time I too am on the path of adventure . . . I am looking for . . . the path you read about in books, the old lane choked with undergrowth whose entrance the weary prince could not discover. You'll only come upon it at some lost moment of the morning when you've long since forgotten that it will be eleven, or twelve. . . . Then, as you are awkwardly brushing aside a tangle of branches, your arms at the same time trying to protect your face, you suddenly catch a glimpse of a dark tunnel of *green* at the far end of which there is a tiny aperture of light (*LGM*, 110–11; emphasis added).

This is the culmination and the explanation of the roads that crisscross this novel and become the means of suggesting an experience that C. S. Lewis describes as a longing for an "unnameable something, desire for which pierces us like a rapier."[17] But even François's trail foreshadows the growing disenchantment of the later portions of the book. When his adventure is forestalled by coming "into a clearing which proves to be an ordinary field," François upbraids himself for being "intoxicated with hopeful fancies," and concludes this episode with the rueful confession "But I hadn't found anything" (*LGM*, 111).

Still, his experience—if he could only interpret it from the perspective of Lewis's "dialectic"—need not conclude on so disillusioned a note. For François has had, like Meaulnes, a genuine glimpse of a dimensionless and unsearchable reality intersecting a moment of time. This is suggested by the fact that the weather parallels the atmospheric conditions of the original fête; that François's excursion, like Meaulnes's meeting with Yvonne, occurs on a Thursday; that the narrative shifts, as in the episodes of the fête étrange, into the eternal now of the present tense; that the "dark tunnel of *green*" not only reminds us of Meaulnes's reverie but summons up an image of a prelapsarian world; and that a nightingale, customarily silent at noon, is singing, in defiance of temporal conditions, among the tangled undergrowth through which Seurel picks his way. There is a possible allusion to Keat's famous ode in which the nightingale embodies a similar meeting point between the finite and the infinite, the actual and the ideal—or, to use Fournier's terms—the "marvelous" and "reality." But when Seurel stumbles into the "dried-up spring" in "old Martin's field," we are again reminded that the sources of life, the baptismal and transforming well from the world's end, remain elusive and inaccessible throughout the novel.

Both Seurel and Meaulnes experience that moment of illumination—and potential initiation—that T. S. Eliot in *Four Quartets* equates with the "hidden laughter / Of children in the foliage" (we again think of the children at the fête) and the "still point of the turning world."[18] But Meaulnes's desire, in especial, to retain this moment of grace in defiance of the laws of Providence, to adhere to it as a stopping point and ultimate peak experience rather than as a catalyst for further growth (for the moment itself points to that unmoving Love, which is outside of time and which can never be seized and manipulated for human convenience) condemns him to that sterile "dialectic" of which Lewis speaks, when the object of our quest is mistaken for the unseen reality which, in a fugitive instant, it discloses. In short, as T. S. Eliot would say both Seurel and Meaulnes have been vouchsafed the "sudden illumination," those "hints and guesses" that trouble the conscience with a dim presentiment of worlds not realized. But though Meaulnes, in his reflections, comes pretty close, neither of them attempts "to restore the experience / in a different form" by an "approach to [its] meaning."[19] The meaning of the experience for both boys is limited to the mysterious château and the young girl who presides, Beatrice-like, over its demesnes. By attempting not only to possess these things but to secure from them the imperishable joy they seem to auger, they confuse creature with creator, symbol with substance, the temporal with the eternal, the beautiful idol with the thing of which it is "only the reminder."[20] The repetitional nature of this quest, the circular round of this dialectic is emphasized again in this episode—another, though still authentic version of the fête étrange. It is interesting, however, that at the precise moment of François's adventure, the other schoolboys are robbing nest eggs and return to the village to hear "a cock crowing" (*LGM*, 112), as if in vocal confirmation of Meaulnes's subsequent spiritual betrayals.

In any event, after François's transfiguring though inconclusive adventure, Meaulnes departs. He determines to search for the young lady at an address obtained from Frantz before his abrupt disappearance. Meaulnes's departure is preceded by a week of rain. Seurel observes at one point that he would like "to go for a long drive like that"—referring to Meaulnes's former flight—"in the pouring rain, *under a big umbrella"* (*LGM*, 113). Again, for Seurel (as for the denizens of Eliot's *Waste Land*), water is a threatening element.

Meaulnes departs on a Thursday for Paris, the same day of the boating expedition at the lost domain (again, the repetitive nature of events is carefully worked out). Though it is spring, the cold in the air reminds the boys of winter (an inauspicious inversion, in short, of the springlike warmth that surrounded Meaulnes's winter sojourn in the lost domain). Meaulnes departs at "the high point of the village where the Four-Roads meet" (*LGM*, 114)—another reminder of his quest. But precisely on the spot where Frantz and Ganache had formerly camped, a rite of passage is finally being completed: a funeral procession toiling through the village momentarily pauses at the "Four-Roads," then recommences its heavy march while, as Seurel observes, "their lugubrious chanting came faintly to our ears" (*LGM*, 115)—an appropriate tonal accompaniment to Meaulnes's failed quest and foredoomed search, which deliberately parallels the aborted baptism at the novel's inception and points toward its tragic conclusion.

Seurel's Regression

When Meaulnes leaves for Paris, Seurel's ambivalence toward his friend becomes increasingly evident. It is as if a heavy weight had been lifted from his spirit, and he is now free to involve himself in the ordinary events and pastimes of the village. But Meaulnes's character had indelibly affected François—try as he will, he can never move again in the same circumscribed world of his unawakened schoolfellows.

In one episode, which sardonically echoes the original fête, Seurel joins Jasmin in a cart (an obvious parallel to Meaulnes's stolen vehicle) that takes them to the back of an inn where they clandestinely share a bottle of liqueur in a feast that cruelly ironizes the festivity at the lost domain. Like a false prophet, Delouche heads the proceedings and makes mock of Meaulnes's former, inexplicable behavior and wild conceits. In an attempt to defend his friend, Seurel reveals the particulars of Meaulnes's adventure. But these particulars are immediately reduced by the other boys to the level of a freakish prank exaggerated out of proportion, a sexual hunger that, sooner or later—perhaps after Meaulnes "has done his military service"—will be consummated in the normal way. Seurel is ap-

palled. He stares abashed at the other boys and, in another allusion
to Defoe, tells us that "I feel like the shipwrecked mariner who,
relieved to find a human to speak to, found himself addressing an
ape" (*LGM*, 119).

For Delouche, as his name implies, is "equivocal," "dubious,"
even "pretentious" in his inability to understand the nature of certain
events. To be sure, he is not all that bad. Meaulnes's hatred of him
is clearly traceable to the fact that it is just Jasmin's accepting
normalcy that he finds so repugnant; but it is this very normalcy
that constitutes a necessary counterpoise to the extravagances of
Meaulnes's own imagination. Despite Jasmin's innocuousness, however, we must not, as C. S. Lewis reminds us, "overvalue the relative
harmlessness of the little, sensual, frivolous people. They are not
above, but below some temptations." We shall return to our examination of Delouche in a later episode, where Meaulnes's reaction
to him reveals a great deal about the spiritual pride of the novel's
would-be hero.

"Three Letters from Meaulnes"

When Meaulnes arrives in Paris, he discovers another person
waiting outside the curtained windows of the closed house where
he expects to meet Yvonne. It is not until the end of part 3 that
we discover that this is Valentine, the former fiancée of Frantz, the
female counterpart to Pierrot ("dressed in black with a little white
collar" (*LGM*, 120), the seductive and dark projection of Meaulnes's
two-sided anima (the other side of which is the ethereal Yvonne).
Yet Valentine is also, like Yvonne, a real character, an independent
female Other unwillingly martyred to a male mentality that sees
the opposite sex as nothing more than a mirror reflection.

Valentine discloses that as far as she knows Yvonne has married
(she is mistaken of course, mislead, as we subsequently discover in
part 2, by Seurel's Aunt Moinel!). Meaulnes reveals all this information to Seurel by way of post—a correspondence that culminates
in a final letter that arrives in February (the month in which Meaulnes
originally disclosed his adventure to Seurel). In this last letter
Meaulnes finally expresses a clear-sighted recognition that his search
is neither for the lost domain nor for a beautiful girl. His consciousness expands to the point of perceiving that the nature of his

quest is metaphysical—he has accurately diagnosed the "dialectic of desire" that formerly animated his movements. As he writes to Seurel, "Our adventure is ended. The winter of this year is as dead as the grave. Perhaps when we come to die, death will provide the meaning and the sequel and the ending of this unsuccessful adventure" (*LGM*, 122). But Meaulnes will not abide in this faithful and clear-sighted recognition. On the threshold of that awareness which Eliot calls "Christian disillusion," Meaulnes apparently knows "not to expect more from life than it can give or more from human beings than they can give; to look to death for what life cannot give."[21] Fournier wisely excised his original plans to render Meaulnes's intentions more explicit: namely his intent to become a missionary. This would, indeed, have been a moral with a vengeance. But Fournier's art is not one of statement, but rather of suggestion.

However that may be, the complications of part 3 bring about a renewed regression on the part of Meaulnes. Again he fails, given his theocentric orientation, to recognize that, in C. S. Lewis's words, "The longings which arise in us when we first fall in love, or first think of some foreign country, or first take up some subject which excites us, are longings which no marriage, no travel, no learning, can really satisfy."[22] This, for Lewis, does not impugn the legitimacy of these things, but rather places them in their proper perspective. But for a character like Meaulnes, committed to the extreme, anything less than dedication to the absolute seems threadbare and poor in comparison. And it is his confusion between the realms of the temporal and the eternal, the natural and the supernatural, the finite and the infinite, that will have such dire repercussions for those around him.

Unlike Dante, who frees himself, following the death of Beatrice, from the "lady at the window," and hence, prepares for the contemplative pilgrimage that culminates in *The Divine Comedy*, Meaulnes first seeks solace in the arms of Valentine and then abandons her after discovering the nature of her former relations with Frantz. Almost immediately thereafter Seurel arranges a meeting between Meaulnes and Yvonne (whom François discovers one day in his uncle's general store). The reappearance of Frantz in the final third of the novel brings all these elements to a head, and the quest, broken and renewed, only to be broken again, repeats itself in an eternal return that leaves a host of victims in its wake.

The Discovery of Yvonne

Part 3 of the novel again doubles backward on itself and makes us aware that each of the characters has experienced, almost syncronously, a temporary lull in their respective quests. A coinherent fate continues to link the characters together in reciprocal alternations of movement and rest, which underline the repetitive and yet identical nature of their respective quests. By this point, too, the image of childhood undergoes a fundamental change for the worse. For, with the exception perhaps of Yvonne, we have come to realize that a full transition to adult awareness is beyond the capacity of the major characters.

The first chapter of part 3 briefly describes a swimming expedition led by Jasmin Delouche whose white donkey (a reminder of Meaulnes's original steed) accompanies Seurel and the other boys to a local bathing hole on a *Thursday* afternoon—again the day of Meaulnes's meeting with Yvonne. For a while Jasmin indulges in lickerish remarks about a local beauty—Gilberte Poquelin—even straying off the path in tentative pursuit of the young lady (accompanied by the whistles and catcalls of the other boys), which clearly ironizes Meaulnes's quest for Yvonne.

When they finally arrive at the pond, Seurel describes, in tones of poignant retrospect, the significance of this bathing spot for his childhood: "it seemed to us, on the hot dry bank of the Cher, that all the coolness of the world was imprisoned in this little pool, and to this day when I hear the word 'spring' my mind returns to linger over it" (*LGM*, 129). Fournier has somehow endowed that "spring" with a metaphorical resonance and plenary grace. It is, at once, a simple village swimming hole, yet also the well at the world's end, a transforming baptismal basin, somehow beyond reach; for no matter how often he tries to taste of its waters, Seurel confesses that he never "succeeded in quenching [his] thirst . . . because the fear of swallowing a woodlouse tightened our throats, or because the transparence of the water made it hard to judge the right distance, with the result that faces plunged in and noses were filled with something so icy it seemed to burn" (*LGM*, 129). This familiar and yet inaccessible spring, transparent source of juvenescence and renewal recalls the cancelled baptism at the novel's beginning. It is "icy" yet it "burns," and purgation by fire and water, ritual passage to another dimension of experience remains, as we have seen, a remote and persistently dangerous option for Seurel.

It is at this point that one of the grand ironies of the book comes to the fore: namely, the revelation by the pedestrian Delouche of the whereabouts of Les Sablonnières, now like a "ruined chapel" (one thinks again of the "ruined chapel" in *Perceval*). In this chapel, an heraldic inscription on a memorial tablet reveals the aristocratic descent of the recent owners: "Here lie the Chevalier Galois / Faithful to his God, his King, and his Lady Love" (*LGM*, 132). Seurel immediately makes the connections, learns the location of Yvonne, and resolves to become the mediary who finally unites her with her modern-day chevalier—Augustin Meaulnes. But in the problematic context of the modern age, the hierarchical and ordered universe of the "Chevalier Galois" is no longer operative. The themes of "God, sin, praise, and disquietude," which engrossed people's minds from Augustine to the height of the Middle Ages have been replaced by preoccupations with "identity, failure, nostalgia, insecurity."[23] And it is Meaulnes's fate (as it was Fournier's) to occupy a no-man's-land, as it were, between these two opposing worlds. The inscription on the tomb, which enables François to identify the domain as belonging to the Galaises (and it is significant that it is a tomb that unpropitiously points the way) has a conspicuously ironic meaning in the context of Meaulnes's later faithlessness—a faithlessness that involves a betrayal of his own metaphysical intuitions as well as his "Lady Love."

It is finally at the general store of his Uncle Florentin that Seurel meets Yvonne and her father (now forced into humbler circumstances by virtue of Frantz's accumulated debts). The whole scene, pitched in a lower but, for all that, most exquisite key, is yet another replication of the original fête. But now it is Yvonne (not Meaulnes) who arrives on a white steed (or rather a broken down cart-horse). Her appearance, preceded by the sound of crunching cartwheels, repeats that auditory device whereby Fournier creates magical expectations and sets the air vibrating with sounds portentous of an unknown joy. And when Yvonne enters, we are not disappointed. The physical description, which, in a less practised hand, could have been fulsome and therefore ruinous of the atmosphere, is handled with extreme delicacy and restraint. There are a few specifics, "the mass of fair hair," the "forehead and face, which was finely

outlined and finely modelled," the "clear complexion" on which
"the summer sun had placed just two freckles." But, on the whole,
the details are broadly sketched in a suggestive pastel that enables
the reader to imaginatively fill in the portrait. When François,
reverting again to those superlatives that are a common feature of
the fairy tale, declares of Yvonne that "I say it in the simplicity of
my heart, well knowing what I say—[that she was] perhaps the
most beautiful young woman that ever existed in the world" (LGM,
135), disbelief is suspended and the reader assents by virtue of the
few, well-chosen details, the lulling cadence of the prose, the simplicity of the diction, the Renoiresque suggestiveness of the whole
portrait.

But when it comes to Yvonne's character—her inner being, apart
from her role as beckoning fair one to a group of generally selfish
boys—Seurel is struck by her "decision" and "earnestness" (LGM,
136). She wishes to be a teacher (like Seurel who is now grown up
and on the point of following in his father's footsteps), and she quite
decisively and unhesitatingly proclaims her philosophy of education.
Seurel notes her astonishing articulateness, which leaves him and
his cousins gaping and "tongue-tied," and we realize that this woman,
who has been kept from pursuing her vocation by her father, conditioned to acquiesce in the silly pranks of her brother, and fascinated
by the memory of a young man who once appeared at her house
and told her, "You are very beautiful," is no dummy, like the doll
Ganache stuffed with bran, but a woman of independent mind and
discriminating judgment. And it is here, in the least exotic of
settings that she enunciates a position that is in every way antagonistic to the romantic excess of her brother and would-be lover.
As she says to François on learning that he intends to teach school
like his father: "But most of all, I would teach those boys to be
sensible. I'd impress upon them a kind of wisdom I do know something about. I wouldn't fill their heads with a desire to go roaming
about the world, as you will probably do, Monsieur Seurel, once
you're an instructor. I'd teach them to find the happiness which, if
they only knew it, is within easy reach" (LGM, 137).

This is the most balanced pronouncement in the whole book, a
clear repudiation of romantic excess and an insistence on the inter-
penetration of the Mystery in the realm of the everyday. It is the
character of Yvonne herself who more than anything else in the
novel, "inserts the marvelous into reality." Her attitude stands in

bold opposition to "the hunger of imagination which preys upon life" and insists upon the inherent dignity of mundane tasks, ordinary pursuits, the laws of human limit. (It is singularly ironic, then, that Meaulnes's first impression of Yvonne, on the day of the boating party in part 1, should be so mistaken. She appears to him as "eccentric," perhaps an "actress" (*LGM*, 63), precisely because, unlike the other revelers, she is dressed in ordinary, everyday clothes. Meaulnes's confusion of the ordinary with the eccentric, the familiar with the fabulous is an indication of his inability to understand Yvonne's character or to accept her as part of anything less than a surreal universe of romantic illusion.)

In any event, Seurel is overawed. When he leaves his uncle's store, he confesses that between him and Yvonne "there was . . . more clearly than if it had been expressed in words, a secret understanding that only death was to bring to an end, and a friendship more moving than a great love" (*LGM*, 138). Seurel's tragedy lies in his inability to recognize Meaulnes's lack of qualification for domestic life, his failure to interpret the veiled hints Meaulnes lets drop on learning of Yvonne's availability, and his reluctance to act decisively in pursuing Yvonne himself. But even Seurel's potentialities must be qualified by the fact that he remains throughout the novel something of a child. Fournier deliberately underplays his responsibilities as a teacher in two or three brief sentences. It is as if Seurel, instead of growing up, is eternally condemned to reenact his childhood in a schoolhouse from which he never frees himself and in which he remains emotionally imprisoned.

Aunt Moinel and the Interview with Meaulnes

The third chapter of part 3 is at first something of a conundrum. On his way to visit Meaulnes with news of Yvonne's availability, François stops to spend the night at his Aunt Moinel's—one of the original invited guests at the fête étrange. Yet it is appropriate and significant to have this episode come before François's revelations to Meaulnes. The chapter is virtually haunted with ghosts: all of Aunt Moinel's children have died and her walls are adorned with "medallions made of their hair" (*LGM*, 140). In a sense, François will become like his aunt by the novel's conclusion—burdened with memories and haunted by ghosts of the past.

But there are even more interesting connections. For it was Aunt

Moinel, who, on the evening of Frantz's attempted suicide, discovered a fleeing figure on the roadway whom she subsequently succored
and brought home. The figure disguised as a man, was none other
than Frantz's distracted fiancée, Valentine Blondeau. (At this point
we are able to deduce that Valentine's rupture with Frantz coincided
significantly with Meaulnes's first meeting with Yvonne—again
underscoring the coinherent destiny and psychological consanguinity
of these characters.)

Valentine lingers with Aunt Moinel as a *seamstress* who, in the
spring seems to attract the swallows—again the nesting and bird
imagery coalesce about her as formerly about Yvonne. We learn,
too, that after her departure, Valentine continued to correspond
with Seurel's aunt—a correspondence that increasingly focused on
her continued love for Frantz and her misgivings as to whether she
should have abandoned him. In a misguided effort to put Valentine's
anxieties to rest, Aunt Moinel—an inveterate pessimist who soon
becomes convinced of her own conjectures—replies that Yvonne has
married and that Frantz has departed never to return. The whole
Valentine affair is, at first, irrelevant to François. Like his aunt, he
too has a proclivity to suppress urgent desires, deny extreme passions, and envelope reality with the sad (and safe) halo of retrospect.
He decides to suppress Aunt Moinel's information and only speak
of Yvonne in his subsequent interview with Meaulnes.

This interview is one of the turning points of the novel: it rei-
terates the theme of the "dialectic of desire" and sows the seeds for
the tragic denouement. And, paradoxically, it is François, the best-
intentioned and most tender hearted of the novel's characters, who,
through his misreading of events and a certain spiritual obtuseness,
helps to bring things to their tragic close. But he, of course, does
not see these tragic ramifications nor realize that he brings to Meaulnes
what are, at best, ambivalent tidings. First, in refusing to supply
Meaulnes with information about Valentine he adds, albeit unconsciously, to his friend's future torment—for François has no idea
that Meaulnes has engaged in a liaison with Valentine for whom he
now feels responsible. (François only learns of this when it is too
late.) Second, he entirely misses the point of Meaulnes's words in
this interview and pushes him in the direction of Yvonne without
detecting Meaulnes's unmistakable apprehensions. Moreover,
Meaulnes's words here are almost an exact repetition of the sentiments he expressed to François in the last of the three letters he

formerly sent from Paris. Though it does not become explicit until later, Meaulnes now feels unworthy of Yvonne. In fact, Seurel's arrival cruelly synchronizes with Meaulnes's intended departure to seek Valentine and redress the wrongs he has showered upon her. By virtue of that self-tormenting affair, Meaulnes has again come to recognize that for him the lost domain must not be construed narrowly as a final resting place or identified simplistically with the figure of Yvonne. A return to the scene of his former afflatus would not produce the desired effect. As his words to Seurel denote, it is only in another dimension that he will find the elusive essence that he seeks: "But how can a man who has once strayed into heaven ever hope to make terms with the earth! What passes for happiness with most people seemed contemptible to me. And when I tried deliberately and sincerely to live like the rest of them I stored up enough remorse to last me a very long time" (*LGM*, 147). He concludes by echoing the words of his former epistle, "Only in death, as I wrote you, can I expect to recapture the beauty of that moment" (*LGM*, 148). Meaulnes has reaffirmed the theocentric orientation of his quest; and his need, perhaps to find Valentine and seek forgiveness and absolution. Now, bang in the middle of this resolution, comes Seurel with news of an imminent country outing at which he has arranged a meeting between Meaulnes and the still available Yvonne (as we learn later, Meaulnes had heard from Valentine, by way of Aunt Moinel, that Yvonne had married). Meaulnes is stunned. All his resolutions fall to pieces—the divisions that formerly possessed him (celibacy contra marriage, the contemplative life contra the domestic life, religious resignation contra pursuit of the past) return with redoubled energy, polarizing his consciousness into contending parts. And so he gives up his plan of searching for Valentine and allows Seurel to convince him that union with Yvonne (not some "peak of perfection, of purity" (*LGM*, 148) is what he really wants. Since Seurel knows nothing of the Valentine affair he cannot be held accountable for Meaulnes's abdication of honor—but even Meaulnes realizes that for him it is too late. Consenting to see Yvonne in what he doubtless thinks of as a last valedictory gesture, he exhorts his mother "not to unpack his trunk, as his journey might only be postponed" (*LGM*, 149). Yet there does seem to be something extravagant and unhealthy in Meaulnes's scruples. They are a consequence not so much of illicit sexuality (which is relatively venial), but spiritual pride—his need to condemn himself for his behavior allows him to think of himself as something of a saint: for who else would experience such exquisite spiritual torments? Moreover, it allows him to avoid the one thing he truly fears: a mature commitment to a responsible adult woman. As we shall see, his desire to find Valentine and save her from her threatened self-destruction is, in part, a rationalization of his need to escape from adult limitations and responsibilities.

The Outing and the Marriage

The outing arranged by François is yet another burlesque version of the fête étrange. Meaulnes's impatience as he waits for Yvonne to arrive is taken out on Delouche. For Delouche is an anti-Meaulnes, a character who, to borrow here an inimitable phrase of Henry James's, possesses "the imperturbable levity of a mind utterly unhaunted by the metaphysics of things."[24] Meaulnes finds him on all occasions an insupportable buffoon. Yet Jasmin's somewhat sycophantic clinging to Meaulnes shows that like Shakespeare's Caliban or Bottom, he, too, has a dim sense that "the isle is full of noises, / Sounds and sweet airs that give delight and hurt not"—in other words, that there is a spiritual reality beyond the normal realm of human affairs. Still, Monsieur de Galais is attracted toward Delouche precisely because he is disabused of all those lofty notions that have ruined his son Frantz. But Jasmin's impoverishment of vision and dearth of imagination are at the opposite extreme of Meaulnes's metaphysical hunger, and the reason Meaulnes despises him is precisely because of Jasmin's unquestioning acceptance of the ordinary—an acceptance Meaulnes himself would do well to acquire. It is important to discriminate, however, between Jasmin's humble earthiness and Yvonne's sense that the sacred itself is a simple produce of the common day. There is all the difference in the world between clinging to the ordinary as a means of staving off uncomfortable or challenging realities and consecreating the ordinary, as Yvonne would have it, from the perspective of those realities.

In any event, when Yvonne arrives on her debilitated cart-horse (a deliberate ironization of the steed bestrode by the proverbial fairy-tale princess and a tacit reminder of Meaulnes's own lame and limping courser), Meaulnes browbeats the girl with a cruel harangue on the Galaises' diminished splendor. Seurel endeavors to intervene, but Meaulnes evokes the razed grounds and lost items of Les Sablonnières (the symbolic mirror, candlestick, and broken lute). Again, it is not so much Yvonne that Meaulnes wants but the original backdrop with its associated emotional thrills against which he first encountered her.

He loses all philosophical perspective, virtually stamps his feet in disappointment at the contrast between a magic then, and an impoverished now, locking himself ever deeper into that "dialectic" which keeps him circling, like a prisoner in his cell, on a continual hunt for a receding felicity from which he is forever cutting himself off. The whole psychological situation is singularly illustrative of Lewis's dialectic. The pearl of great price that Meaulnes associates with the fête étrange thus becomes, as Lewis would rightfully prognosticate, increasingly remote in proportion as Meaulnes "sits down on the desire and attempts to cherish it."[25]

Seurel marvels at Meaulnes's rude behavior and asks himself, "Why then this present emptiness, this aloofness, this inability to be happy?" (*LGM*, 157). If he were only better read in Pascal (whose words Fournier may be deliberately echoing here), the answer would be clear and incontestable: "What is it then that this desire [for happiness] and this inability to achieve it proclaim to us?" asks Pascal in words that recall Seurel's. His answer is not devoid of significance to this particular dramatic moment in *Le Grand Meaulnes*. For what it proclaims, according to Pascal, is "that there was once in man a true happiness of which there now remain to him only the mark and empty trace, which he in vain tries to fill from all his surroundings, seeking from things absent the help he does not obtain in things present. But these are all inadequate, because the infinite abyss can only be filled by an infinite and immutable object, that is to say, only by God Himself."[26]

But this goes unrecognized and the sea imagery when it returns, is laden with the darkest of undertones. As Seurel comments, Yvonne "was unable to produce a single bit of wreckage to prove they hadn't both been dreaming, like a diver who brings up a mere handful of seaweed and stones from the depth of the sea" (*LGM*, 156). Meanwhile the children at the picnic torment the animals (in a way that belies their former role as personifications of an untarnished innocence and emphasizes Meaulnes's degeneration from the childlike to the childish). When, in the distance, Meaulnes hears someone singing the refrain of the "red shoes" that he had heard on the last night of his stay at the domain (now a painful reminder of an imperfect world, or more specifically, of Meaulnes's liaison with Valentine), he runs off seeking he knows not what, and stumbles upon Jasmin attempting to untether the Galaises' feeble cart-horse. In an ecstasy of anger (for the limping horse is an outward and tangible emblem of Meaulnes's own spiritual lameness) he lashes out at Jasmin and on discovering that the horse belongs to Yvonne becomes even more furious. Someone suggests that the animal (severely hurt by having been hitched negligently to a tree) might recover by a douche of "cold water . . . if you stood him in the ford" (LGM, 159)—but the idea is abandoned, the animal presumably beyond help, and the "cold water," like François's pool or the cancelled baptism, again serves to remind us of Meaulnes's failed rite. Yvonne is mortified beyond expression and departs solemnly with her father. Nevertheless, that night, in a fit of remorse, Meaulnes arrives at the Galaises' cottage and asks Yvonne to be his wife. (Yet it is interesting that it is only after the actual Yvonne is gone that Meaulnes decides to marry her. Her presence had compelled him to recognize her irreducible otherness—but that is not what he wants. What he wants, as we have seen, is an exact repetition of his first encounter with her. Her absence enables him once again to surround her with that imaginative halo which is the real object of his pursuit. This further confirms Meaulnes's unenlightened entrapment in Lewis's "dialectic," and perfectly illustrates Pascal's collateral insight into human nature: "The consciousness of the falsity of present pleasures, and the ignorance of the vanity of absent pleasures, causes inconstancy."[27] And Meaulnes, as we shall see, is nothing if not inconstant.)

The opening of the chapter entitled "The Wedding Day" is one of the most evocative in the whole book. "In each house a fire in the dining room throws a sheen over varnished toys set out as if on an altar," observes Seurel—an altar, we might add, about to be desecrated. For again the warm firelight glow contrasts with the "icy afternoon" and "strong wind," and Seurel, as if in anticipation of the ensuing disaster, observes, in a haunting return of the marine imagery, "for a man who prefers not to be happy, there is the attic where he can listen till nightfall to the creakings and groanings of shipwrecks" (LGM, 161). The repetitive cycle (suggesting that the marriage will fail) is signaled by the fact that it is again a Thursday in February—"the month of Meaulnes's projected second flight from

Sainte-Agathe," and, as we later learn, "the month of the Paris adventure" with Valentine.[28]

When, following the wedding ceremony Meaulnes and Yvonne are together in their cottage, François, fearing some nameless treachery, stations himself outside their dwelling, and, in one of the most tender and evocative of the musical passages we have thus far examined, describes the sound of Yvonne's piano:

The music coming from the depths of the inscrutable house is at first like some far-away tentative voice intimidated by an excess of joy, or the laughter of a child who has gone to fetch all her toys and spread them out before a new playmate. . . . It is also like the timorous, questioning regard of a woman who has put on her finest gown but is not sure it will find favor. . . . This melody, which I've never heard before, is a kind of prayer to happiness, an entreaty asking fate not to be too cruel, a salutation to happiness and at the same time a genuflection (*LGM*, 162–63).

But the confusion of this frail and fugitive happiness is almost immediately indicated by another sound—the piercing cry of Frantz to whom François and Meaulnes, in an early gesture of schoolboy bravado, had unconditionally promised to respond. François recognizes it at once, and in an attempt to forestall the harassment of the newlyweds, searches for and confronts the pitiable Frantz. For Frantz has entirely lost his former luster; he is now a young man in his early twenties, still attempting to live life as a storybook and, in consequence, all the more pathetic and contemptible. As Seurel observes, "he was more of a child than ever: imperious, whimsical, and suddenly deflated" (*LGM*, 166).

It is at this point that we realize the extent to which Frantz represents the atavistic elements in Mealunes's ego. His return, on the night of Meaulnes's wedding, portends a disruption of the newlywed's happiness, indicated again in a significant return of the window imagery, by "the scratching sound made against a pane by the leafless branch of a rose-bush" (*LGM*, 167). Meaulnes, endeavoring to close the shutters (like Monsieur Seurel in the opening chapters), is distracted by a noise, runs off in pursuit of Frantz (who has been persuaded to leave by François) and, psychologically speaking, reverts back to his former childish self. The entire episode mirrors and echoes Frantz's disruption of the original fête étrange.

When Yvonne, disturbed at her husband's prolonged absence, rushes out to search for him, she stumbles and sustains a wound on her forehead, thus replicating her brother's headwound and Meaulnes's original wound on getting down from the cart. This wound, which spreads outward from Meaulnes like a spiritual infection, is the tangible emblem of the devastation wrought by his own psychological unbalance.

Seurel's Fidelity and Meaulnes's Betrayal

The next day, when Seurel pays a visit to the newlyweds, he hears, prior to his arrival, "the sound of distant bells . . . ringing for Vespers" (*LGM*, 172). The bells recall the opening failed baptism and are another instance of the way in which Fournier uses sounds to mysteriously foreshadow important events—in this case, the death of Yvonne. Seurel learns that Meaulnes has fled without giving any hint of his destination or indicating the time of his return. Clearly, Fournier's attitude toward his "hero" is one of distant and devastating irony—a point that needs emphasis to counteract the mistaken notion that the author (as Byron with Manfred) identified fully with his "hero." Yet in a letter of November 1912 to Bichet, Fournier's attitude toward Meaulnes is quite unmistakable: "The great imbecile runs away for the first time at nightfall and they bring him back. He runs away a second time before daybreak and this time he gets clean away."[29] The note of ironic contempt is clear and perspicuous.

Of course, as we later learn, Meaulnes's ostensible reason for leaving Yvonne is to fulfill his childhood pledge to Frantz, to find the erring Valentine whom he has unwittingly seduced from Frantz, and to salvage his honor through this act of rectification. In T. S. Eliot's words, however, Meaulnes's is the "treason / of doing the right deed for the wrong reason." For the real purpose behind Meaulnes's leaving Yvonne is his desire to return to an easier, less complex stage of his existence in which his "purity" is unmolested and he can still imagine Yvonne as the beckoning fair one—virginal, veiled, and forever chaste. Since marriage has made this impossible and Meaulnes cannot forego his infatuation with his own past, Yvonne, and the child (conceived on the night prior to Meaulnes's departure) are the victims. By failing to differentiate his desire for the absolute from the mortal Yvonne, Meaulnes destroys his prospects of earthly comfort and divine consolation. He is condemned to remain a "childe" in both the ordinary and medieval sense of the term—namely, a novitiate knight who has not yet completed the full term of his initiation.

Hence, it is Seurel who takes over Meaulnes's role during his absence. As surrogate husband to Yvonne and substitute father to Yvonne's child, Seurel comes closest to fulfilling his existence—but, of course, he is, as he realizes, nothing more than a substitute, albeit a loyal and devoted one. Both Martin Sorrell and Robert Gibson have noted how, at this point, François begins to increasingly dominate the narrative, placing himself and Yvonne in the foreground in a kind of aesthetic revenge against the friend who has in a sense ruined his life.[30]

In the long colloquies between François and Yvonne that follow, we learn more about the novel's enigmatic heroine. As previously noted, Yvonne is at once a breathing incarnation of the absolutes of purity and grace, a Dantesque mediary between the divine and the human, and very much a well-meaning, responsible, though patriarchally oppressed girl who is never fully disabused of the image to which she is forced by father, brother, husband, and, yes, even Seurel, to correspond—the image, that is to say, of a selfless, ethereal, almost disembodied mother, sister, angel, and beloved all rolled into one.

To the end, our estimate of Yvonne is ambiguous. On the one hand, as in Simone Weil's description of God as a "beggar waiting for our love," she waits patiently and without censure for the love that neither Frantz nor Meaulnes are mature enough to give. It must be admitted, however, that it is this uncritical acceptance of her brother's petulance and her husband's shortcomings that assists in her demise. Whether we regard her as a pathetically exploited victim or a Christ figure she is, at any rate, oppressed by a male mentality that distorts the interpersonal situation of love by regarding the woman exclusively from an aesthetic point of view. Only Seurel can see her, and then but intermittently, from a perspective other than his own.

Her vicarious suffering and death deliberately recalls Christ's; while the episode where Yvonne succors the exposed baby chicks whose nests (in a recurrence of this important motif) have been overturned consciously echoes the Gospel of Saint Matthew: "how often would I have gathered thy children together, even as a hen gathereth her chickens under her wings, and ye would not!" (Matt. 23:37).

When Yvonne dies and Seurel carries her down the steps in a cruel ironization of the traditional image of the bridegroom carrying the bride over the threshold (an episode with macabre sexual overtones—for Seurel, afflicted like Meaulnes with fear of a mature female Other, can embrace her safely only in death), we are also reminded of traditional images of the Pieta, with Yvonne as female Christ and Seurel as male virgin. Of course, this whole scene is determined by the fact that the stairs are too narrow to accommodate Yvonne's coffin. When one of the pall-bearers suggests that it may be hoisted up through the window and lowered in the same way, François intervenes and enacts this symbolic descent (which is not only a descent from the cross but another instance of a ravaged innocence clasped to a sympathetic breast).

Thus, even in death, Yvonne repudiates the emotional restlessness of the male protagonists and symbolically reaffirms the conviction that authentic existence is not to be grasped in some remote and alluring never-land, but in the world of diurnal relationships and sacramental commitments; for, by the end of the novel, the window imagery loses its initial connotations of mystery, transcendence, and wonder and declines into a motif associated with an irresponsible escapism. Given her scale of values, then, it is impossible for Yvonne to pass through a window even in death.

How shall a contemporary reader interpret Yvonne's character? Is she an unenlightened and oppressed member of an exploited sex discriminated against by a partriarchal society of selfish males or an authentic and self-sacrificing witness to transcendent values? Each reader must answer this question for himself or herself. But perhaps Seurel's own words come closest to capturing the fundamental ambivalence evoked by the character of Yvonne: "I felt," he observes, "she had made a great mistake [with regard to her brother and her husband] out of generosity, in a spirit of self-sacrifice. . . . But how could I find fault with so much goodness, so much love?" (*LGM*, 180).

Yvonne's Daughter

Yvonne dies as a result of the complications of childbirth, but it is suggested that Meaulnes's absence and silence—for he fails even to write—are, at least, indirectly responsible. It is significant that the child, after a difficult delivery, sustains a headwound from the doctor's forceps—again, the sins of the father are being visited upon his child.

One of the central ironies of *Le Grand Meaulnes* is the fact that Meaulnes in his vain and ill-conceived intent to restore Valentine to Frantz has missed the most mysterious and miraculous event offered to him in his existence: namely, the birth of his daughter. In attempting to sustain the ideal world of childhood, "trailing clouds of glory," he misses another rite of passage that would have enabled him to recover the very thing he seeks. For it is there, in the birth-room, that a new rite of passage, namely, the reception of an infant soul into the community of the living, takes place. As François observes, "I discovered a world quite unknown to me, and my heart was swelling with a new kind of joy." "Conscious of a strange presence in the room" (*LGM*, 182), François has at least been granted a vision of the way in which, as Yvonne herself has stipulated, the glory and the dream—to wit, the beginnings of a new human life—enters mysteriously into the realm of the everyday.

For although the freshness and fantasy of childhood are no longer available to Meaulnes, his child herself is a fresh incarnation of the mystery that his distracted desire to return to the past prevents him from seeing. For the way in which adults normally renew contact with the magic wellsprings of childhood is by nurturing the next generation of children. Thus the child is precisely a visitant from that other mysterious landscape that Meaulnes desires; but his selfish enthrallment with a moment in his past, his fear of a mature relationship that would bring Yvonne into the realm of the accessible, and his refusal to relinquish his own claims to childhood prevent him from participating in that mystery which is a simple produce of the common day or in preparing the conditions that would allow a new generation of children to grow into an awareness of the values that Meaulnes associates with the lost domain.

Meaulnes and Valentine

Several months after Yvonne's death, Seurel discovers the diary that contains a full account of Meaulnes's relations with Valentine. Again we become aware of a strange consanguinity among the characters: for just as Seurel has assumed Meaulnes's role in relation to Yvonne, so Meaulnes has assumed Frantz's role in relation to Valentine.

Through this affair, Meaulnes completes at least part of his rite— but his sexual initiation is, at best, a fragmented experience. For from the beginning the whole affair is fundamentally unpalatable to him. "The red designs on the black curtains" (LGM, 194) in the bedroom he shares with Valentine portend the imminent disruption of their illicit idyll. Significantly, as he looks with tender pathos at the sleeping Valentine, Meaulnes muses, "that's how birds must sleep" (LGM, 195). But within two days Meaulnes will ravish, as it were, Valentine's nest. The discovery that she was Frantz's former fiancée, the fact that they had been living together under false pretenses, the disclosure that her scruples are not as "fine" as his, issue in an utter rejection of the hapless girl who becomes an object of contempt to this inveterate idealist. Yet again it is important to note that Meaulnes's sin is not that of concupiscence, as he conceives it, but rather of pride. After he rejects Valentine and she runs off, threatening him, in her last angry reprisals with her imminent ruin, he is overcome by remorse and searches for her in a red-light district of Bourges. It is a complete inversion of the green lantern in the window of the lost domain.

At this point the novel deepens in moral complexity. Are we to believe, as Meaulnes would have it, that if Valentine had remained faithful to Frantz (instead of retreating in the face of his far-flung ideals), an unbroken felicity would have been guaranteed for all? When Meaulnes discovers Valentine's true identity, he throws this accusation in her face and abandons her to what, in the context of the period's double standard, is her only alternative: a life of prostitution. Yet Meaulnes's accusation is more accurately applicable to himself. If he had remained faithful to his former impulses, if he had clearly discriminated between the love of woman and the search for the absolutes of perfection, if he had been able to recognize the difference between emotional restlessness and divine discontent (for as Pascal observes, "it is natural for the mind to believe, and for the will to love; so that for want of true objects, they must attach themselves to false"),[31] then neither Valentine, Yvonne, Seurel, nor Meaulnes himself would have been subject to the disequilibrium of Meaulnes's undisciplined will.

The Return of Meaulnes

Meaulnes returns to Les Sablonnières more than a year after Yvonne's death. He has successfully searched out and reunited Frantz and Valentine. But, as we have seen, his exertions on Frantz's behalf are self-deceiving. The short-lived nature of Frantz's union with Valentine becomes apparent when, on their return to Les Sablonnières, they enter the playhouse formerly constructed by Monsieur de Galais for his errant son. They are no more than two children playing "house" before the onset of a mutual, estranging tantrum. On the pretext of aiding his friend, Meaulnes has been able to circumvent his greatest fears: a humble recognition of his own short-comings, an acceptance of Yvonne's (and by implication) God's forgiveness and love, a daily and painstaking renewal of the sacrament of marriage in the context of the ordinary struggles, numberless failings, and rekindled aspirations of common humanity—in short, the ceaseless wear and tear of daily life on two individuals who endeavor to transcend its pettiness through renewed pledges, mutual forgiveness, and deepening love.

In any event, Meaulnes's return on a Sunday in autumn (it is on a Sunday in autumn that the novel opens) betrays the repetitional nature of his misdirected quest. Significantly, he cannot get back into his own house. For his behavior has in a sense indefinitely exiled him from the human community. It is Seurel who sees him in the distance, runs to his side, and finally unlocks the door to reveal the tragedy that Meaulnes has left in his wake. But the final turn of the screw occurs when Meaulnes departs the next day with his daughter clasped to his breast, "wrapping [her] in a cloak" (*LGM*, 206). Seurel has been robbed of his last comfort, and Meaulnes's gesture, which recalls the opening gesture of Millie as she clasps her hat to her breast, or the awkward embrace by Ganache of the self-mutilated Frantz, or the heavy burden of Yvonne as Seurel carries her down the stairs, portends a dark and questionable future for this last helpless victim of an insensate quest doomed, it seems, from the start.

In the final analysis, *Le Grand Meaulnes* is a cautionary tale: it embodies a sense of reality that is distinctly antiromantic and implicitly warns against the extravagances to which an untempered romanticism is prone. Its hero, Meaulnes, is a conspicuous example of bad faith. He leaves Yvonne for the putative purpose of reuniting Valentine with Frantz, but we know and so must he, that such a union is ill-advised and without substance. He seeks for a purity that is not of this world, but he marries a woman who exists for him exclusively as a symbol of that purity. He both solicits and recoils from the demands of marriage and the responsibilities of parenthood, confusing heaven with earth, the natural with the supernatural, the divine with the human. Desiring all or nothing, he wrecks the happiness that comes from the acceptance of human limit, yet lacks the self-dedication, the disdain for comfort, and the single-minded tenacity of the hero or the saint.

Yet for all this our final estimate of Meaulnes is leavened with compassion. He is one of the last characters in twentieth-century fiction possessed of an Augustinian longing (and there is no pun here; the namesake is deliberate) for a happiness that is not of this world. And, indeed, those memorable words from Augustine's *Confessions* may be applied to Meaulnes without hesitation: "I loved not yet, yet I loved to love. . . . I sought what I might love, in love with loving."

But it is above all Seurel's grave and musical prose, his sense of the sadness and inscrutability of the human condition, his tender fidelity to the memories of Meaulnes and Yvonne, that create a gentle palliative to the novel's grim conclusion and temper the tragedy with grace notes.

In its delicate and perceptive undercutting of an unenlightened romanticism, its organic use of imagistic and symbolic motifs, its superb architectonics, constrained lyricism, and controlled pathos, Alain-Fournier's novel is one of the seminal achievements of modern French literature. Moreover, for those readers who remain enchanted by its central themes and enthralled by its nostalgic spirituality, *Le Grand Meaulnes* must ever be among those few rare books that sagaciously chart and justly delineate that "sweet desire" which, in C. S. Lewis's words, "is only a foretaste of that which the real Desireable will be when [we] have found it."[32]

Chapter Six
Conclusion

Hitherto we have been able to trace Fournier's spiritual and artistic development, to examine the evolution of his style, the nature of his themes, and the quality of his achievement. At this point, however, we enter a dangerous no-man's-land of critical conjecture, supposition, and surmise.

Fournier's early death at the age of twenty-eight is as poignant and irreparable a loss for those who feel a strong and steadfast interest in the development of French literature as are the early deaths of Keats and Shelley for those who wonder with sad dismay how the progress of English literature might have been altered by the longevity of two of its finest poets. Moreover, just as we imagine what the response of Keats or Shelley would have been to the complex and bewildering world of Victorian industry, science, and thought, so may we equally wonder at what Fournier's response might have been had he survived, to the blind mechanism of modern warfare, the cynical relativism of the lost generation, the formidable cerebrality of modern literature, and the utter destruction of that prewar innocence, that enviable though illusory idyll in which the men and women of the first decade of this century lived and moved and had their being.

As one of the first casualties of the Great War, "the war to end all wars," as it was thought by the people of his generation, Fournier did not live to see the gradual but unrelenting brutalization of battlefield experience, to undergo the insidious attrition of hope and faith that one survivor, Anthony Eden, Lord Avon, speaks of as follows: "The stench, the mud, the corpses, the destruction everywhere, the torn and twisted guns and limbs, the shattered wagons, the mutilated horses and mules, creat[ing] a scene of desolation beyond description."[1] Blessedly or not, for Fournier the end was quick, presumably instantaneous, and perhaps—occurring as it did before "the mechanical nature of modern warfare had neutralized both men and values"[2]—grandly chivalric. As François Mauriac recollects in a bittersweet passage from *Mémoires intérieurs*, "with his

145

starched collar and his neat tie, Alain-Fournier . . . his back turned
on all that was sordid, vulgar, tainted, moved through his elaborate
and magic world to the holocaust of 1914."[3]

But what if he had survived this holocaust? Like Rivière he would
doubtless have remained haunted by nightmare horrors of unspeakable deprivation and human barbarism. Would these have pushed
him, as presumably in the case of Rivière, into an open avowal of
religious faith? Or, on the contrary, would he have turned bitter,
hardened, and resentful, embracing one of the many dubious ideologies—Marxism, existentialism, a militant nationalism—that pro-
liferated in the postwar years? Would the religious examples of
Jacques Maritain, Gabriel Marcel, Simone Weil, T. S. Eliot, and
a maturer François Mauriac, have provided a counterpoise to the
shell shock, depression, and loss caused by trench warfare and an
alternative to the militant and unbending Catholicism of apologists
such as Claudel or the followers of Charles Maurras? And how would
Fournier have responded to the new wave of modernism—to Joyce,
Kafka, Proust, Mann, and the later Gide whose experiments rev-
olutionized the world of letters (a revolution Fournier himself prefigured in the deft architectonics of *Le Grand Meaulnes*)? These
questions must forever remain open, unanswered and unanswerable.
Still, there have been not a few intrepid critics who have ventured
suggestions as to Fournier's potential development (or regression)—
a venture in which we cannot forbear to participate.

One thing is clear. Unlike his hero Augustin Meaulnes, Fournier
could not have been deluded with the hope of going backward. As
we have seen in our discussion of *Le Grand Meaulnes*, Fournier's hero
is a "romanticist"—one who, to define the term in the words of
Irving Babbitt, "revels in the mere picturesqueness of the facts or
else takes refuge in the past from the present, uses it . . . to create
for himself an alibi." But the ironic elements in *Le Grande Meaulnes*
already reveal, to continue with Babbitt's words, "that the past
should be regarded primarily neither as a laboratory for research nor
as a bower of dreams, but as a school of experience."[4]

Furthermore, in his last letters to Rivière, Fournier admits that
the first fine careless rapture of his youthful lyricism was on the
wane and that a new "school of experience" lay ahead of him: "I
am alone. And despite my stiffled heart, although I am quite crushed,
I must get up again. I need glory. I must win souls. I must rise
above it all . . . My country scenes no longer have their hidden

face, mysterious and adorable. My roads no longer lead toward the kingdom of the heart, a kingdom as strange and mysterious as she [Yvonne] herself. I have lost those bitter-sweet imaginings she inspired in me, which were all my life. Now I am alone in the middle of the world" (*Corr. R-F* 2:262).

The state Fournier describes here with such candor and directness is not at all dissimilar from that moment in Dante's *La Vita nuova* where the poet dreams that his lady has died and agonizes, in inexpressible torment, over the vulnerability of the woman he loves. Yet for Dante this proved to be a turning point in his relations with Beatrice—the self-regarding sorrows and pitiful laments give way to a firm inner conviction that his lady is, indeed, the bearer of a benison that transcends the spatio-temporal limits of human experience. In a certain sense, *Le Grand Meaulnes* is Fournier's *La Vita nuova*. Even the meditation cited above where he speaks to Rivière of that lamentable state so well known to both Coleridge and Wordsworth, is itself a dialectical moment in the writer's progress toward that instant of gracious release where the soul recognizes that the whole of its longing and the ground of its beseeching point to an infinite object of unutterable love.

In the interwar years and following, Joyce, Eliot, and Mann were constrained to dramatize and give order to the chaotic multiplicity of contemporary life and the spiritual desuetude of modern culture by appealing to the mythic structures and poetic fabulists from the ages of legend and romance. The wanderings of a Ulysses, the gropings of a Perceval, the demonology of a Faust return in modern guise to comment obliquely but incisively on the loss of traditional wisdom, the capitulation to moral anarchy, the absence of dependable guideposts, the refusal of proffered grace. The "immense panorama of futility, anarchy, and chaos" that Eliot saw as modern civilization required even greater and more heroic efforts on the part of those men and women of letters who refused to succumb to the directionless drift, false prophets, and ascendent materialism of an abandoned and destitute age. Their works became broader in scope, more monumental in structure, profounder in theme, and darker in latent prophecy. Would Fournier have joined with these experimenters, using the knowledge he had gained in the composition of *Le Grand Meaulnes* to construct a work of even greater magnitude, using perhaps the organizational patterns of *The Divine Comedy* (as Joyce used Homer's *Odyssey*) to chart the contemporary reaches of human degradation and hope? Or would he, in the face of postwar disillusion and with the knowledge that all he had loved had been transformed, once and forever, by the irreversible tread of that "rough beast" which Yeats imagined as the incarnate image of the anti-Christ, have acted on his earlier impulses, to enter a monastery and devote himself to a life of religious consecration? Though asked in vain, these tantalizing questions linger in the silence of Fournier's early and unjust death. Even the fragments Fournier wrote in the midst of his liaison with Simone provide no real clue—for neither of them bears the impress of the postwar years with which Fournier would have had to grapple spiritually and contend aesthetically. To these fragments, however, we shall turn, in a brief analysis of their potential direction and latent themes, before concluding with a general estimate of Fournier's achievement and influence.

Colombe Blanchet and *La Maison dans la forêt*

Given Fournier's method of composition, a process of slow accretion, revision, revaluation, and developmental change, both *Colombe Blanchet* and *La Maison dans la Forêt* are modeled, at best, on inchoate plans that would doubtless have undergone modification during the tenure of their growth. As in *Le Grand Meaulnes* the disparity between the original conception of these works and their final realization would probably contradict anything we can presently imagine. Harold March, looking at these fragmentary plans and tentative notes, concludes that both the novel and the play would have demonstrated an "improved technique; but their insistence on the irreparable character of lost purity sounds more like a backward look than progress."[5] Karen D. Levy, examining these same materials, comes to the opposite conclusion. For her both works "deal with situations where the protagonists attain fulfillment through reciprocal love and the prospect of a future together."[6] In short, the aborted rite of passage in *Le Grand Meaulnes* would have been reenacted and successfully dramatized at a higher level of awareness that would have led to Fournier's personal liberation and artistic redemption. Moreover, for Levy, and despite Isabelle Rivière's assertions to the contrary, Simone Casimer-Périer, for whom the play was originally conceived, would have enabled Fournier to eschew "a love that fed on absence" and "realize that today and tomorrow are more important than yesterday."[7] Here, then, are two conclusions, based on the same materials, by two critics of penetrating mind whose opinions are diametrically opposed. In any case, March's conjecture that Fournier "might have found peace in God and in the arms of the church, as his sister was convinced he would and as Rivière did"[8] stands at the opposite pole of Levy's supposition that Fournier would have shed the spiritual agitations that disturb the characters in *Le Grand Meaulnes* and would have accepted a less lofty and more accommodating vision of love such as that offered by Simone.

At all events, both *Colombe Blanchet* and *La Maison dans la Forêt* are less subjectively conceived. While they reflect, as *Le Grand Meaulnes,* the personal conflicts and contradictions of the author, they seem to widen outward in their embrace of multiple, distinct, and humorously realized characters less obsessed and self-tormenting than the three protagonists of the earlier novel. The potential for comic contrast, domesticated romance, and self-deprecating irony deepens even as it contrasts with a residual yearning to maintain, at least in memory and with a poignant backward glance, an emotional attachment to those "echoes that die away just as they [catch] your ear"—what C. S. Lewis speaks of as "the secret signature of each soul, an incommunicable want, the thing we desire [before all else] and which we shall still desire on our deathbeds."[9]

Still, in both works Fournier seems to be engaged in an attempt to tame his youthful romanticism, to enlarge the area of his dramatic concerns, and to accept the compromises maturity brings without altogether abandoning the perceptions, the "hints" and "guesses," that disturbed and transfigured his youth. Gibson notes that as early as 1908, Fournier was already involved in a strategy to expand his sense of human drama beyond the territorial and psychological confines of *Le Grand Meaulnes.* As he wrote to Rivière at this time: "I want to do for Paris a little of what I shall have done for the countryside. I would find the landscapes and souls behind those sordid and sentimental Parisian scenes . . . I would find the landscape behind the settings in the music halls as the prostitutes look at them. It would be a world as mysterious and terrifying as that of my first book" (*Corr. R-F*, 2:262)

Evidence of what this new world may have been like is available to us in a chapter Fournier deleted from *Le Grand Meaulnes*—"La Dispute"—that appeared posthumously in *Miracles.* Here Fournier writes, as has been observed of Flaubert, with a scalpel rather than a pen, describing in penetrating detail the psychosexual nature of Meaulnes's liaison with Valentine, treating such things as menstruation, sexual frustration, the mutual recrimination of two lovers who have embraced the projected phantoms of one another as in a distorting mirror only to realize the disparity between those projections and the real person they hold in their arms. Gibson feels that the excision and taming of the chapter in *Le Grand Meaulnes* narrowed the range of the novel's final achievement, but Fournier's sister has plausibly argued that the excision was sagely done and based on a perception that its tone contrasted too flagrantly and inharmoniously with the delicate atmosphere Fournier, even in the last third of the book, maintains with the expertise of an unerring artisan.

Herbert Howarth, however, sees in this cancelled chapter a significant portent of things to come:

Although *Le Grand Meaulnes* shows that his best gift lay in purity, in the far clear voice of *l'innocent paradis*, Fournier began to experiment in the atmosphere of evil and its flowers. His story, "La Dispute," an alternate version of an episode in *Le Grand Meaulnes*, described an "odeur de sang corrumpu, de femme malade," rising from the bed of quarreling lovers. He played with fancies of a new novel, the urban counterpart of *Le Grand Meaulnes*, to be set in Paris instead of the countryside. From sketches, from the Paris chapters of the rural novel, and from glimpses of the city in the correspondence with Rivière, one can guess how he would have filled it with the taste of fog, the shining squares of windows, rain-wet benches, the violence of street quarrels, the intimations of a repugnant secret. It would have been [akin to the spirit of Eliot's *Waste Land*] . . . softened—perhaps weakened, perhaps refined—by his compassion and by his delicacy. [10]

However that may be, we are still in the realm of conjecture. To return to more solid ground, it is necessary to fix our attention on the actual fragments Fournier left behind and allow these to speak for themselves.

The fragments of *Colombe Blanchet* do seem, at first blush, to confirm Karen Levy's sense that Fournier was engaged in an attempt to reach a synthesis between the conflicting poles of his personality. A young schoolteacher, Jean-Gilles Autissier, is assigned to a small French village where he becomes involved in the acrimonious world of small-town politics—the nature of this acrimony is unspecified, but the very fact that Fournier intended to include a political element in the formation of the plot shows a movement outward and away from the brooding introspection of Seurel's narrative in *Le Grand Meaulnes*. The chief interest, however, would have centered on Autissier's successive entanglement with three young women: Laurence (whom he ultimately abandons, in Meaulnes-like fashion, on hearing of her indiscreet past); Colombe (who abandons him and enters a convent after learning, in the midst of their liaison, that Autissier had acted unscrupulously in his earlier affair with Laurence); and Emilie (Colombe's sister with whom Autissier would presumably have achieved a stable, steady, less exhalted but more accepting relationship on the level of workaday reality). Moreover, these affairs would have been counterpointed with the political squabbles between Autissier and the father of the Blanchet sisters who is mayor of the town and dedicated to keeping the local teachers in their place. Another character—Marazano—Autissier's landlord, an inveterate cutpurse and kleptomaniac, would have provided extensive comic relief and joined a host of other characters, schoolteachers and people of the village, whom Fournier intended to develop with an expansive Dickensian gusto. Does the novel signal, as Levy suggests, a way out of the dilemma that divided Fournier's consciousness in *Le Grand Meaulnes*? Is Emilie based on the real-life character of Simone (who had, incidentally, written a play on the life of Emily Brontë)? Would the novel have revealed itself as a turning point in Fournier's own rite of passage into the adult world of pluralistic human activity, limited goals, and attainable ideals? If so, why then did Fournier prefix the words from the *Imitation of Christ* as an epigraph to his novel—"I seek a pure heart and there I will dwell"— an epigraph that remained to the end, as Gibson observes, "at the head of his draft"?[11] The ultimate working out of this apparent dichotomy between idealism and compromise was destined to remain unresolved.

La Maison dans le Forêt was, in part, intended as a showcase for the acting talents of Simone. Fournier completed only a single scene, but like *Colombe Blanchet* it seems to point in the direction of a more dispassionate and balanced examination of romantic love that undercuts lofty pretentions and emphasizes the mutual accommodation of Fournier's protagonists to the exigencies of daily routine. To be sure, the world of moral absolutes would have been brought to bear on the foibles, idiosyncrasies, and fallacies of two bemused, imperfect, but well-meaning lovers. The result might have been com-

parable in effect to the delicate pathos, gentle humour, and warm
human sympathy that radiates from the cinematographic moral fa-
bles of the French Catholic movie director, Eric Rohmer. The central
character of the play, a well-off though embittered countryman
named Harold, has returned to his native village following a series
of disillusioning affairs in Paris. He has lost all hope of attaining a
viable relationship with a woman of genuine substance. Unlike
Meaulnes, however, he recognizes that his temperament has been
largely responsible for his past unhappiness and that his conception
of love is incommensurate with the actualities of the real world. He
endeavors to forget his Parisian experiences in company with a
misogynistic though avuncular servant with whom he retreats to
the family's private hunting lodge. Both have forsworn the company
of women and hope that the rigors of the hunt will mute the
memories of the past.

While Harold and his servant Phillipe are in the midst of the
chase, two women appear at the lodge. One of these is a young girl
named Eléonore, a friend of Harold's sister who has run away from
a local private school in order to avoid a marriage being pressed
upon her by her parents. She is accompanied by her teacher Sainte-
Pourçain, who observed her escape and accordingly followed in an
effort to remonstrate with her young charge. As the two women
discuss the situation, they hear the sound of men's voices and,
becoming frightened, hide in different parts of the lodge. This is
where the fun begins. Both Harold and Phillipe begin to grow
suspicious of one another on discovering unmistakable signs of a
feminine presence in the house. When Phillipe discovers to his own
dismay, that he is stuffing his pipe with a bobby pin, he endeavors
to hide the fact from Harold who has begun to suspect that Phillipe
has secreted a woman in the house in defiance of their pledge. When
Phillipe discovers Saint-Pourçain he hides her, fearing that Harold
will come to the wrong conclusion. Harold, in the meanwhile, has
begun to suspect more than one female presence in the house, and
rushes upstairs after hearing a suspicious noise from the second floor.
The enterprising Eléonore has removed the two top steps, however,
and Harold falls through to the first floor in a state of mental
confusion. Slapstick from Alain-Fournier? Incredible, but true. The
playwright presumably intended to follow up Harold's misadventure
with scenes, both tender and comic, in which the growing love of
Eléonore and Harold would have been counterpointed with Phillipe's

wooing of Saint-Pourçain. The conception of the play owes some-thing perhaps to Shakespeare's *Love's Labour's Lost*, and confirms the opinion of Edward Sackville-West: "If he had lived, Alain-Fournier would certainly have written other books . . . and I think it prob-able that he would have outgrown the phase of adolescent melancholy and frustration which produced his first book."[12]

Despite the novel direction, widening concerns, and reconciling humor that may be detected in his posthumous fragments, Fournier's fame and reputation finally repose upon the consummate aesthetic achievement of *Le Grand Meaulnes*. Throughout this study we have endeavored to emphasize the impact and significance of that achieve-ment as attested in the words of this century's foremost writers and critics. "More robust and at the same time more mystical than Proust," as Cyril Connolly observes, Fournier created a novel com-parable to some of the finest classics of literary modernism. "It is," Connolly further avers, "a world of symbolism suddenly immersed under a cold douche of reality and emerging strengthened, as in the work of [Fournier's] two contemporaries, Eliot and Kafka."[13]

But there is an extraliterary dimension to Fournier's achievement as well. For a generation that seems to be engaged in a blind rush into the future, trusting in technology, scrambling for success, ignorant of the historical past, indifferent to metaphysical axioms, bereft of aesthetic standards, ungraced by "immortal longings," and uncaring of spiritual recollection, *Le Grand Meaulnes* can awaken an immaterial need in sharp contrast to the appetency and competi-tiveness of these times.

It is not only an outstanding example of fictional craftsmanship, rich in character, theme, and structure—and therefore an ideal springboard for the discussion of literary and artistic standards—it is also, as Ralph Harper avers, "in a time like ours, when spiritual quests are rather pushed aside by the clamor of public events and technological achievement," an indispensible reminder of "the lost path" to "the lost paradise" that dominated Fournier's imagina-tion.[14] Let us recall again the words of François Seurel: "I am searching for something far more mysterious. It is the path told of in books, the ancient obstructed path to which the weary prince could find no entrance" (*LGM*, 110). As Harper notes, apropos of this passage, "Alain-Fournier's conscious effort to retain, for the sake of intellectual continuity, the symbolism of [that lost paradise]

should not be forgotten." Moreover, by leaving a "symbol of [him]
self, and [his] vision of the mystery of love," Alain-Fournier has
done what "very few men in history are destined to do." And, as
Harper further proclaims, "the rest of us would do well to try to
assimilate his dreams into our own range of love."[15]

Notes and References

Preface

1. Robert Champigny, *Portrait of a Symbolist Hero* (Bloomington, 1954), 7.
2. M. A. Ruff et al., *Hommage à Alain-Fournier* (Paris: NRF, 1930), 113.
3. Harold Nicolson, *Observer*, 19 April 1953.
4. Robert Gibson, *The Quest of Alain-Fournier* (New Haven, 1954), 271.
5. Cyril Connolly, *Previous Convictions* (New York, 1963), 214.
6. C. S. Lewis, *Surprised by Joy* (New York, 1955), 16.
7. Ibid., 17.
8. Ibid., 17.

Chapter One

1. Eliot's characterization of Alain-Fournier is cited by Robert Gibson in *The Land without a Name* (London, 1975), 184.
2. Jacques Rivière and Alain-Fournier, *Correspondance 1905–1914*, 2 vols.(Paris: Gallimard 1966), 2:395. (Subsequent references to vols. 1 and 2 of this work will be noted in text with the abbreviation *Corr. R-F*, 1 or 2, followed by the specific page numbers.)
3. Henri Peyre, Introduction to *The Wanderer* (New York: 1958), xiv.
4. Cited by Mechthild Cranston in " 'La Marquise Sortit À Cinq Heures . . . ' Symbol and Structure in Alain-Fournier's *Le Grand Meaulnes*," *Kentucky Romance Quarterly* 26 (1979): 385.
5. David Ewen, *The World of Great Composers* (Englewood Cliffs, N. J., 1962), 449.
6. Fredrika Blair, Introduction to *The Wanderer* (Garden City, 1953), 13.
7. André Billy, *Histoire de la vie littéraire* (Paris, 1956), 163.
8. The epithets are those of George A. Panichas who in "The End of the Lamplight" reflects on the prewar atmosphere of western Europe. See *The Reverent Discipline* (Knoxville, 1974), 55.
9. John Fowles, Afterword to *The Wanderer* (New York, 1971), 217.
10. Champigny, *Symbolist Hero*, 101.

11. Cited by Gibson in *The Quest,* 39.

12. Ibid., 12.

13. *Le Grand Meaulnes,* trans. Frank Davison (Harmondsworth, England, 1978), 132. This translation in the Penguin Modern Classics series is the most poetic and accurate of the three presently available. Subsequent citations in text to this edition will be marked by the abbreviation *LGM* followed by the appropriate page number.

14. David Paul, "The Mysterious Landscape," *Cornhill Magazine* 162, no. 972 (Autumn 1947): 449.

15. Gillian Avery, "The Quest for Fairyland" *Quarterly Journal of the Library of Congress* (Fall 1981): 221.

16. David Paul, "The Mysterious Landscape," 442.

17. Ibid., 440.

18. "The Green Paradise of a Child's Affections"—a line from one of Fournier's favorite poems, Baudelaire's "Moesta et Errabunda." See Charles Baudelaire, *Les Fleurs Du mal* (Boston, 1982), 244.

19. Cited by Gibson in *The Land without a Name,* 43.

20. Jacques Rivière, Introduction to *Miracles* (Paris, 1924), 14–15.

21. Fowles, Afterword, 212.

22. Cited by Gibson in *The Quest,* 45.

23. Marcel Proust, *Remembrance of Things Past,* trans. C. K. Scott Moncrieff and Terrence Kilmartin (New York, 1981) 1:49–51.

24. Fowles, Afterword, 212.

25. George A. Panichas, ed., *A Simone Weil Reader* (New York, 1977), 360 and xxii.

26. Jacques Maritain, *Creative Intuition in Art and Poetry* (Ohio, 1954), 284.

27. Robert Liddell, *Some Principles of Fiction* (Bloomington, 1953), 158.

28. Cited by Gibson in *The Quest,* 113.

29. For a discussion of the tension between art and morality, see my essay "The Spiritual Significance of the French Symbolists in the Aesthetics of Jacques Maritain," *Studies in the Literary Imagination,* (Spring 1985): 33–48.

30. Cited by Fowles in Afterword, 219.

31. Cited by Gibson in *The Quest,* 254.

32. Rachilde, *Mercure de France,* 16 December 1913, 783.

33. Charles Péguy, in *Penguin Book of French Verse,* ed. Anthony Hartley (Harmondsworth, 1959), 90 (translation mine).

34. Panichas, *The Reverent Discipline,* 52.

35. The words here are from Shelley's comment on his poem *Epipsychidion.* See *The Letters of Percy Bysshe Shelley,* ed. Frederick C. Jones (Oxford, 1964), 2:434.

36. Champigny, *Symbolist Hero*, 155.

37. Cited by Gibson in *The Quest*, 257.

38. Cited by Gibson in *The Land without a Name*, 279.

39. Frederick W. Locke, "*Le Grand Meaulnes*: the Desire and the Pursuit of the Whole," *Renascence* 11 (Spring 1959): 136.

40. Paul, "The Mysterious Landscape," 449.

41. Fowles, Afterword, 208.

42. Edmond Jaloux, *Les Nouvelles littéraires*, 16 January 1939.

43. Leonard Woolf, *Downhill All the Way* (London, 1967), 9.

44. Harry Goldgar, "Alain-Fournier and the Initiation Archetype," *French Review* 43, no. 1 (1970): 99.

Chapter Two

1. Paul, "The Mysterious Landscape," 443.

2. Fowles, Afterword, 212.

3. Cited by Henri Peyre in *The French Literary Imagination and Dostoevsky* (Alabama, 1975), 23.

4. Paul, "The Mysterious Landscape," 447.

5. Stephen Ullmann, *The Image in the Modern French Novel* (Cambridge, 1963), 110.

6. For a thorough discussion of Fournier's affinities with his musical contemporaries see Christopher Palmer, "Debussy, Ravel and Alain-Fournier," *Music and Letters* 50, no. 2 (April 1969): 267–72.

7. Paul, "The Mysterious Landscape," 447.

8. Alex Aronson, *Music and the Novel* (Totowa, N. J., 1980), 137.

9. Erich Heller, *The Disinherited Mind* (Cleveland, 1969), 265.

10. C. S. Lewis, *Christian Reflections*, (Grand Rapids, Mich., 1967), 23.

11. C. S. Lewis, Preface to *Essays Presented to Charles Williams* (Grand Rapids, Mich., 1966), vi.

12. C. S. Lewis, *The Pilgrim's Regress* (Grand Rapids, Mich., 1977), 10.

13. Ibid., 9.

14. C. S. Lewis, *Mere Christianity* (New York, 1972), 128. A further discussion of this theme in Fournier's oeuvre may be found in my article, " 'The Dialectic of Desire' in *Madame Bovary* and *Le Grand Meaulnes*," *Romanticism Past and Present* 7, no. 1 (Winter 1983): 37–62.

15. Lewis, *The Pilgrim's Regress*, 7.

16. Gibson, *The Land without a Name*, 13–14.

17. R. T. Sussex, *The Sacrificed Generation* (Townsville, Australia, 1980), 106.

18. Q. D. Leavis, "The Englishness of the English Novel," *Modern Age* 26; no. 3–4 (Summer/Fall 1982): 359.

19. Paul, "The Mysterious Landscape," 446.

20. John Fowles, Afterword, 221.

21. Herbert Howarth, *Notes on Some Figures behind T. S. Eliot,* (London, 1965), 218, 155–56.

22. Yves-Gérard Le Dantec, in *Homage à Alain-Fournier,* 74.

23. Sussex, *The Sacrificed Generation,* 72.

24. Mary Duclaux, *Twentieth-Century French Writers* (London, 1919), 250.

25. Havelock Ellis, Introduction to *The Wanderer* (Boston, 1928), xxvii.

26. Melvin J. Friedman, Introduction to *The Vision Obscured: Perceptions of Some Twentieth Century Catholic Novelists* (New York, 1970), 5.

Chapter Three

1. Jack Stillinger, ed., *The Poems of John Keats* (Cambridge, 1978), 72.

2. Ibid., 125.

3. Ibid., 72.

4. Gibson, *The Quest,* 73.

5. *Miracles,* ed. Jacques Rivière (Paris, 1924), 95. Subsequent references in text will be indicated by the abbreviation *M* with the appropriate page number.

6. T. S. Eliot, *Collected Poems: 1909–1962,* (New York, 1963), 175.

7. U. C. Knoepflmacher, "Projection and the Female Other . . .," *Victorian Poetry* (Fall 1984): 142–43.

8. Gibson, *The Quest,* 76.

9. Jean Bastaire, *Alain-Fournier, ou la tentation de l'enfance* (Paris, 1964), 125.

10. Gibson, *The Quest,* 105.

11. Cited in ibid., 124.

12. Stillinger, ed., *The Poems of John Keats,* 119.

13. Lord David Cecil, ed., *The Oxford Book of Christian Verse* (Oxford, 1940), 272–73.

14. Sussex, *The Sacrificed Generation,* 102.

Chapter Four

1. Cranston, " 'La Marquise Sortit À Cinq Heures . . . ,' " 390, 378. My discussion of *Le Grand Meaulnes*—especially its structural organization—is deeply indebted to and strongly influenced by this seminal essay. Though I do not entirely agree with Cranston's conclusion that

"Meaulnes's is a world unredeemed by love," her essay is one of the soundest and most rigorous examinations of the novel yet to appear.

2. Locke, *"Le Grand Meaulnes,"* 138.

3. For a thorough discussion of marine imagery in *Le Grand Meaulnes* see Ullmann, *The Image in the Modern French Novel,* 99–123.

4. Mircea Eliade, *The Sacred and the Profane* (New York, 1959), 209.

5. Again see Ullmann, *The Image in the Modern French Novel,* 122.

6. See Joseph Campbell, *The Hero with a Thousand Faces* (Princeton, 1973), 49–238. Though Campbell does not discuss Fournier's novel, the reader will be able to discern some distinctive analogies between Meaulnes's adventure and the archetypal quest-romance analyzed by Campbell.

7. See Cranston, " 'La Marquise Sortit À Cinq Heures . . . ,' " 379.

8. Ibid., 380.

9. Eliade, *The Sacred and the Profane,* 196.

10. See Cranston, " 'La Marquise Sortit À Cinq Heures . . . ,' " 381.

11. Eliade discusses this pattern at length in *The Sacred and the Profane,* 184–201.

12. Ibid., 189.

13. Eliot, *Collected Poems,* 200.

14. Aronson, *Music and the Novel,* xiii.

15. Cited by Gibson in *The Quest,* 113.

16. Mircea Eliade, *Myths, Dreams, and Mysteries* (New York, 1967), 196.

17. Aronson, *Music and the Novel,* 113.

18. Stillinger, ed., *The Poems of John Keats,* 375.

19. Bruno Bettelheim, *The Uses of Enchantment* (New York, 1960), 268.

20. Aronson, *Music and the Novel,* 41.

21. Ibid., 41

22. Cited by Jessie L. Weston in *From Ritual to Romance* (1913; Garden City, N. Y. 1957), 16. This, of course, is the book that had such a profound impact on Eliot's composition of *The Waste Land.* Though Fournier would not have been familiar with Weston's study (though it was published in the same year as *Le Grand Meaulnes,* 1913), his acquaintance with the Perceval legend is unmistakable. Chapter 2 of Weston's book (pp. 12–24) entitled "The Task of the Hero" enables us to discern some remarkable affinities between Meaulnes and Perceval.

23. See Bate, Bronson, Brower, et al., eds. *Major British Writers II* (New York, 1959), 2: 453.

24. Ibid., 457.

25. Eliade, *The Sacred and the Profane*, 211.
26. Jacques Rivière, *The Ideal Reader* (New York, 1960), 126.
27. Kathleen Raine, *Defending Ancient Springs* (Oxford, 1967), 132.

Chapter Five

1. Denis Sauret, *Modern French Literature, 1870–1940* (London, 1946), 105.
2. Leon Cellier, *"Le Grand Meaulnes" ou l'initiation manquée* (Paris, 1963), 39 and 42.
3. André Gide, *Journal 1889–1939* (Paris, 1948), 1150.
4. C. S. Lewis, *The Weight of Glory* (Grand Rapids, Mich., 1965), 4.
5. Lewis, *The Pilgrim's Regress*, 161–62.
6. Lewis, *The Weight of Glory*, 4.
7. Ibid., 5.
8. Panichas, ed., *A Simone Weil Reader*, 424–25.
9. Blaise Pascal, *Pascal's Pensées* (New York, 1958), 55.
10. Meister Eckhart, *Meister Eckhart: A Modern Translation* (New York, 1941), 32.
11. Cited by Matthew Arnold in his essay "Maurice de Guerin," in *Lectures and Essays in Criticism* (Ann Arbor, 1962), 23.
12. Connolly, *Previous Convictions*, 215.
13. Freida Fordham, *An Introduction to Jung's Psychology* (Middlesex, 1968), 54.
14. Ibid., 53.
15. Ibid., 54.
16. Ibid., 54.
17. Lewis, *The Pilgrim's Regress*, 9.
18. Eliot, *Collected Poems*, 181 and 177.
19. Ibid., 199 and 194.
20. C. S. Lewis, *Mere Christianity*, 119.
21. T. S. Eliot, *Selected Essays* (New York, 1950), 235.
22. Lewis, *Mere Christianity*, 119.
23. In a comparative study of Augustine and Proust, Ralph Harper notes that it is the opposition between these themes that constitutes the principal difference between the literature of the Christian past and the secular present. Harper has also written eloquently on Alain-Fournier whose work similarly illustrates the thematic tensions that Harper discerns in Proust. See "The Weight of Our Time," *Modern Age* (Spring/Summer 1984): 117–120.
24. Henry James, *European Writers and the Prefaces* (New York, 1984), 354.

25. See C. S. Lewis, *The Problem of Pain* (New York, 1967), 148.

26. Pascal, *Pensées*, 113.

27. Pascal, *Pensées*, 35.

28. See Mechthild Cranston, " 'La Marquise Sortit À Cinq Heures . . . ,' " 390.

29. Cited by Gibson in *The Land without A Name*, 222.

30. See Martin Sorrell, "François Seurel's Personal Adventure in *Le Grand Meaulnes*," *Modern Language Review* (January 1974): 79–87, and Gibson, *The Land without A Name*, 297–304.

31. Pascal, *Pensées*, 24.

32. Lewis, *The Pilgrim's Regress*, 161.

Chapter Six

1. Cited by George A. Panichas in *The Courage of Judgment* (Knoxville, 1982), 234.

2. Panichas, *The Reverent Discipline*, 51.

3. François Mauriac, *Mémoires intérieurs* (New York, 1961), 71–72.

4. Cited by Panichas in *The Courage of Judgment*, a63.

5. Harold M. March, "The 'Other Landscape' of Alain-Fournier," *PMLA* 56 (1941): 279.

6. Karen D. Levy, "Alain-Fournier and the Surrealist Quest for Unity," *Romance Notes* 18 (1978): 307.

7. Ibid., 310.

8. "The 'Other Landscape,' " 279.

9. Lewis, *The Problem of Pain*, 146–47.

10. Howarth, *Notes on Some Figures behind T. S. Eliot*, 159.

11. Gibson, *The Land without a Name*, 253.

12. Edward Sackville-West, *Listener*, 12 February 1948, 269.

13. Connolly, *Previous Convictions*, 214.

14. Ralph Harper, *Human Love: Existential and Mystical* (Baltimore, 1966), 161.

15. Ibid., 161 and 166.

Selected Bibliography

This bibliography is confined only to studies that can be of most help in introducing a reader to Fournier's work. With the exception of the original texts, all works mentioned are in English. For a specialized bibliography, one should consult Alden and Brooks's *Critical Bibliography of French Literature*, vol. 6 (Syracuse: 1980), 660–78. See also the *Bulletin des Amis de Jacques Rivière et d'Alain-Fournier,* nos. 30, 31, and 33 (1983 and 1984).

PRIMARY SOURCES

1. Books

Le Grand Meaulnes. Edited by Robert Gibson. London, 1968. An authoritative French edition with a valuable introduction and notes by the editor.

Le Grand Meaulnes. Translated by Frank Davison. 1959. Reprint. Harmondsworth, England: Penguin Books, 1984. This is the best of the English versions.

Miracles. Edited by Jacques Rivière. Paris, 1924. Rivière's introduction is, perhaps, the single most important study in any language.

2. Correspondence

Péguy, Charles and Alain-Fournier. *Correspondance 1910–1914.* Paris: Fayard, 1973.

Rivière, Jacques, and Alain-Fournier. *Correspondance 1905–1914.* 4 vols. Paris: Gallimard, 1926. New edition in 2 vols. Paris: Gallimard, 1948.

Alain-Fournier. *Lettres au petit B.* Paris: Emile-Paul, 1930.

Alain-Fournier. *Lettres d'Alain-Fournier à sa famille 1905–1914.* Paris: Emile-Paul, 1949.

SECONDARY SOURCES

1. Books

Blair, Fredrika. Introduction to *The Wanderer.* Garden City, N. Y.: Doubleday, 1953. A concentrated and sympathetic discussion of the tonality of *Le Grand Meaulnes*—the qualities it shares with Keats and the suggestiveness of its imagery.

Cancalon, Elaine. *Fairy-Tale Structures and Motifs in "Le Grand Meaulnes."* Bern, Switzerland: Herbert Lang, 1975. A thorough and painstaking analysis of fairy-tale allusions in *Le Grand Meaulnes* and the manner in which these illumine and give universality to Fournier's principal themes.

Champigny, Robert. *Portrait of a Symbolist Hero*. Bloomington: Indiana University Press, 1954. An uneven, eccentric, and dogmatic study that emphasizes the psychological consanguinity of the three male characters but erroneously concludes that Meaulnes achieves self-emancipation by regarding life as an aesthetic phenomenon. By-passing the implicit self-criticism and irony in Fournier's novel, Champigny sees the author as a surrealist visionary indifferent to the claims of religious or ethical convention.

Connolly, Cyril. *Previous Convictions*. New York: Harper & Row, 1963. Contains a brief but significant discussion of *Le Grand Meaulnes* that stresses the structural continuity of its three parts and defends the latter half of the book as a deliberate critique of romantic excess.

Fowles, John. Afterword to *The Wanderer*. New York: New American Library, 1971. An infectiously enthusiastic essay in which Fowles acknowledges Fournier's influence on his own work, commends Fournier's acumen as a critic, celebrates the achievement of *Le Grand Meaulnes,* and graphically retells the story of Fournier's life. Fowles derides a critical approach to the novel, arguing that its atmosphere and magic are untranslatable into discursive language.

Gibson, Robert. *The Land without a Name*. London: Paul Elek, 1975. Perhaps the single most important work on Fournier in English. A marvelously evocative recreation of Fournier's life and times that brings Fournier, his friends and associates, to compelling and dramatic life. Updates Gibson's earlier study by including a long discussion of Fournier's liaison with Simone and concludes with a brilliant discussion of Suerel's crucial role as narrator of *Le Grand Meaulnes.* Generous and accurate translations from the correspondence and other minor works make this a treasure house for English readers.

———. *The Quest of Alain-Fournier*. New Haven: Yale University Press, 1953. An earlier study that contains important discussions of the minor works and stresses the autobiographical resonances in *Le Grand Meaulnes.*

Harper, Ralph. *Human Love: Existential and Divine*. Baltimore: Johns Hopkins University Press, 1966. Contains a single but indispensible chapter on Fournier that analyzes *Le Grand Meaulnes* from the perspective of the mystic's preoccupations with love as both transcendent and immanent.

Houston, John. *Fictional Technique in France 1802–1927.* Baton Rouge: Louisiana State University Press, 1972. Contains a short but incisive reading of Seurel's limitations as narrator of *Le Grand Meaulnes.* Seurel fails to fathom the religious dimension of Meaulnes's quest and, hence, misinterprets the motives behind his friend's erratic behavior.

Howarth, Herbert. *Notes on Some Figures behind T. S. Eliot.* London: Chatto & Windus, 1954. Discusses Fournier's influence on and relationship with T. S. Eliot in the years before the First World War.

Jones, Marian Giles. *A Critical Commentary on Alain-Fournier's "Le Grand Meaulnes."* New York: St. Martin's Press, 1968. A rather oversimplified account of Fournier's images and themes that fails to present a coherent and organized view of the novel. Incidental observations are helpful, however.

Liddell, Robert. *Some Principles of Fiction.* Bloomington: Indiana University Press, 1964. Though largely biographical in scope, Liddell's discussion of Fournier contains some interesting and valuable comparisons with Proust.

Peyre, Henri. Introduction to *The Wanderer.* New York: Heritage Books, 1958. A cogent and laudatory introduction that traces the coalescence of symbolist technique and homely rusticity in Fournier's novel. Regards *Le Grand Meaulnes* as equal to Proust's *Swann's Way* in form, influence, and content.

Sussex, R. T. *The Sacrificed Generation.* Townsville; Australia: University of North Queensland Press, 1980. Sees Fournier as a representative figure of idealistic French youth on the threshold of the First World War. Contains some valuable observations on the correspondence and minor works.

Turnell, Martin. *The Rise of the French Novel.* New York: New Directions, 1978. One of the best overall introductions to Fournier's novel. Clearly delineates the novel's themes and structures as it explores the contrast between Meaulnes's failure to grow up and Seurel's sober assessment of human possibility. Turnell adumbrates the notion of the medieval quest theme in *Le Grand Meaulnes* and traces the thematic opposition between interiors and exteriors, home and world, danger and security.

Ullmann, Stephen. *The Image in the Modern French Novel.* Cambridge: Cambridge University Press, 1960. A brilliant study in the tradition of New Criticism that examines the significance of sea imagery in *Le Grand Meaulnes.* Fournier's poetic use of imagery is at once evocative and organic, subtly related to the exigencies of the plot and revelatory of the novel's central issues.

2. Articles and Periodicals

Cranston, Mechthild. " 'La Marquise Sortit à Cinq Heures . . . ' Symbol and Structure in Alain-Fournier's *Le Grand Meaulnes*." *Kentucky Romance Quarterly* 26 (1979): 377–95. A brilliant structural analysis of *Le Grand Meaulnes* that explores the formal integrity of Fournier's composition. Concentrates largely on the novel's mathematical organization—the use of numbers, dates, and times to create a sense of circularity, stasis, and repetition.

DeLutri, Joseph R. "The Adult World and the Romantic Quest in *Le Grand Meaulnes*." *Language Quarterly* 18, nos. 1 and 2 (1980): 35–38. Argues that the adolescents in *Le Grand Meaulnes* fail to reach maturity because of the lack of viable adult role models. Gives concentrated attention to the novel's secondary adult characters, revealing their shortcomings and regressive yearnings for childhood.

Goldgar, Harry. "Alain-Fournier and the Initiation Archetype," *French Review* 43, special issue, no. 1 (1970): 87—99. A Jungian analysis of *Le Grand Meaulnes* that discusses the mythopoeic elements in Fournier's work. Highlights archetypal mythic patterns in the book's design and examines the overall initiation patterns that connect Meaulnes with legendary figures such as Perceval.

Gurney, Stephen. "The 'Dialectic of Desire' in *Madame Bovary* and *Le Grand Meaulnes*." *Romanticism Past and Present* 7, no. 1 (Winter 1983): 37–62. A comparative study of Flaubert and Fournier from the perspective of C. S. Lewis's "dialectic of desire." Discusses the implicit moral issues associated with the invasive romanticism of these works.

Lainey, Y. "*Le Grand Meaulnes* as a Romantic Novel." *Theoria* 29 (1967): 33–43. One of the many biographical approaches to the novel, which fails to discern the ironizing distance that the author places between himself and his creation.

Levy, Karen D. "Alain-Fournier and the Surrealist Quest for Unity." *Romance Notes* 18 (1978): 301–10. One of the few articles that explore the question of Fournier's potential development after *Le Grand Meaulnes*.

Locke, Frederick W. "*Le Grand Meaulnes*: The Desire and Pursuit of the Whole." *Renascence* 11 (1959): 135–46. *Le Grand Meaulnes* possesses the organic unity and inexhaustible richness of a scrupulously designed poem. Notes similarity to other quest romances including the *Conte du Graal* of Chrétien de Troyes.

March, Harold M. "The 'Other Landscape' of Alain-Fournier." *PMLA* 56 (1941): 266–79. Sees Fournier as possessed of mystical longings but unable to realize either in his life or his work the faith toward which he aspired.

Palmer, Christopher. "Debussy, Ravel, and Alain-Fournier." *Music and*

Letters 50 (1969): 267–77. Concentrates on Fournier's knowledge of and indebtedness to the music of his contemporaries: Debussy and Ravel. Traces affinities between *Le Grand Maulnes* and the programmatic music of the impressionists. Both instance a preoccupation with the sea and childhood. A suggestive and stimulating article.

Paul, David. "The Mysterious Landscape." *Cornhill Magazine* 162, no. 972 (1947): 440–49. An affective essay that warmly expresses this critic's appreciation of Fournier's achievement. Sees Fournier as belonging to the English tradition of Arcadian romance and childhood poetry as exemplified in Traherne, Vaughan, Wordsworth, and Blake.

Savage, Catherine. "Nostalgia in Alain-Fournier and Proust." *French Review* 38 (1964): 167–72. A sensitive study that compares the element of retrospective pathos in Fournier and Proust. Fournier's quest for a genuine lost paradise that has an objective and external reality is contrasted with Proust's subjective evocation of an ideal past that exists only in memory and art.

Sorrell, Martin. "François Seurel's Personal Adventure in *Le Grand Meaulnes*." *Modern Language Review* 38 (1964): 167–72. Discusses *Le Grand Meaulnes* as a portrait of the artist in which Seurel achieves self-definition through an aesthetic recreation of the past. Argues that Seurel's domination of the narrative becomes the means whereby he transcends and controls the willful personality of Meaulnes.

Stubbs, Marcia. "The Pilgrim Spirit." *Accent* 18 (1958): 121–33. An illuminating and fastidious study of the novel's characters, language, themes, and structure. Regards Meaulnes as susceptible to the sin of pride—obstinately clinging to a peak experience at the risk of destroying his own and others' happiness.

Woodcock, George. "Alain-Fournier and the Lost Land." *Queen's Quarterly* 81 (1974): 348–56. A distillation of the prevailing critical responses to *Le Grand Meaulnes*. Sees the characters as conflicting sides of Fournier's personality, the plot as a modern adaptation of the medieval quest, and the image of the lost land as a symbolic adumbration of the absolute.

Index

DATE DUE
